IMAGES
of America

NIXA

IMAGES *of America*

NIXA

Michelle Korgis-Fitzpatrick

ARCADIA PUBLISHING

ISBN 978-0-7385-3327-8

Published by Arcadia Publishing
Charleston, South Carolina

Printed in the United States of America

Library of Congress Catalog Card Number: 2004112019

For all general information contact Arcadia Publishing at:
Telephone 843-853-2070
Fax 843-853-0044
E-mail sales@arcadiapublishing.com
For customer service and orders:
Toll-Free 1-888-313-2665

Visit us on the Internet at www.arcadiapublishing.com

Contents

ACKNOWLEDGMENTS

The photographs and information found in this book were collected over the past few years from out-of-state ancestors, local residents, and ancestors with websites. Each family member that sent me photos and information has kindly granted permission for their use in the book.

I wish to express my great gratitude to the following people:

Boyd, Larry	Brand, Kathy	Case, Martha
Colli, Rosalie	Dunn, Harley	Fitzpatrick, Chris
Fitzpatrick, Joretta	Gay, Steve	Hightower, Rosa
Hudson, C.A.	Inman, Fred Winston	Jaramillo, Clara
Johnson, James C.	Johnson, Victoria	Johnston, Jerry
Lawson, Jerry	Marler, Gale	Nance, Ed
Noe, Stan	Norris, Nancy Jane	Pearce, Donald
Pegram, Bruce	Scott, H.E.	Stewart, Kathy
Weaver, June		

A special thanks to Jessica Jones for help with scanning and creating digital images from old photographs. Her help in creating this book has been invaluable.

And to the following organizations:

Christian County Library	City of Nixa	Springfield Writers Guild
Arcadia Publishing	Nixa Gun & Pawn Shop	John Thomas Elementary

And last but not least, to my family and friends:

My parents Russell & Margaret Korgis; My siblings Tom Winge and Jeannette Korgis; My kids Zackory Korgis and Allen Fitzpatrick; My husband and his family Chris Fitzpatrick, Bill and Joretta Fitzpatrick, Rick and Shirley Fitzpatrick, and Daren and Lillian "Muffy" Fitzpatrick, and my friends Theresa and Cliff King, as well as my fellow writing group members and friends of the SWG. This includes all those who buy my books. Thank you all!

Introduction

"Nixa is one of the fastest growing cities in Missouri," according to Nixa's Chamber of Commerce. Nixa can be found as far back as the mid-1800s, when farmers and traders came to the area for the fertile soil of the Southwest Missouri region. Farming settlers were some of the first to arrive to this region. Many of them settled along the wooded streams of the area. After other settlers quickly began to arrive, the community started growing and the area became known as a "Crossroads" site. It was about a half-day ride for travelers hauling supplies by a team of horses from Arkansas to Springfield, Missouri and Nixa was a convenient stopping point to water their horses and rest.

In 1852, Nicholas Alexander Inman came to the area from Tennessee and established a blacksmith shop with Joe Weaver. When he returned to the area after the Civil War, he opened another blacksmith shop in Nixa. "Inman's family home site of 160 acres adjoins the present day corporate boundaries of Nixa," states Nixa's Chamber of Commerce. A town meeting was held to officially name the area for the community and post office. One suggestion was made after the German word "nix" meaning "nothing" and another suggestion was made to add the letter "a" from Inman's middle initial creating the community's new name—Nixa. On June 10, 1902 Nixa was officially incorporated as a village.

Dear Readers

To my readers: I would like to say how grateful I am for those of you who have generously contributed photographs and information. Preserving history is important for us today and for generations to come.

As I continue to write and research the history of this area, I welcome additional photographs as well as any information anyone has to offer.

I have compiled the information in this book over the past two years, and together with my first book with Arcadia Publishing, *Ozark*, I hope I have put together a good photographic snapshot of the history of Christian County. But there is always more to learn, and as I continue to research and write about Christian County history, I am always thankful to those who share their stories and history with me. You can learn more about me and my research and writing at my website, http://freepages.history.rootsweb.com/~mkfitz/. You may contact me at:

Michelle Korgis-Fitzpatrick
PO Box 553
Nixa, MO 65714
Storywriter1976@aol.com

Again, I thank all of you who have contributed to this book.

Michelle Korgis-Fitzpatrick

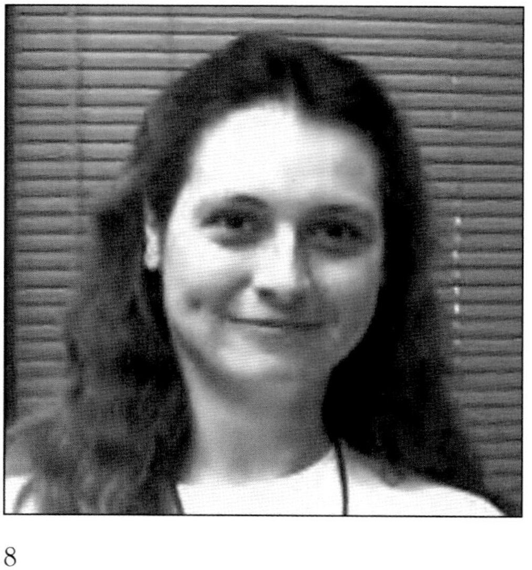

One

Early Settlers of Nixa and Sparta

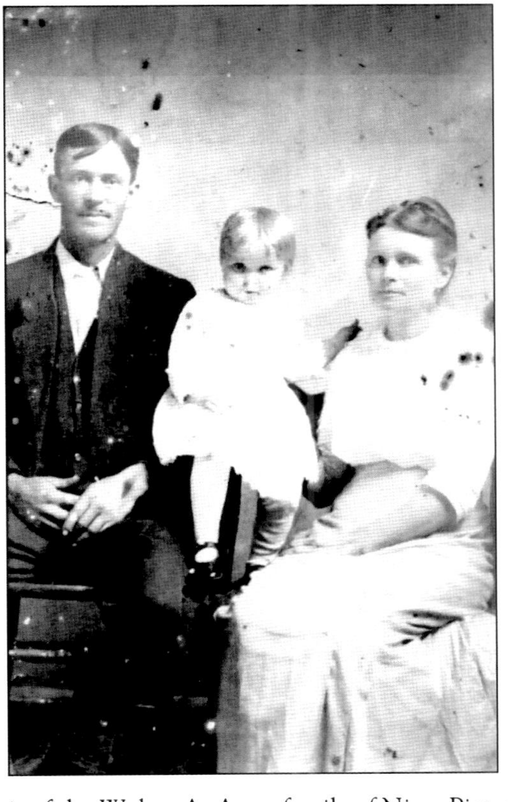

This photo from c. 1914 is of the Walter A. Aven family of Nixa. Pictured from left to right are Walter A. Aven, Hester Ann (Aven) Jackson, and Josephine R. (Hedgpeth) Aven. Walter was born in August 1873 and died in 1948. Hester was born on March 3, 1912 and died on April 27, 2001. Josephine was born on April 4, 1875 and died in 1967.

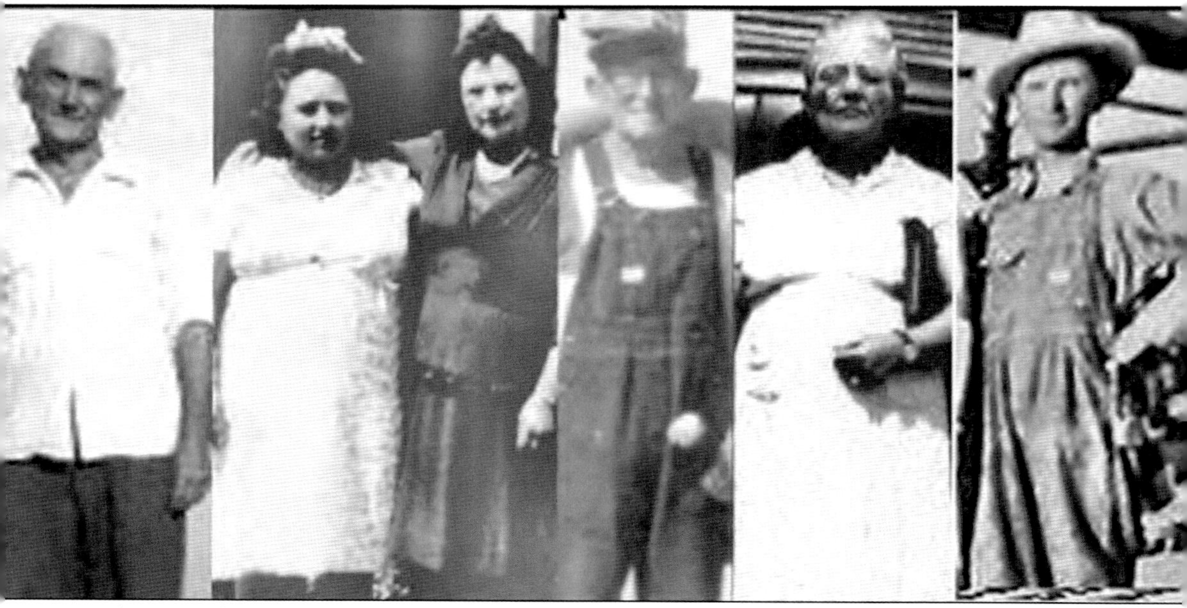

These are the children of Isaac Wilson and Susan (Johnson) Bledsoe. Their great grandparents were John Lowery and Mary Bacon Bledsoe. Pictured from left to right are Sam Bledsoe, Josephine Bledsoe, Pearl Bledsoe, Bill Bledsoe, Minniebell Bledsoe, and Fred Bledsoe. According to Mike Cotter, a resident and descendent of the Bledsoe family, the name Bledsoe use to be spelled Bedsoe.

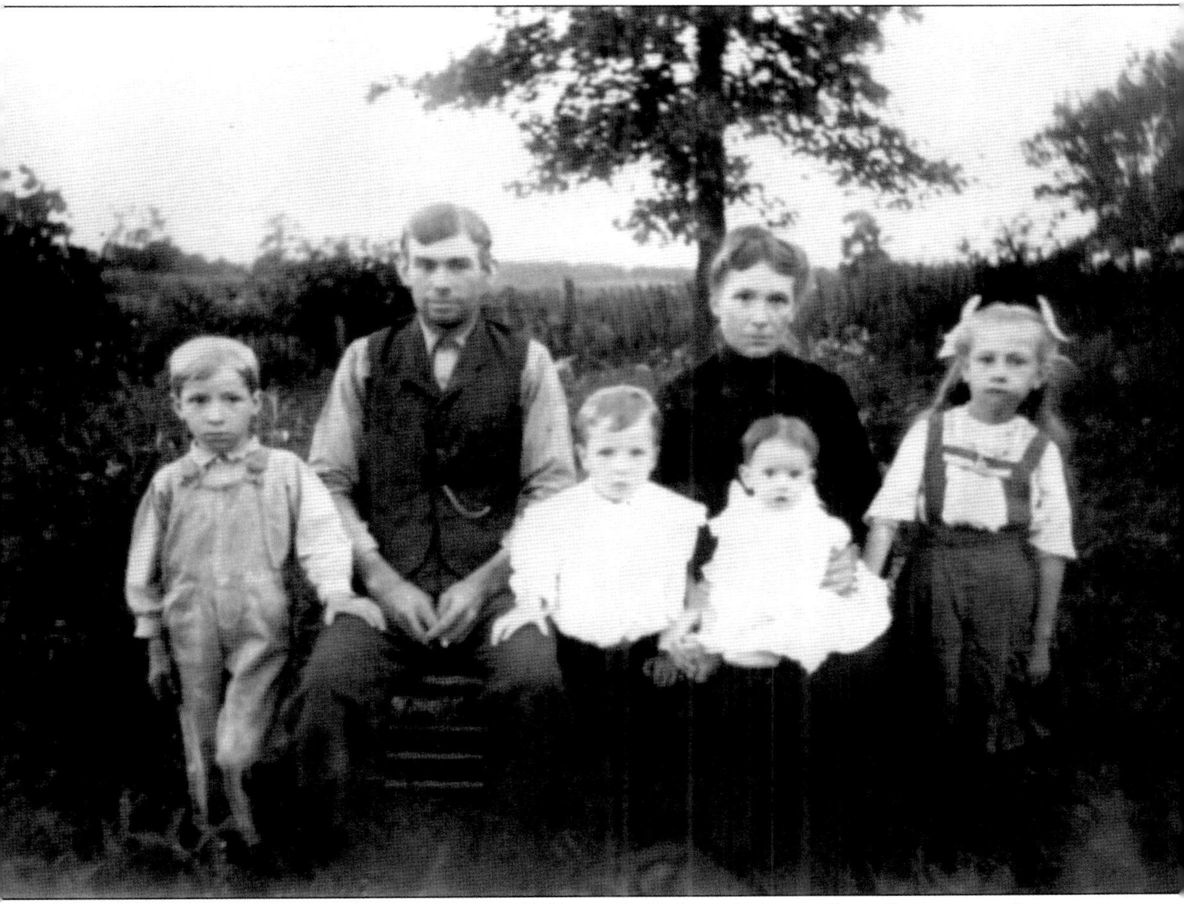

Pictured here are the family members of William D. Bolin of Nixa. This photo was taken c. 1908. The two adults sitting in the back behind the children are William D. and Addie E. Bolin. The children in this photo from left to right are Lester H. Bolin; Orville L. Bolin; Merl L. Bolin, and Ersha Eva Bolin. Lester married Lola Loreen Jones, the daughter of Charley W. and Clara M. (Sparkman) Jones. Orville L. married Eula Agnes Glidewell, daughter of William D. and LaVada E. (Stiffler) Glidewell. Ersha Eva never married. Merl L. Bolin married Jesse F. Jones, son of Charley W. and Clara M. (Sparkman) Jones. Clara M. (Sparkman) Jones is a sister to Martha Jane (Sparkman) Inman.

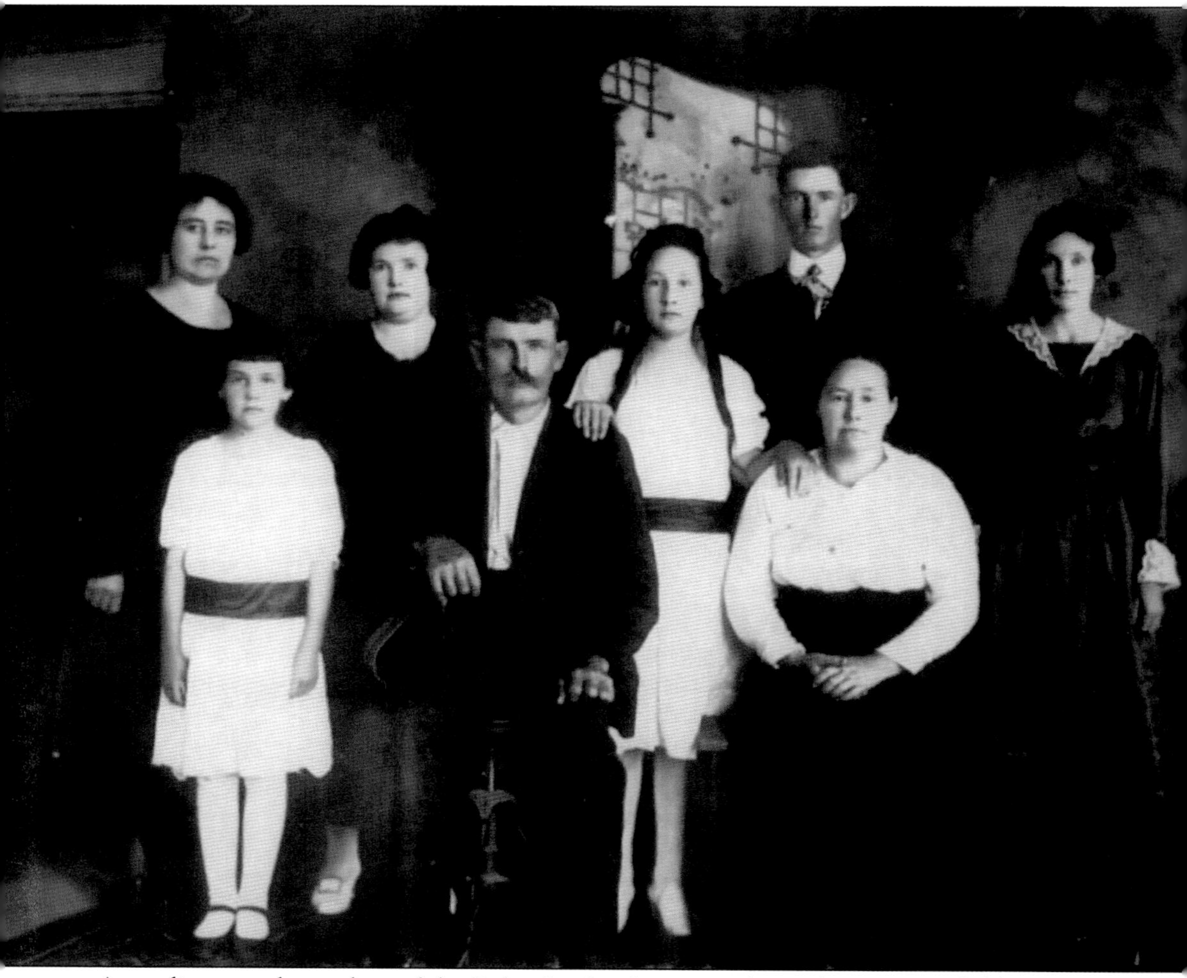

According to a descendent of the Bolin family who currently resides in Springfield, MO, this photo of the Bolin family is from Nixa. The date of the photograph is unknown. However, another descendent of this family believes this photo is of the Robert James Bolin family. Robert James Bolin is the second son of Elisha B. Bolin and Elisha is a brother of Granville Bolin and also the son of William and Millie (Cates) Bolin. Robert James was born in Springfield, MO, in 1870 to Elisha B. and Paralee A. (Ruyle) Bolin. She was the daughter of a John W. and Sarah C. (Pruitt) Ruyle and also the sister to the well-known Cassinda "Aunt Cindy" (Ruyle) Bolin, who was the wife of Granville Bolin. Robert James Bolin died in Collin County, Texas, in 1947. He had married Mary Elizabeth Turner, of Collin County, TX, in 1892. Pictured from left to right are: (front row) Blanche Ruby Bolin, Robert James Bolin, and his wife Mary Elizabeth Bolin; (back row) Almanta Bolin, Stella M. Bolin, Ressie V. Bolin, Samuel William Bolin, and Oleta Earl Bolin.

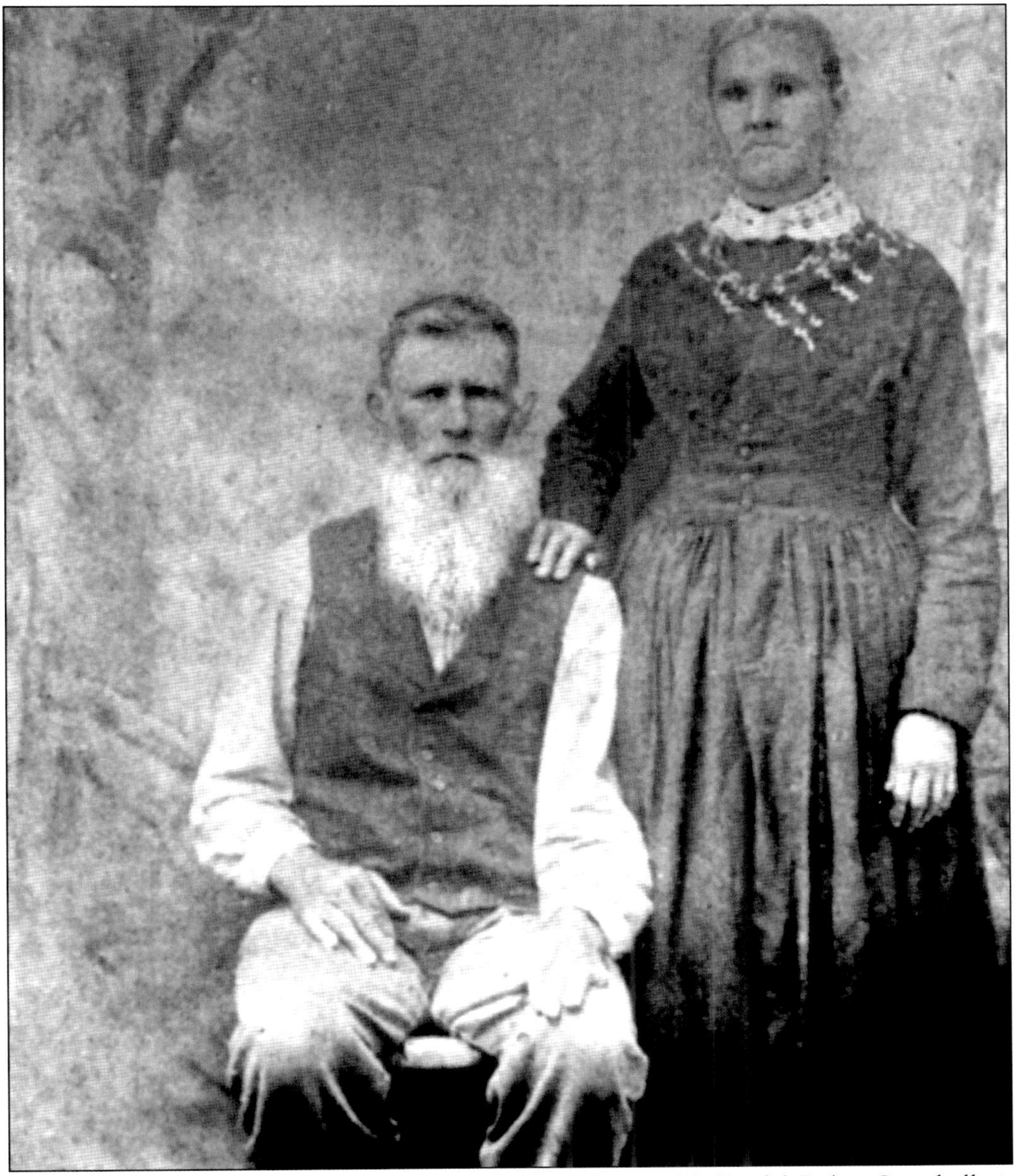

This photo is of Grandville and Martha Cassinda "Aunt Cindy" (Ruyle) Bolin. Grandville is the son of William and Millie (Cates) Bolin. Cindy was known in the Nixa community and Christian County area as "Aunt Cindy." Cindy is the daughter of John W. and Sarah Catherine (Pruitt) Ruyle who all lived in the Nixa area. Cindy treated the residents of the area with her home remedies and was known as an herb doctor. She had also delivered many babies. She was born in Greene County, Illinois. It is a question if Cindy's mother, Sarah, was a sibling to Jacob L. Pruitt, who was married to Nancy Morrisett. Jacob was born in Tennessee and Sarah was born in Illinois but Sarah had lived in Tennessee at one time. Grandville's younger brother was Elisha Bolin and his younger sister was Mary Ann Bolin. Elisha married Paralee A. (Ruyle) Bolin and Mary Ann Bolin married Isaac Ruyle. Elisha and Mary Ann's family moved from this area after 1870 to Collin County, Texas.

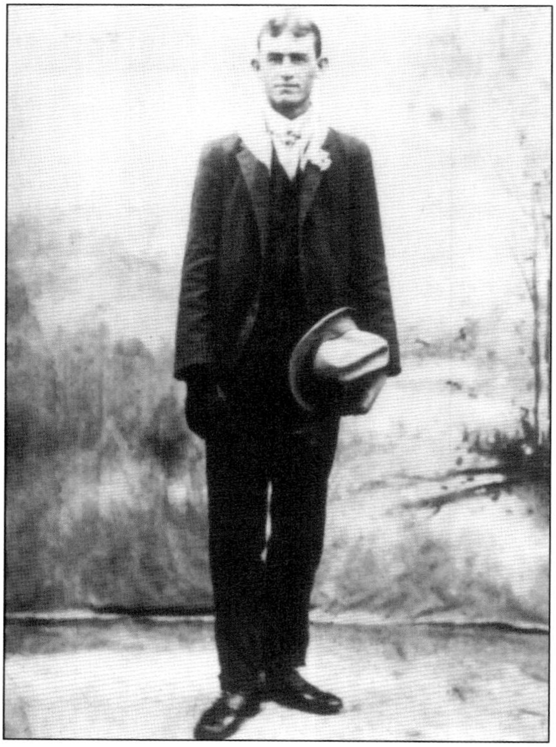

This is William D. Bolin as a young man. Born in Nixa, he was the son of John L. and Margaret M. (Ray) Bolin. William is the father of Opal Mae (Bolin) Inman.

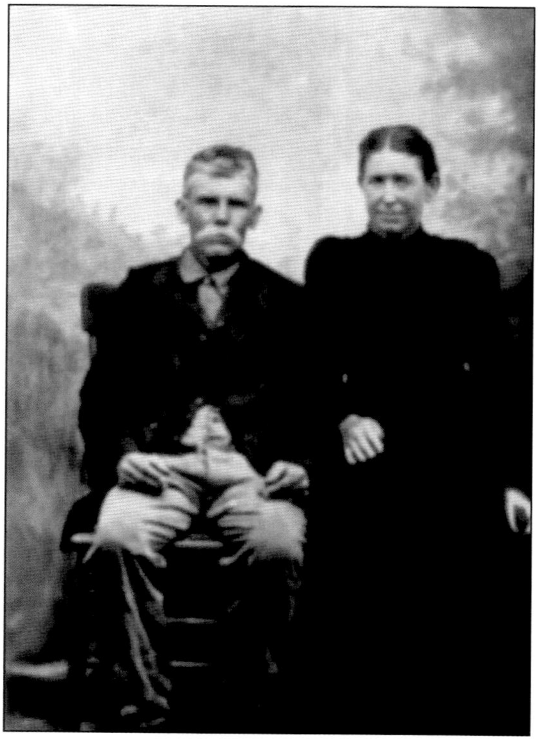

John L. and Margaret M. (Ray) Bolin are pictured here. Margaret smoked a corncob pipe and occasionally chewed tobacco. John is a son of Granville and Cassinda "Aunt Cindy" (Ruyle) Bolin. Margaret is the daughter of James and Margaret N. (Maze) Ray.

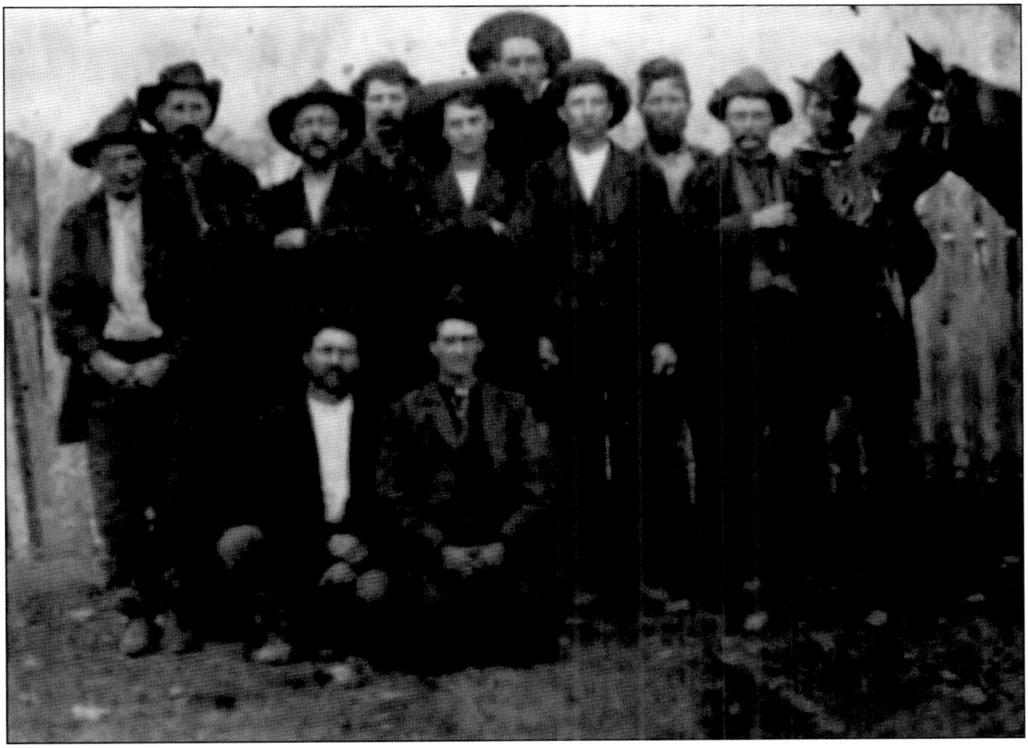

Nothing is known about this family; it is an old tintype photo found in Frances (Davis) Brown's collection.

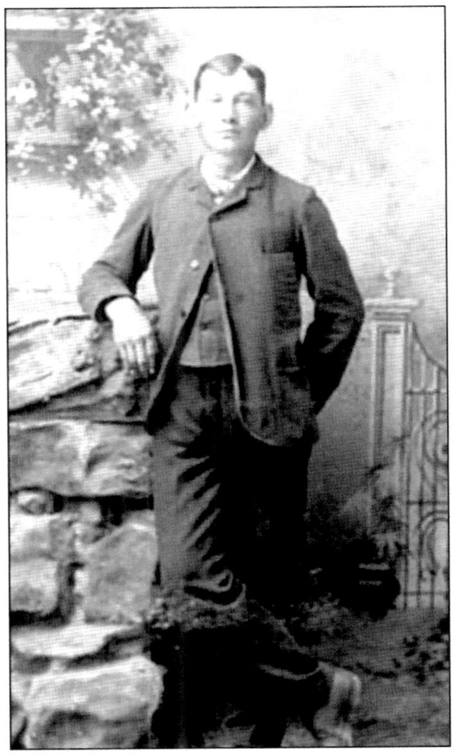

This photo is of David H. Carroll, who died at a young age, approximately 23-years-old. He is buried in the Payne Cemetery of Nixa.

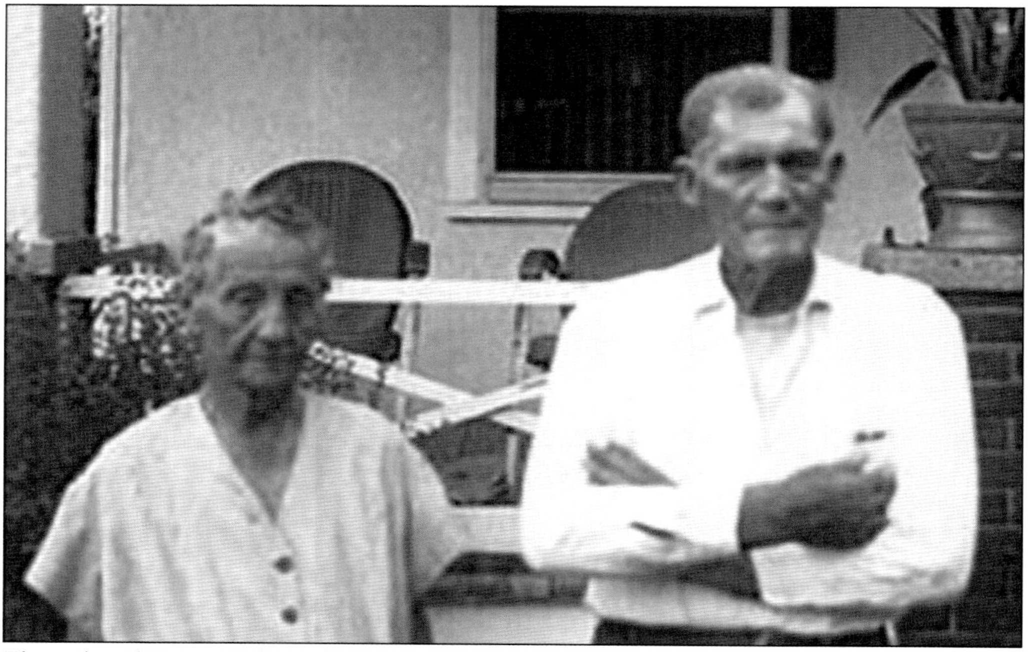

The only information about this photo is that this is John and his sister, Lizzie Carroll. John is also the grandfather of C.A. Hudson.

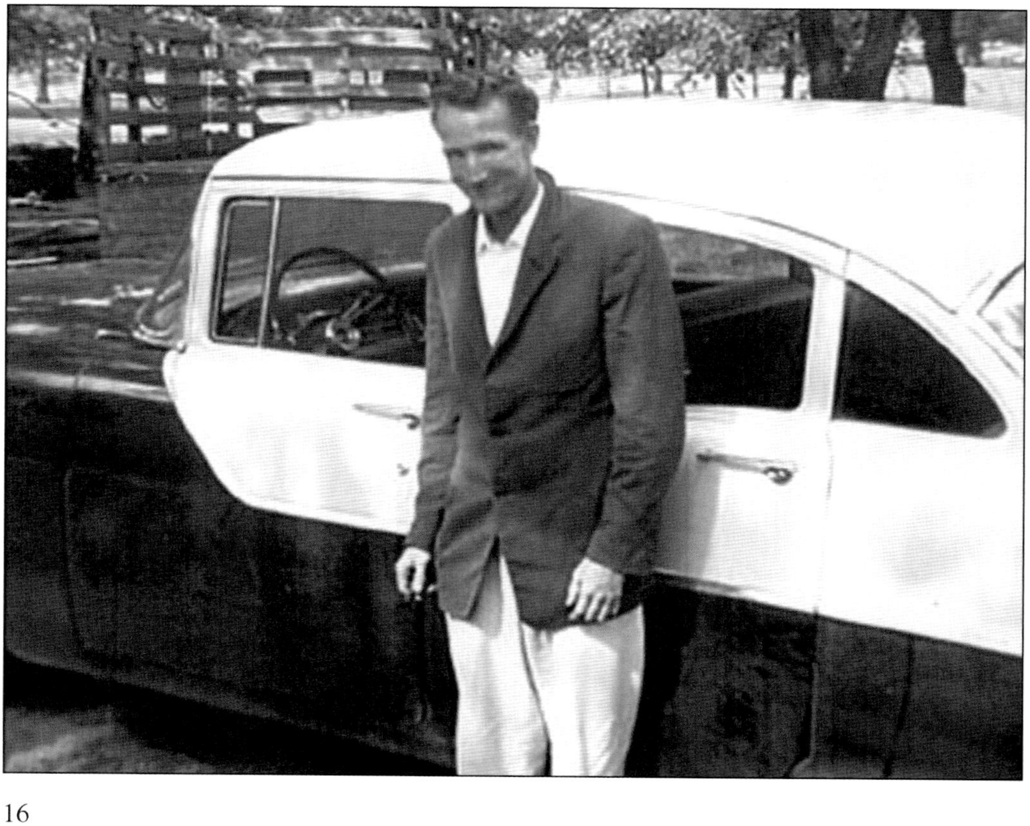

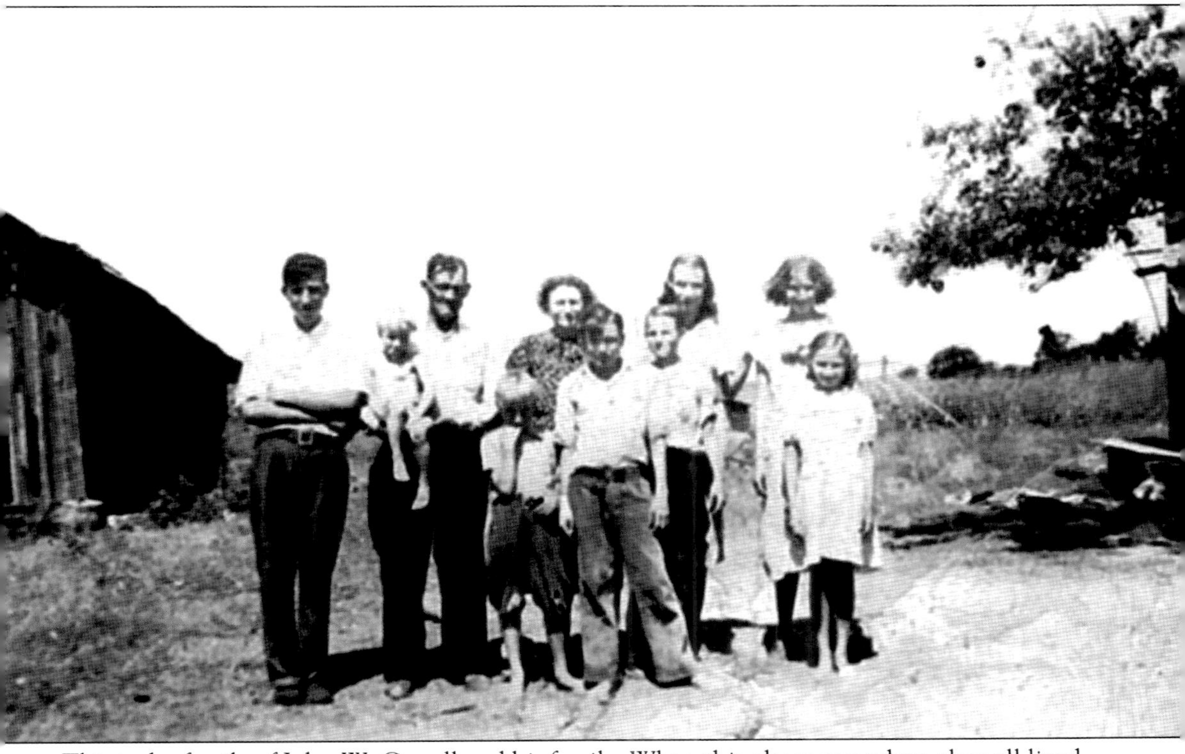

This is the family of John W. Carroll and his family. When this photo was taken, they all lived in eastern Dallas. John W. Carroll was a correctional office for Dallas County. He came to Christian County because his first wife was dying of tuberculoses. It is believed she died in El Paso. He then married a young girl who was C. A. Hudson's grandmother from Buckner Orphvs Home in Dallas. However, the people seen in this photo are unknown except for John W. Carroll, and it is not known which man in the photo is John.

Opposite: John William Carroll was born in Monroe County, Tennessee, and moved to Nixa. John worked for the sheriff's department in Springfield, Missouri as a young man. Ernest was a messenger in downtown Dallas. He worked for a company called Blanks Engraving and made the deliveries on a bicycle for forty years. Ernest was born in 1935 and died in 1985. He never married or had any children. Ernest lived his life in Dallas, Texas. His father, John William Carroll, lived in Nixa. Ernest is the man in the photo standing by this 1955 Pontiac. The photo was taken in the 1960s in Mesquite, Texas.

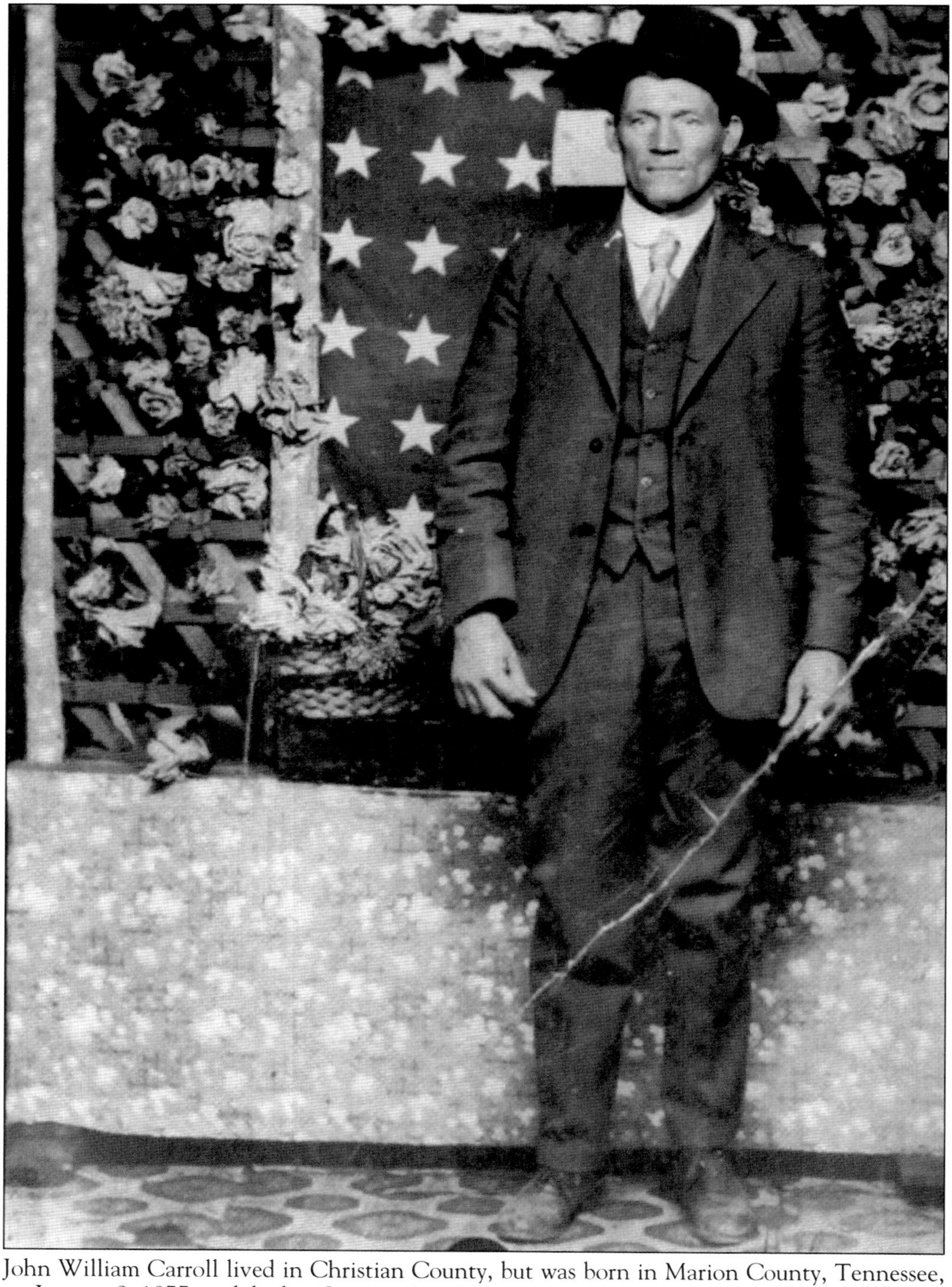

John William Carroll lived in Christian County, but was born in Marion County, Tennessee, on January 9, 1877, and died on January 6, 1967, in Dallas, Dallas County, Texas. It is believed that he married Toney D. Mensor of Christian County, Missouri in 1901. He later left Christian County, likely due to Toney's death, and remarried Viana Elizabeth Campbell of Dallas, Texas in 1919.

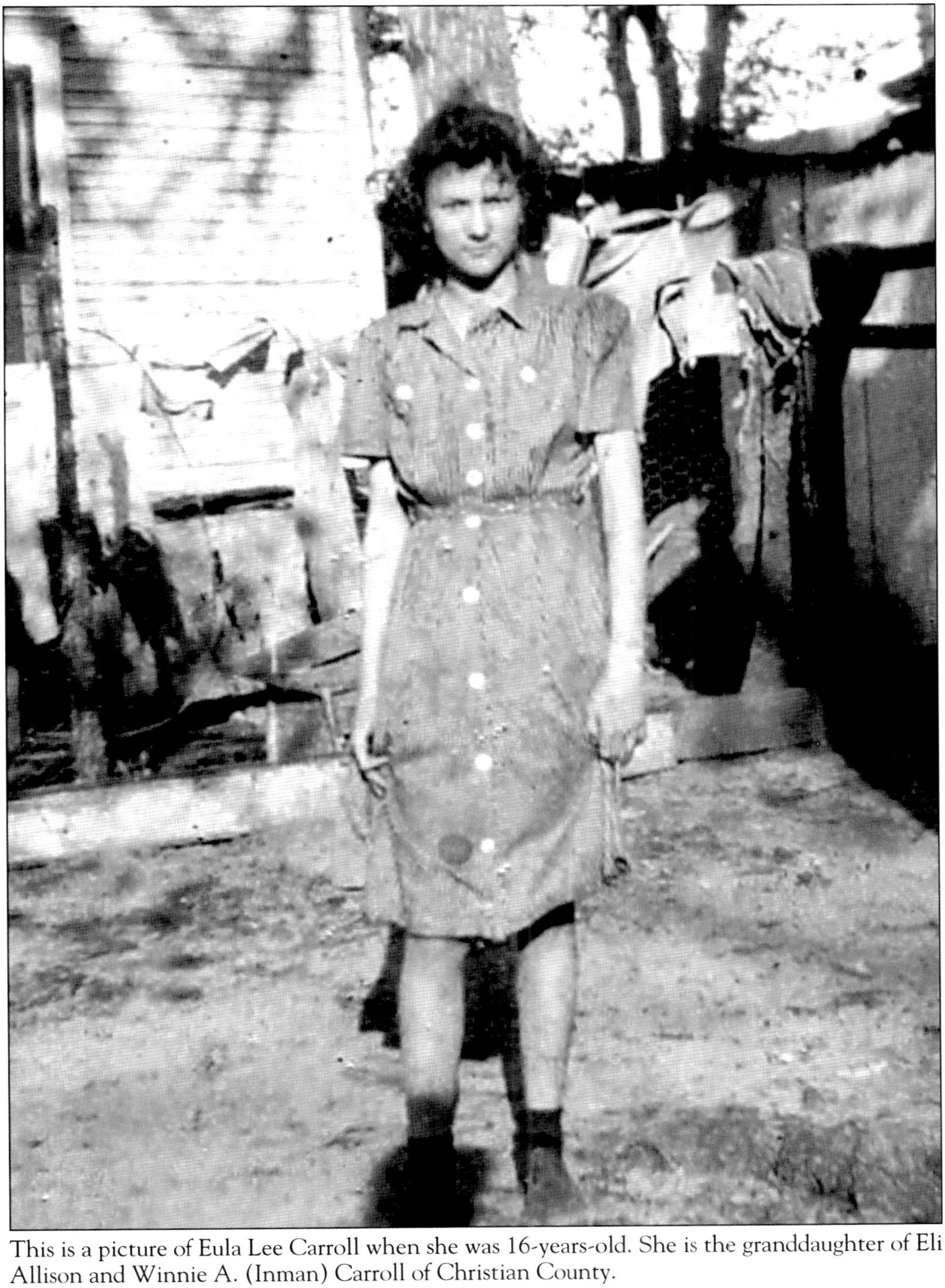

This is a picture of Eula Lee Carroll when she was 16-years-old. She is the granddaughter of Eli Allison and Winnie A. (Inman) Carroll of Christian County.

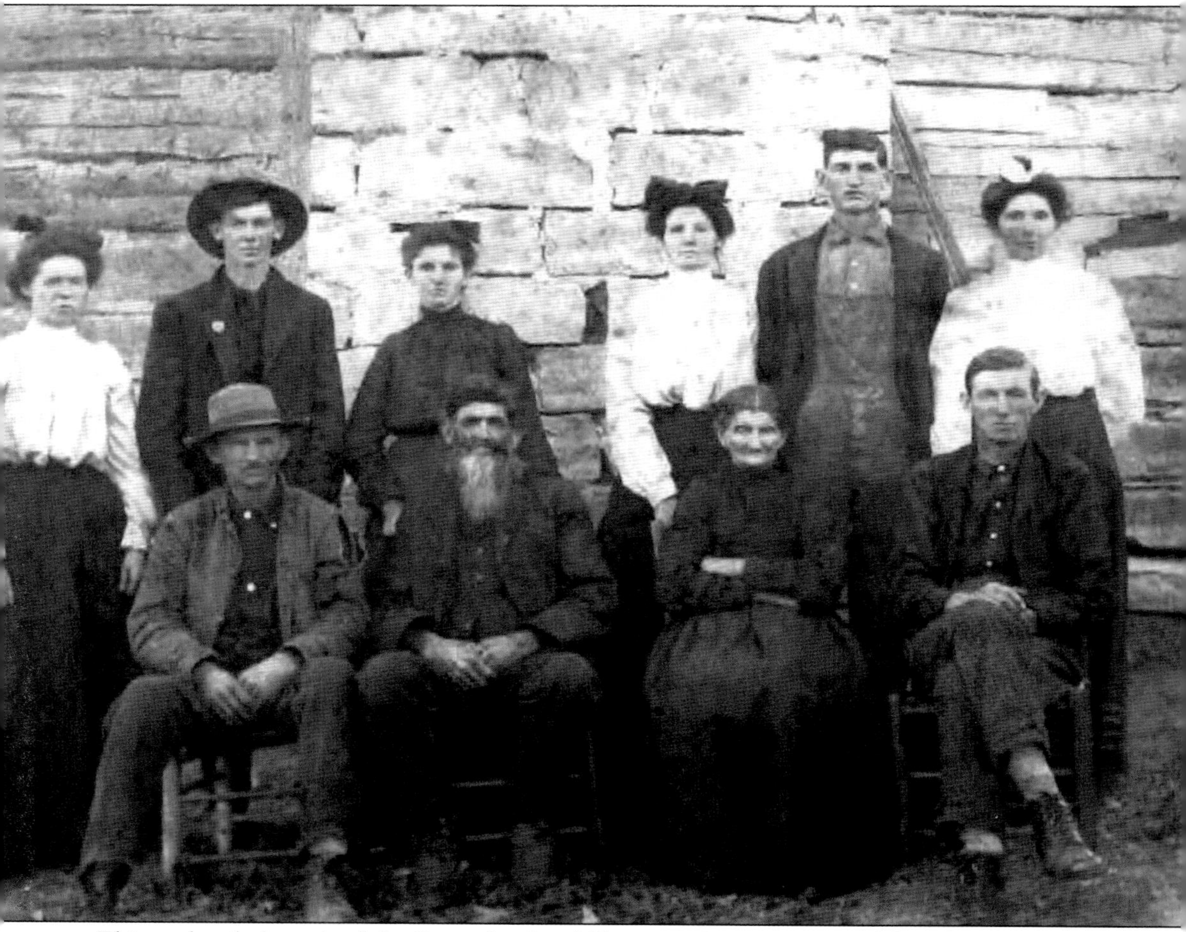

This undated photo is of the Davis family of Christian County. Pictured from left to right are: (front row) Frank Davis, Jim Davis, Mary Elizabeth (Melton) Davis, and Steve Davis; (back row) Frances (Davis) Brown, Matt Davis, Eliza Dicey (Davis) Lee, unidentified, Reuben Davis, and Margaret (Davis) Mills.

This photo, taken c. 1915, might be Mary Emily Day of Sparta on the Day family farm.

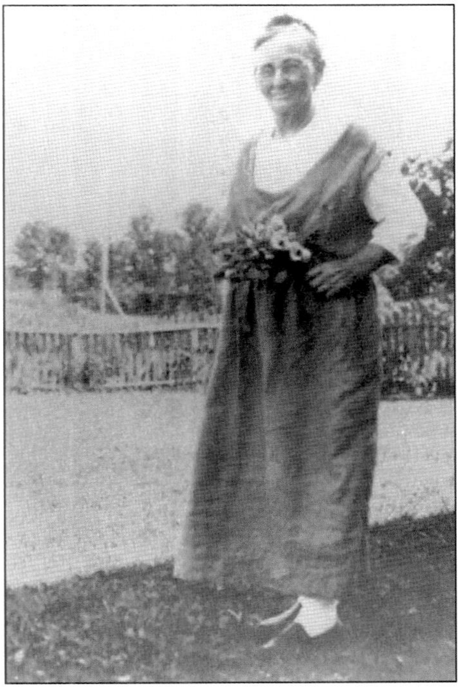

This photo shows the marriage license of Thomas Benton Day, of Sparta, and Mary E. Elderidge, of Sparta; they were married on July 25, 1877.

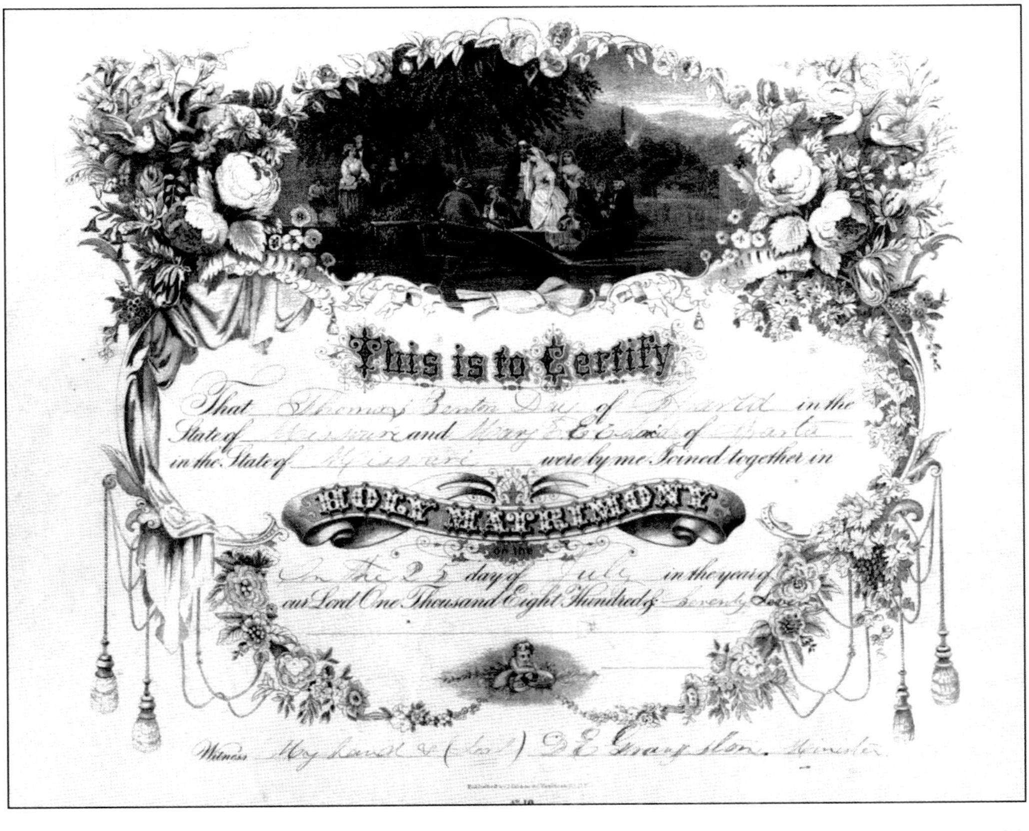

This is to Certify

That in the State of and of in the State of were by me Joined together in

HOLY MATRIMONY

on the day of in the year of our Lord One Thousand Eight Hundred &

Witness

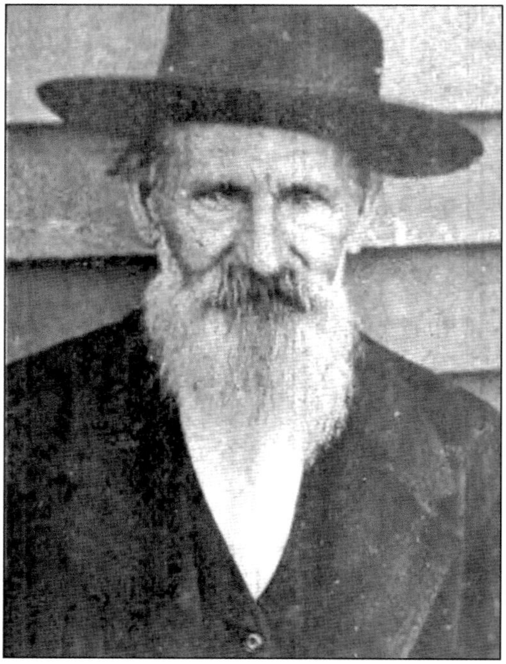

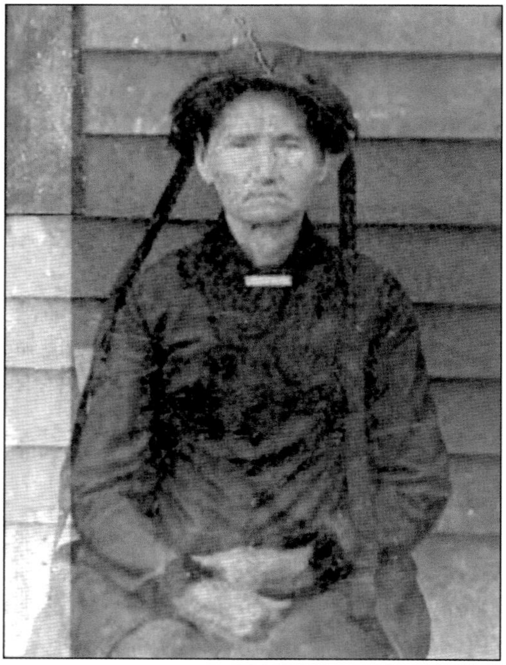

This man and woman are unknown, but for the fact that they are the first Day family who had settled in the Sparta area. The photo was taken *c.* 1900.

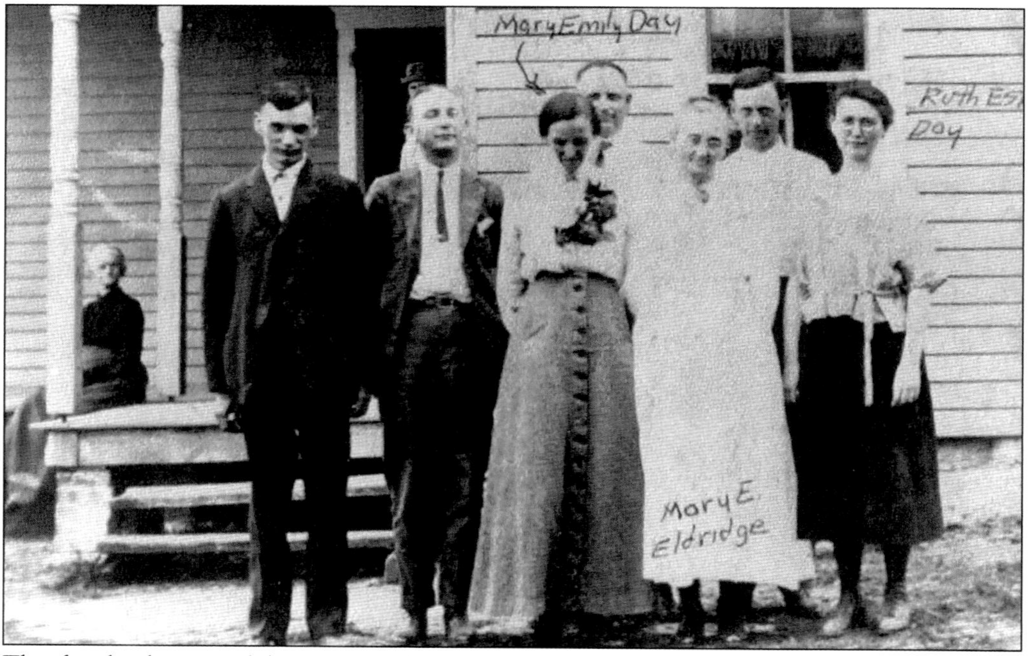

This family photo is of the Day and Eldridge families, taken in Sparta. The two men standing in back are both unknown as well as the man standing on the front porch by the door entrance and the older lady sitting on the porch. However, picture from left to right are two unknown men, Mary Emily Day, Mary E. Eldridge, and Ruth Ester Day.

Two

Prominent Nixa Families

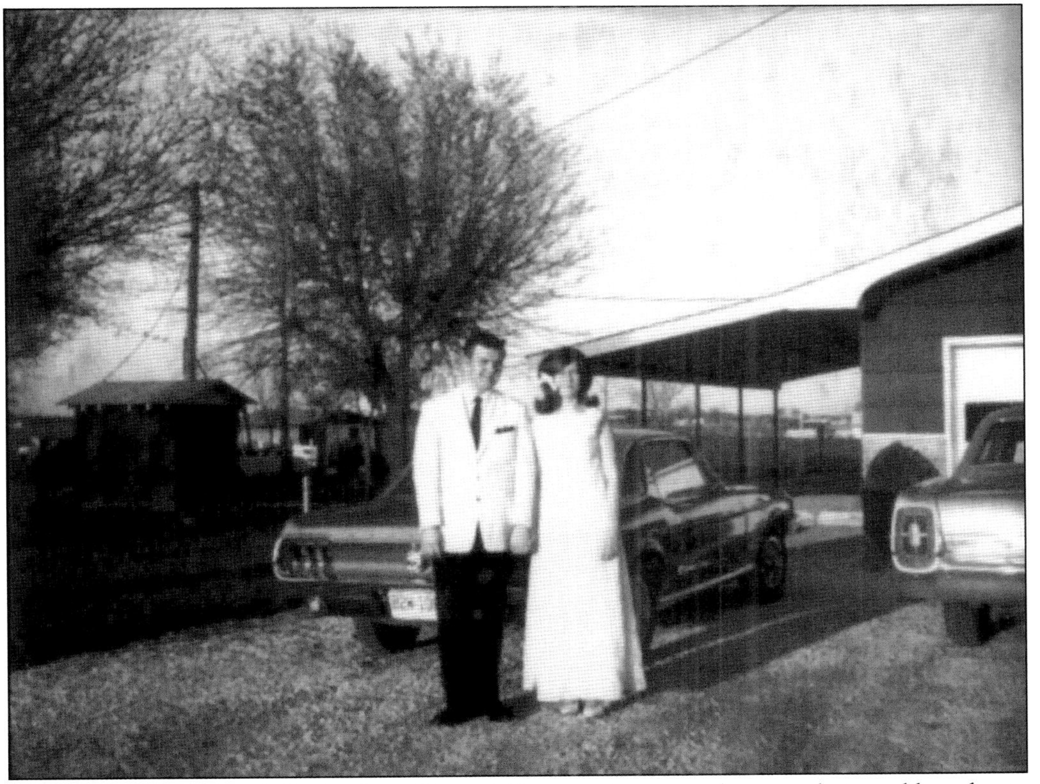

Rickey "Rick" Gene and Shirley Jean (Range) Fitzpatrick are seen here on their wedding day in February 1973 in Nixa at the home of Billy "Bill" Gene and Joretta "Jo" (Jackson) Fitzpatrick.

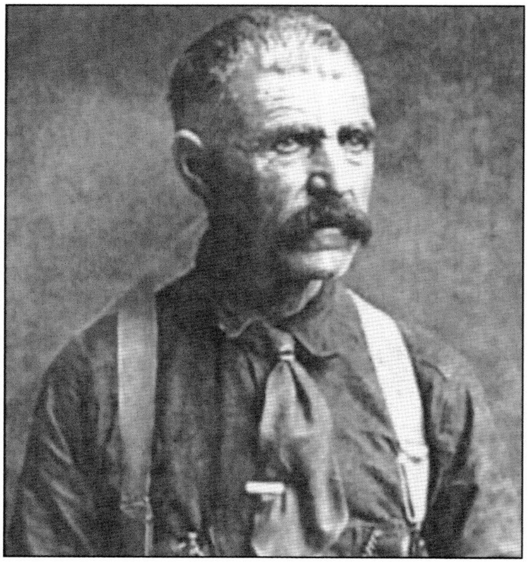

Isaac Friend sports the thick mustache that was popular in his day.

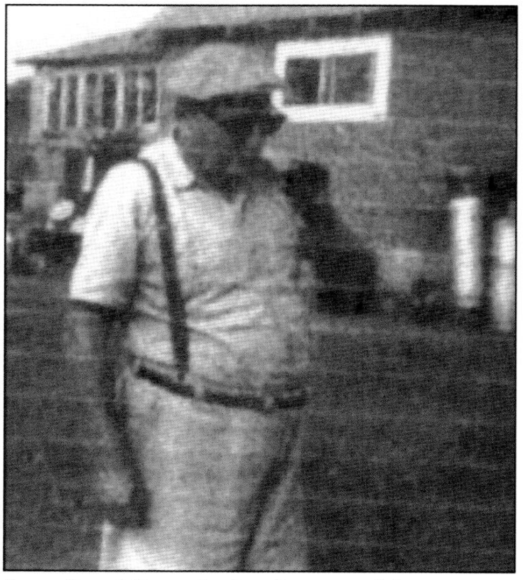

Jesse Boyd Friend, the the son of Isaac Friend, became blind at the age of 3. Jesse also played the fiddle and entertained extensively in the Ozark region. It is also said that he could tell what color a horse was by wetting his hands and touching it. Jesse was born on June 29, 1896 in Sherman, Grayson, Texas and died August 2, 1977. He married Vida Shaver.

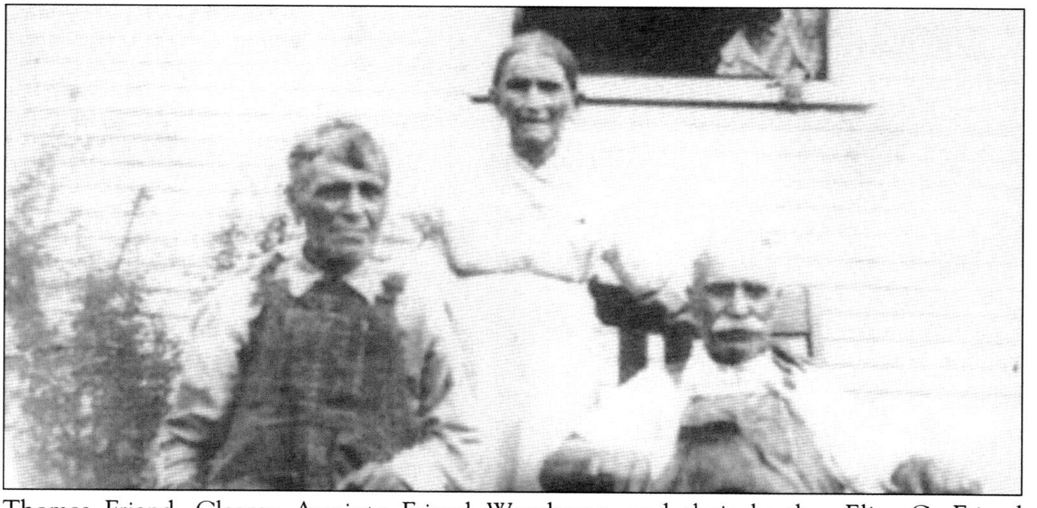

Thomas Friend, Clearcy Arminta Friend Woodrome, and their brother Elias G. Friend are pictured here. Clearcy was born on August 18, 1864 in Linden and died on February 2, 1947 in Kansas City. Elias G. Friend was born on July 27, 1858 and died January 1940. He married Isabella Tyndall, born in 1858 and died on April 4, 1941. According to one history of Springfield, Missouri, William Friend was in the battle of Tippecanoe in 1811, when the Indian Chief Tecumseh was killed. Other accounts say that Tecumseh was not at that battle, but that he died in 1813 at the Battle of the Thames in Ontario, north of Detroit.

Isaac Friend, pictured here, is the son of Reason and Elizabeth (McCarty/McCarthy) Friend. Isaac was born on June 1, 1854 and died on November 25, 1934. He was from Linden.

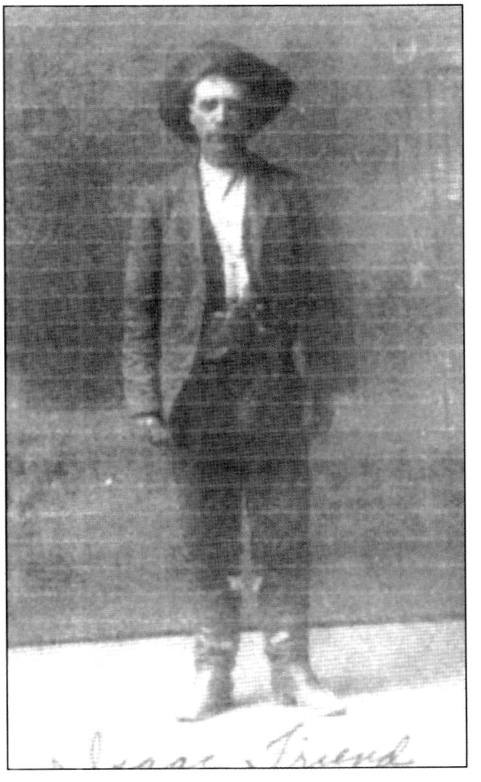

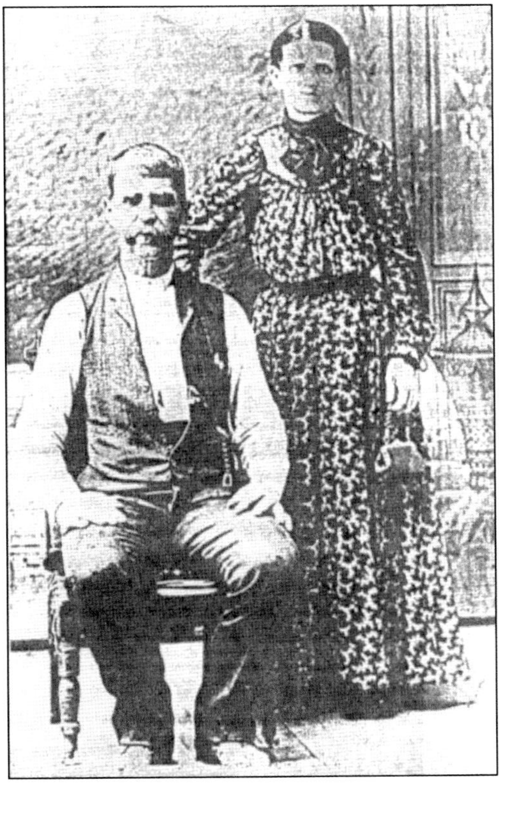

Isaac Friend is pictured here with his wife Diselizabeth (Holt) Friend standing by his side. Diselizabeth was born in Stockton, Cedar County, Missouri, on February 15, 1861 and died on April 23, 1917 in Pansy, Douglas County, Missouri, and is buried in the Goodhope Cemetery in Ava. It's believed Isaac was a mail carrier in Douglas County.

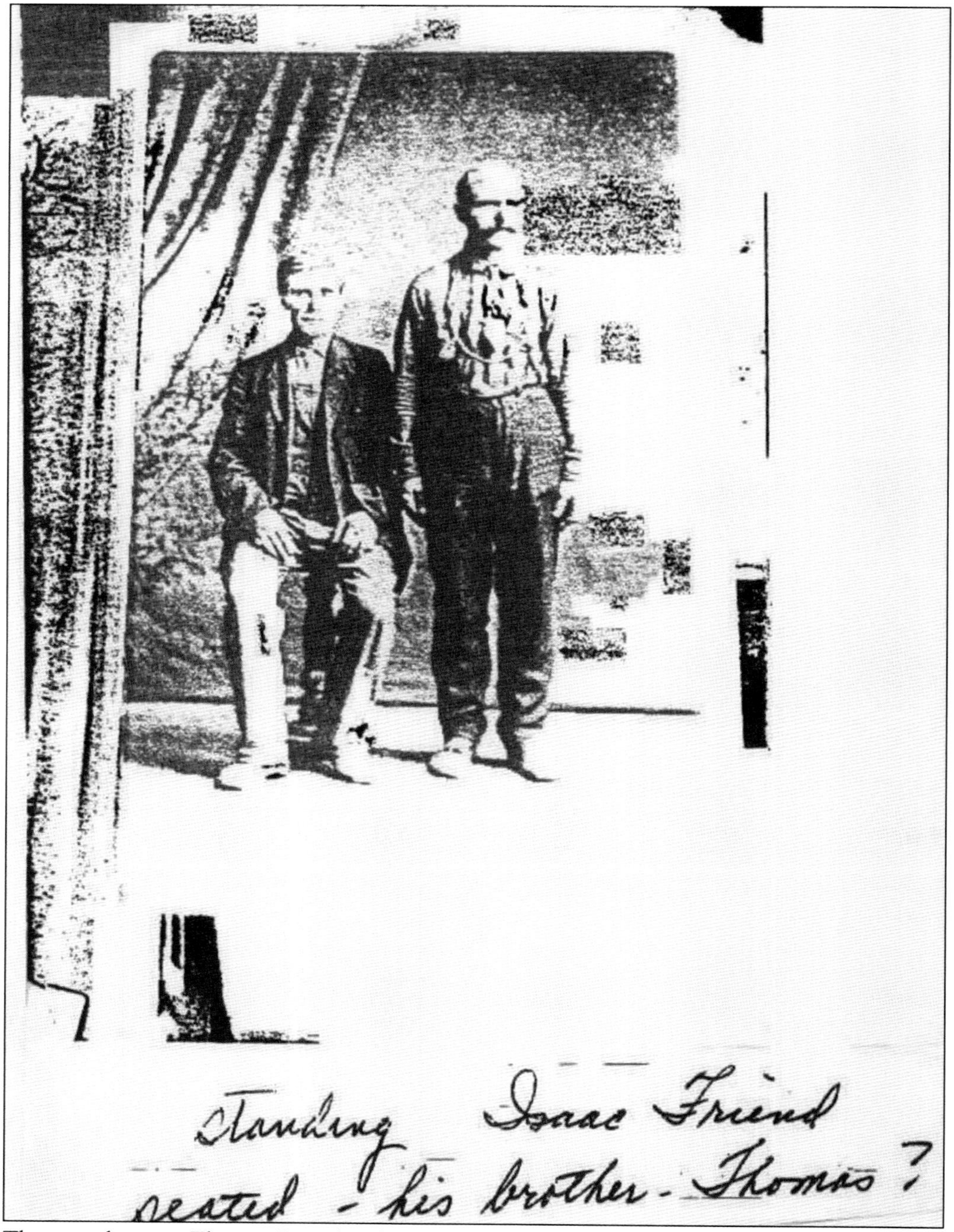

The seated man is Thomas Friend and the standing man is Isaac Friend. They were the sons of Reason Friend and Elizabeth (McCarty/McCarthy) Friend. Reason is the son of William and Elizabeth (Grimes) Friend. Isaac was born June 1, 1854 in Linden and died on November 25, 1934. He is buried in the Goodhope Cemetery in Ava, Douglas County, Missouri. Thomas was born on June 14, 1867 in Linden and died on October 13, 1954. He is buried in the Hazelwood Cemetery in Springfield, Greene County, Missouri.

Pictured here is Orlena Elizabeth Pruitt Ricketts Gooch, who was born on July 5, 1850 in Linden.

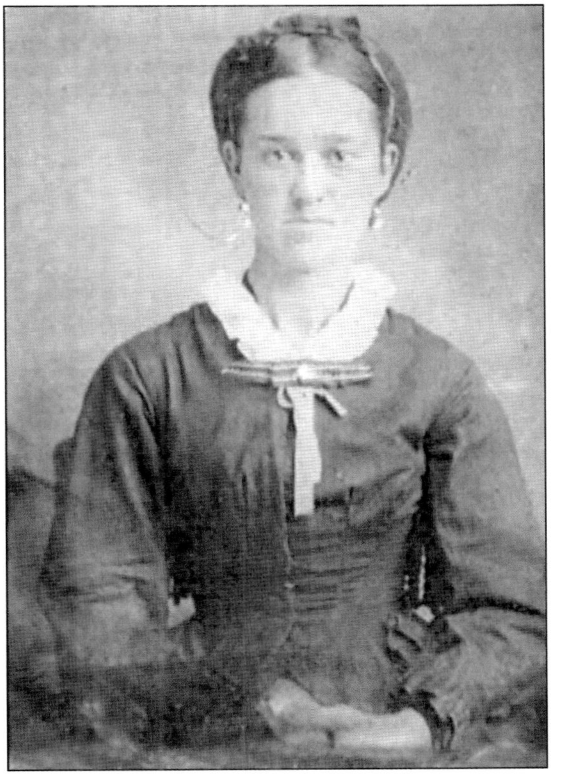

This is Joe Hall as he rested beside Sprout Spring in Nixa. Travelers in these days would stop at this spring and water their horses and themselves. The spring has withstood many changes over the years. Presently, the spring is much smaller then what it was in this photo due to Highway 14, which leads from Nixa into Ozark, and the additional building and construction that has occurred over the years.

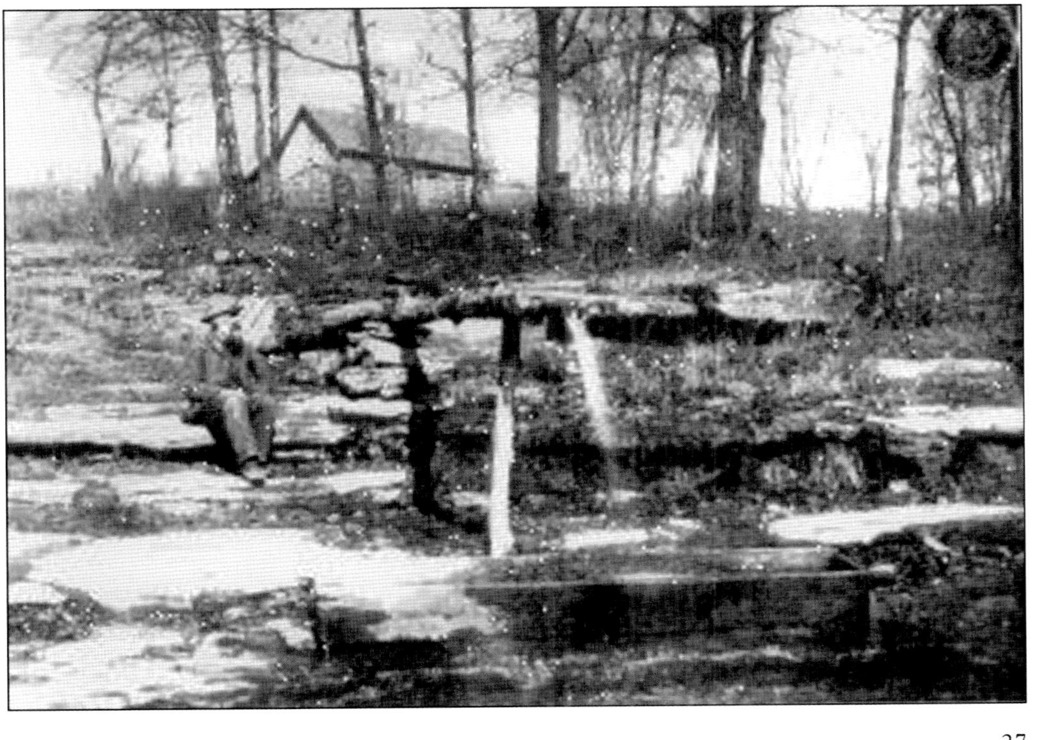

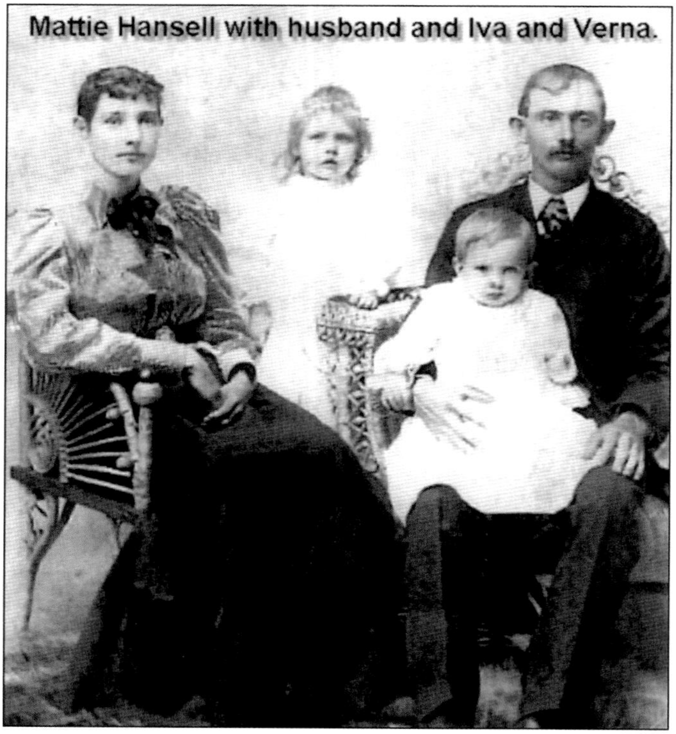

This photo shows the Hansell Family from Nixa. Pictured from left to right are Mattie (Thacker) Hansell, Iva Hansell, unidentified Hansell (husband), and the baby is Verna Hansell.

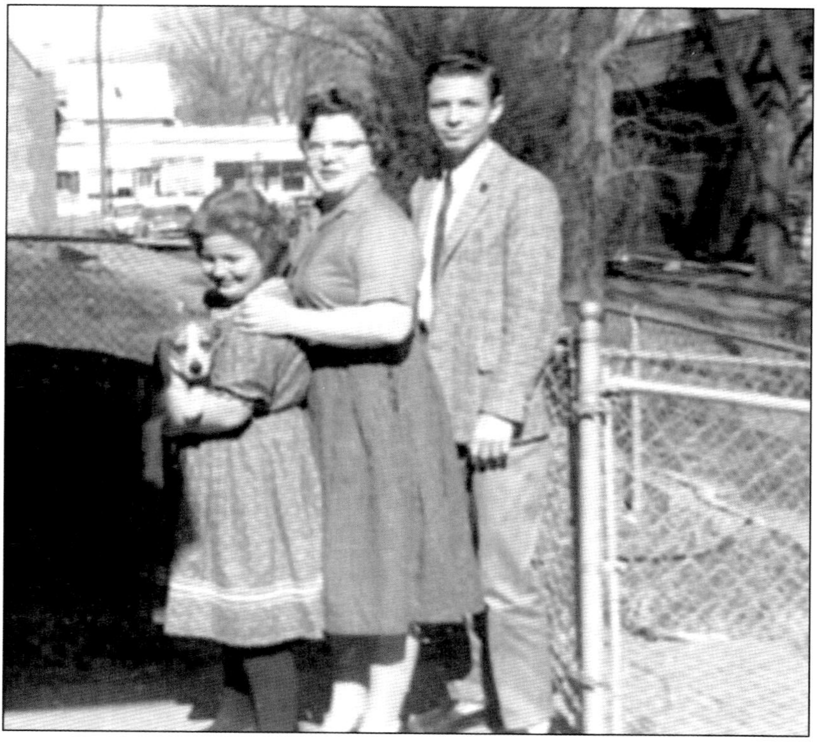

The young girl holding the puppy is believed to be Bernice Hasting and the lady is Oleta (Jackson) Hasting. The boy is unknown. Oleta is the daughter of Leota (McCafferty) and Fred Jackson. Leota was the daughter of James F. and Annahline "Ann" (Carroll) McCafferty.

Pictured from left to right are Zena Hodges, Ike Hodges, and Nettie Wisenburg of Christian County.

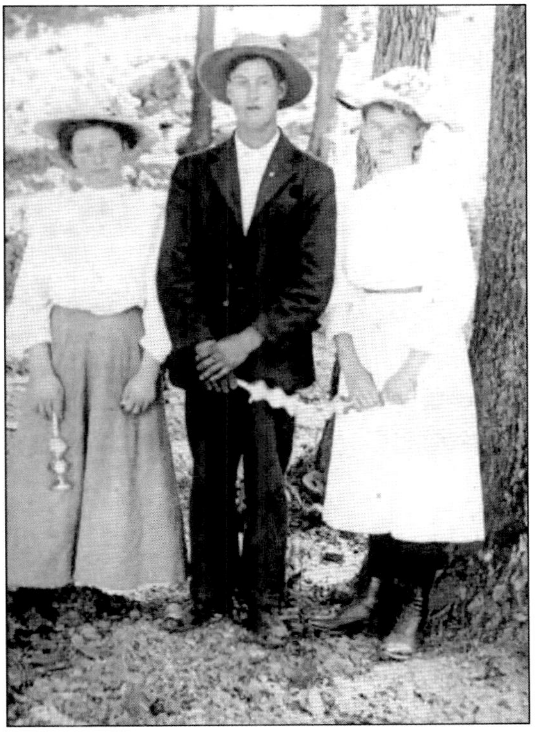

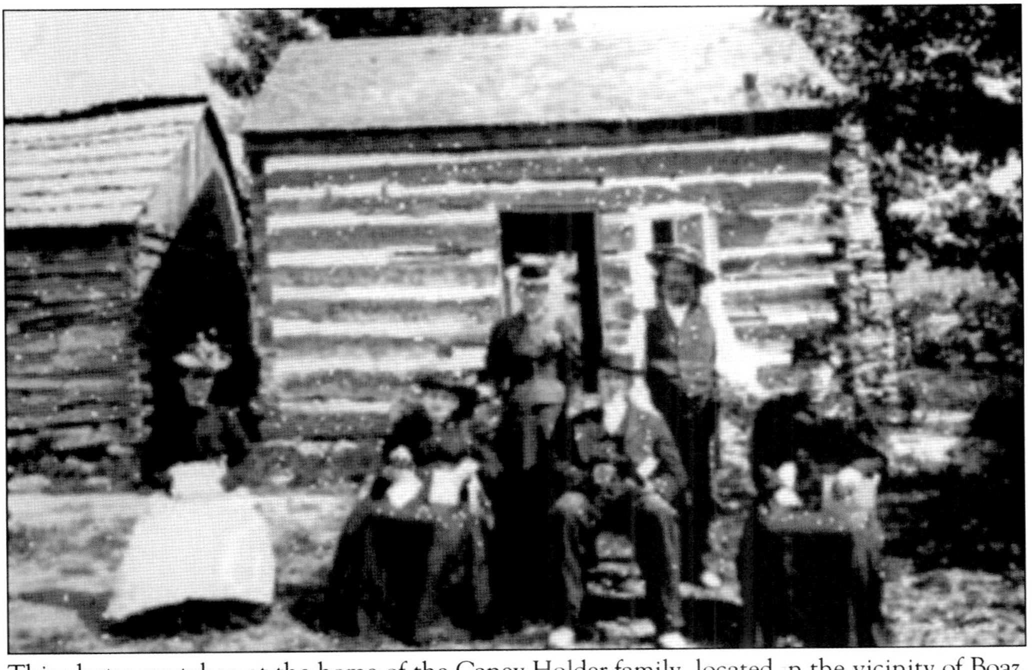

This photo was taken at the home of the Caney Holder family, located in the vicinity of Boaz, which is not far from Nixa. Caney was a veterinarian during the late 1800s. Pictured from left to right are: (front row) Mrs. George Cavenor, Becky Hatridge, Caney Holder, and Mrs. Caney Holder; (back row) Mrs. Josh Pearce and William Holder.

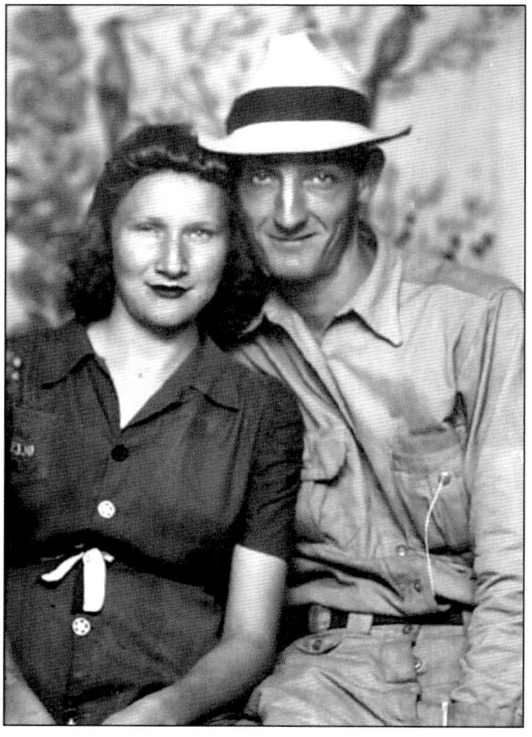

Pictured here is Marvine and her husband Jimmy Horton.

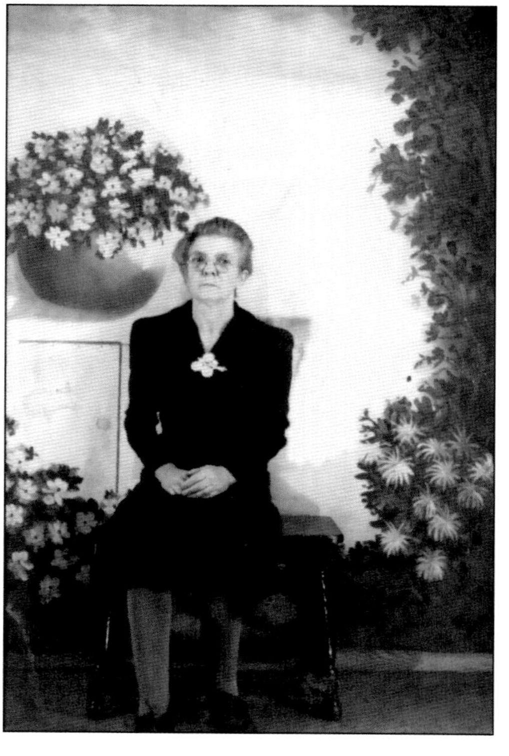

This c. 1945 photograph is of Nixa resident Martha Jane (Sparkman) Inman. Martha was the daughter of James Alexander and Ophelia Virginia (Pruitt) Sparkman and the wife of James Elkanah Inman. He was the son of John Wesley and Nancy Lavanda (Wilson) Inman.

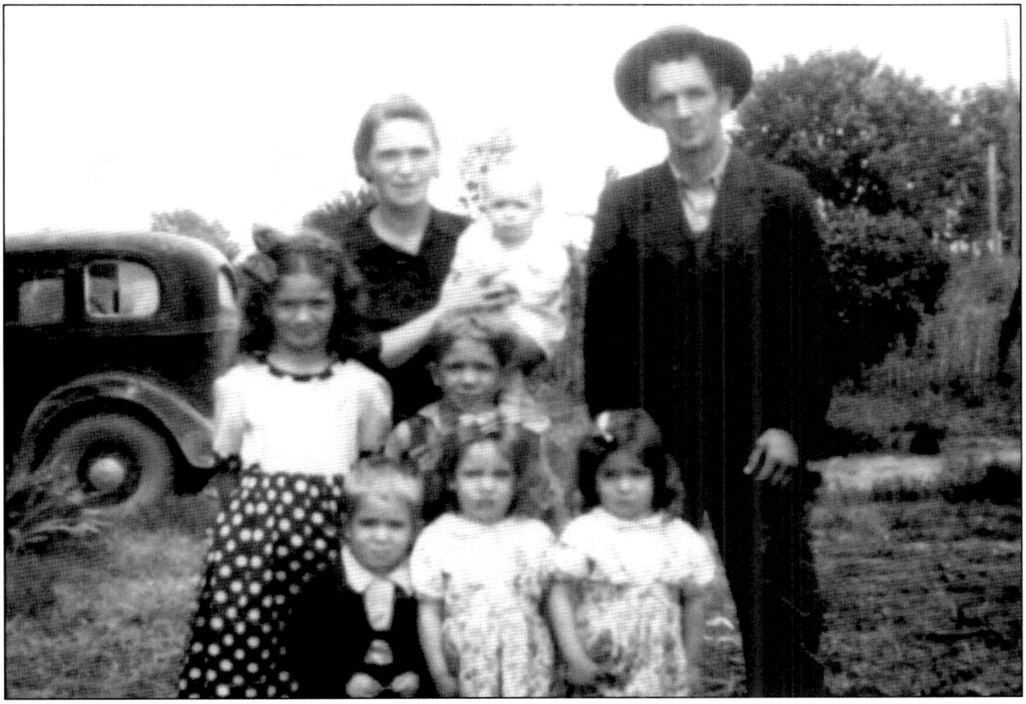

Taken *c.* 1945, this photo is of the Ira P. and Opal M. Inman family of Nixa. Pictured from left to right are: (front row) Eldon Dean Inman, Rosa Mae (Inman) Hightower and Donna Faye Inman; (second row) Mary Elizabeth Inman and Jerry Gene Inman; (back row) Opal Mae (Bolin) Inman, Nettie Lou Inman, and Ira Porter Inman.

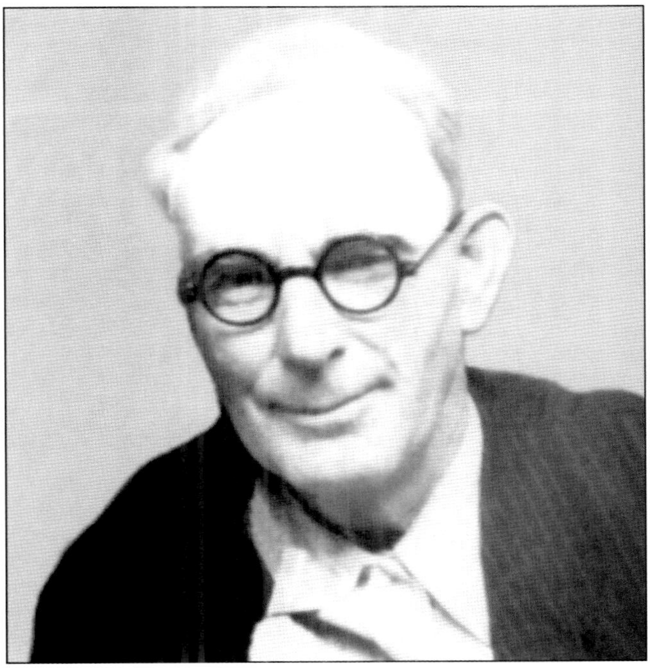

James Elkanah Inman is seen here *c.*1940 in Nixa. On his headstone, his name had been listed as James L. Inman. It was believed that James's middle name, "Elkanah," was spelled with an "L" instead of "E." As a young man, James was known as "Caney." He was the son of John Wesley and Nancy Lavanda (Wilson) Inman.

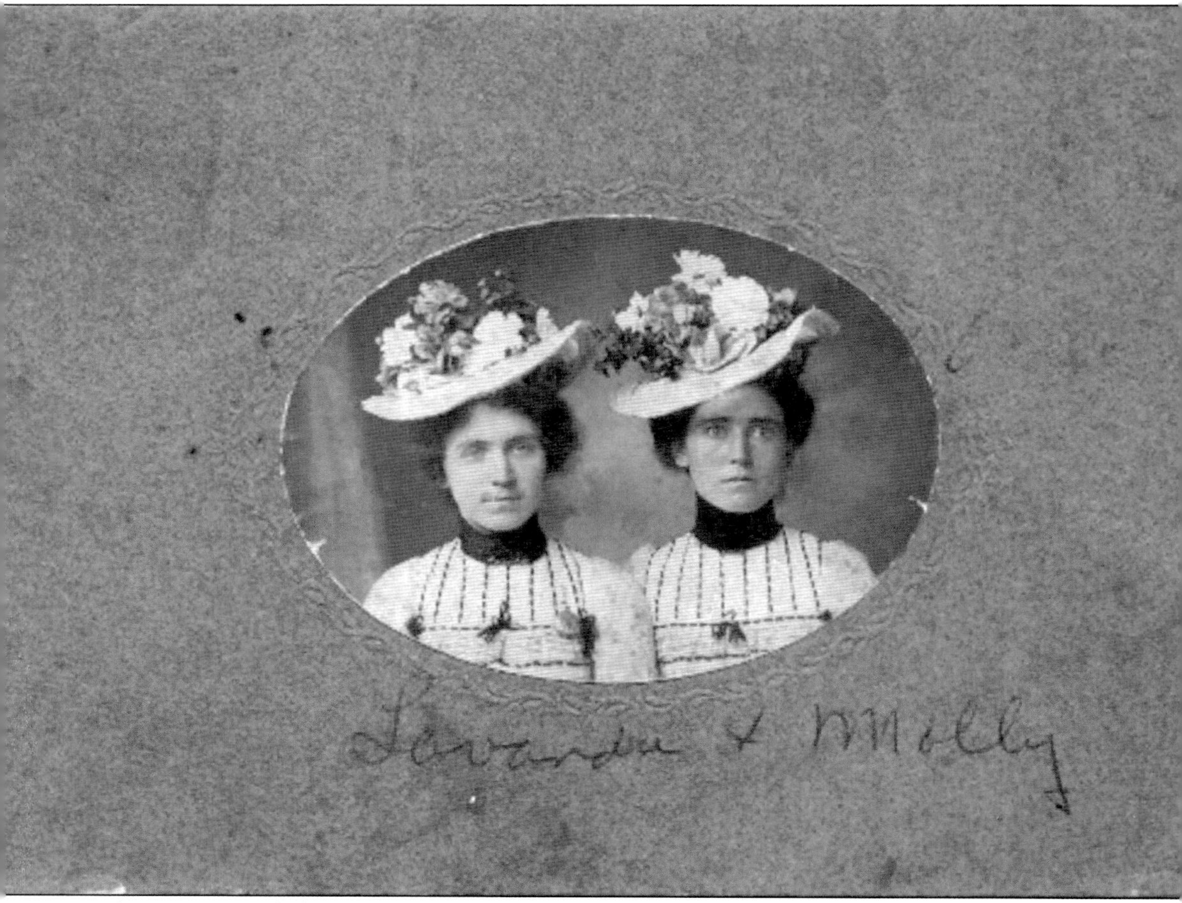

The two pretty ladies in this photo are believed to have been from the Nixa area. They are Lavanda (left) and Molly Inman. They were the daughters of Joseph Porter and Sarah Catherine (Wilson) Inman. Joseph was the brother of John Wesley Inman who was married to Nancy Lavanda Wilson. Joseph was married to Nancy's Sarah. Joseph and John were the older brothers of James L. Inman who had been married to Sarah and Nancy's sister, Mary N. (Wilson) Inman. Later, the name Inman was changed to Inmon.

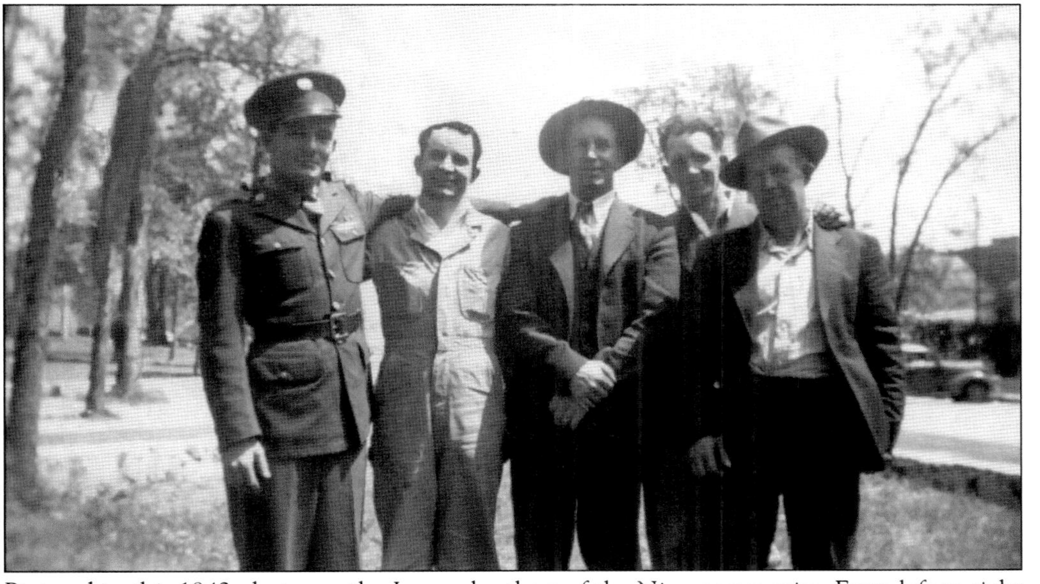

Pictured in this 1942 photo are the Inman brothers of the Nixa community. From left to right are Seth Eldon Inman, William Jack Inman, Lewis Carl Inman, and James Homer Inman. The man standing behind Lewis Carl and James Homer is Ira Porter Inman. These men are all the sons of James E. and Martha J. Inman.

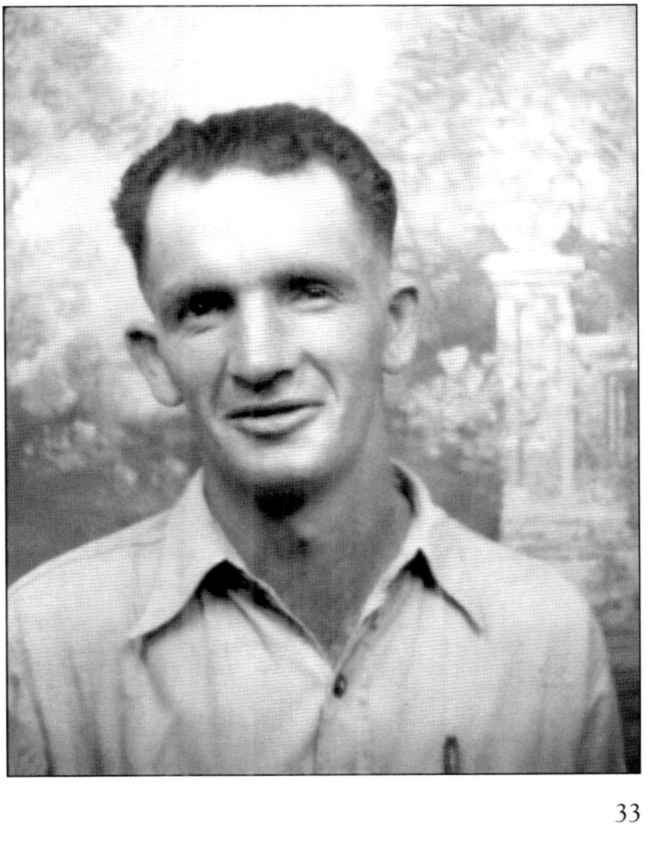

This photo of Ira Porter Inman was taken in either 1933 or 1938. Ira, from Nixa, didn't like his real name, so he decided to go by Porter Isaac Inman. After his wife's death, he had purchased a double headstone for himself and his wife and made sure his name was carved as Porter Isaac Inman, rather than his birth name—Ira Porter Inman.

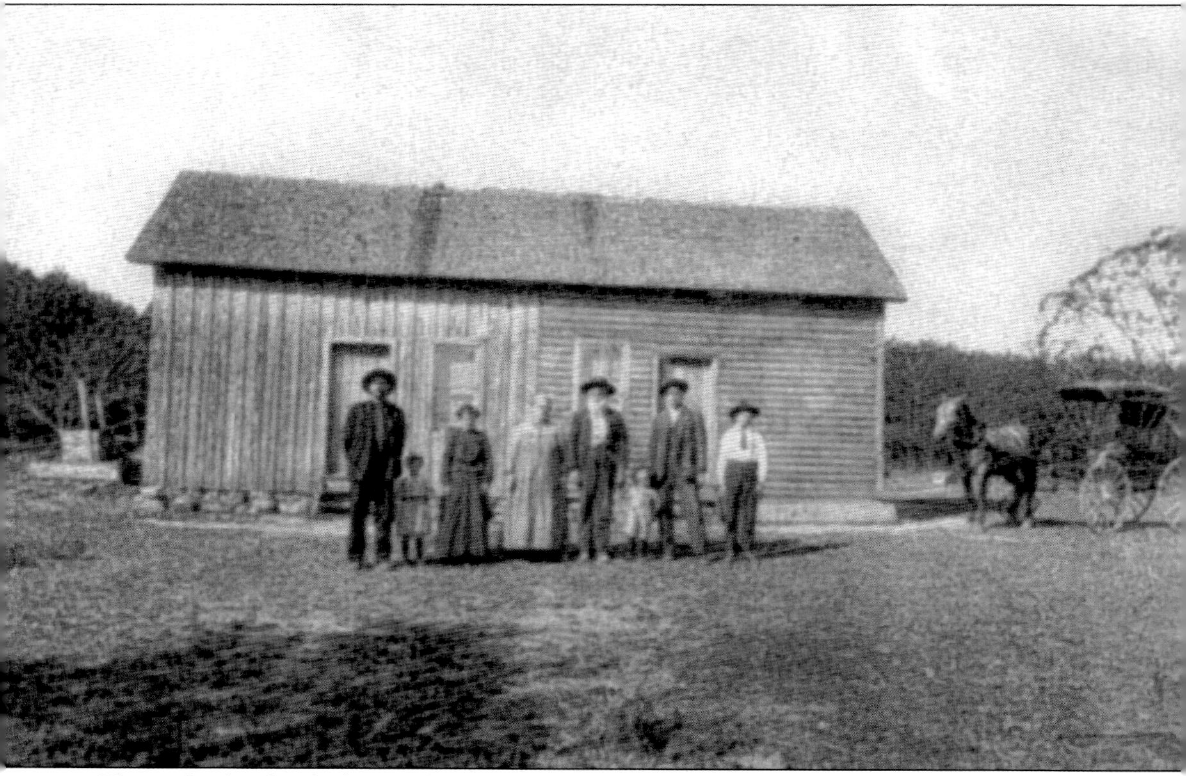

This is the family of John Wesley Inman standing in front of their homestead in Nixa. Pictured from left to right are James L. (Elkanah), Mary Frances, Martha J. (Sparkman) Inman, Nancy Lavanda (Wilson) Inman, John Wesley Inman, James Homer Inman, and William Daniel Inman. The last man is only known to be Martha's brother. Rosa Hightower said, "Elkanah and Sarah's last two children were born in Porter Township (Nixa), Christian County. Elkanah and Sarah had been living in Giles County, Tennessee in 1850, but were living in Nixa during 1860. So the house was built sometime before their son David was born. He was born in 1853 and his sister Sarah was born there in 1856." Rosa continues, "That's why I think the older people on the porch are Elkanah and Sarah and the children are three of their children, but I don't know which ones. And if I'm right about this, then, the elderly lady on the right has to be Elkanah's mother, Martha (Wilson) Inman."

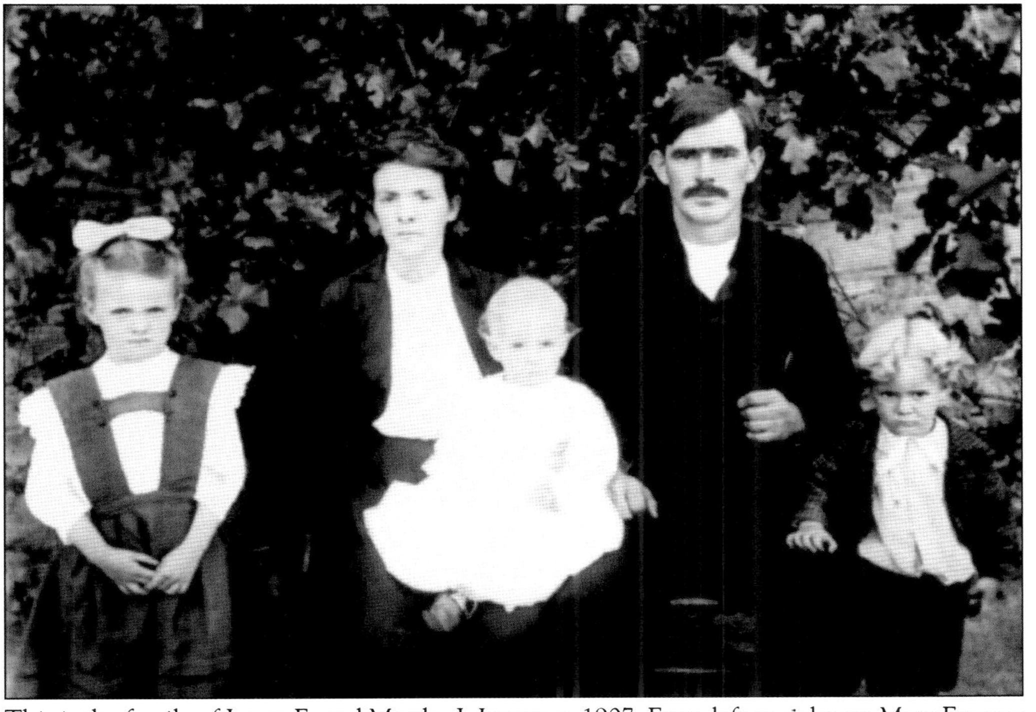

This is the family of James E. and Martha J. Inman *c.* 1907. From left to right are Mary Frances Inman, Martha Jane Inman, Florence Elizabeth Inman, James E. Inman, and James Homer Inman. Mary married Alva R. Young, Florence married Harvey Jones, and James Homer married Laura M. Norman.

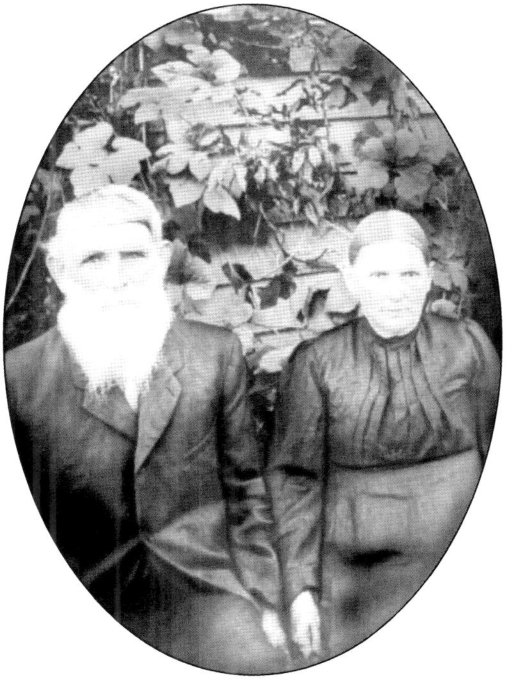

John Wesley and Nancy Lavanda (Wilson) Inman of Nixa were the great-grandparents of Rosa Hightower.

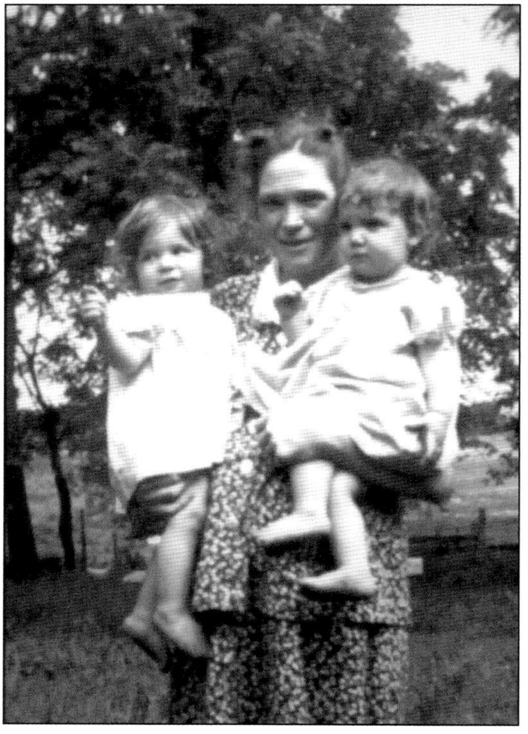

This is Opal Mae (Bolin) Inman holding her beautiful twin girls. Donna Faye Inman is on the left side and Rosa Mae Inman is on the right of Opal.

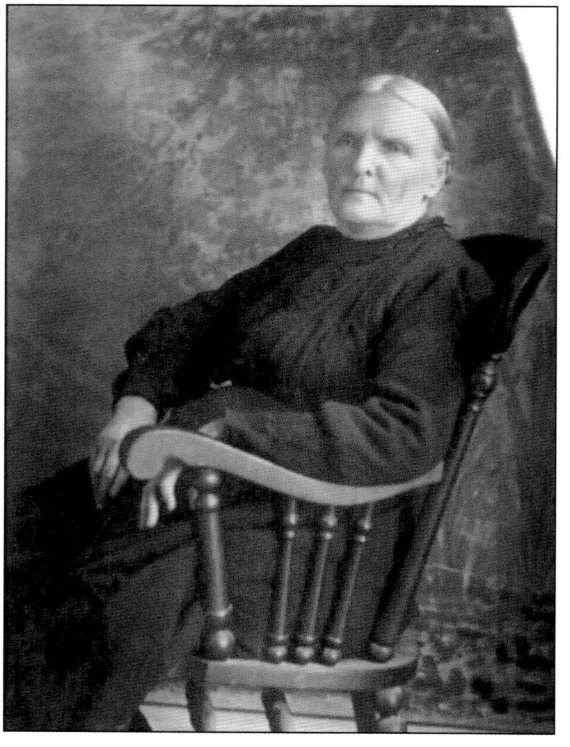

Mary N. (Wilson) Inman was the wife of James L. Inman, who was the brother to Joseph Porter and John Wesley Inman. James, Joseph, and John Inman are all sons of Elkanah D. and Sarah (Moore) Inman.

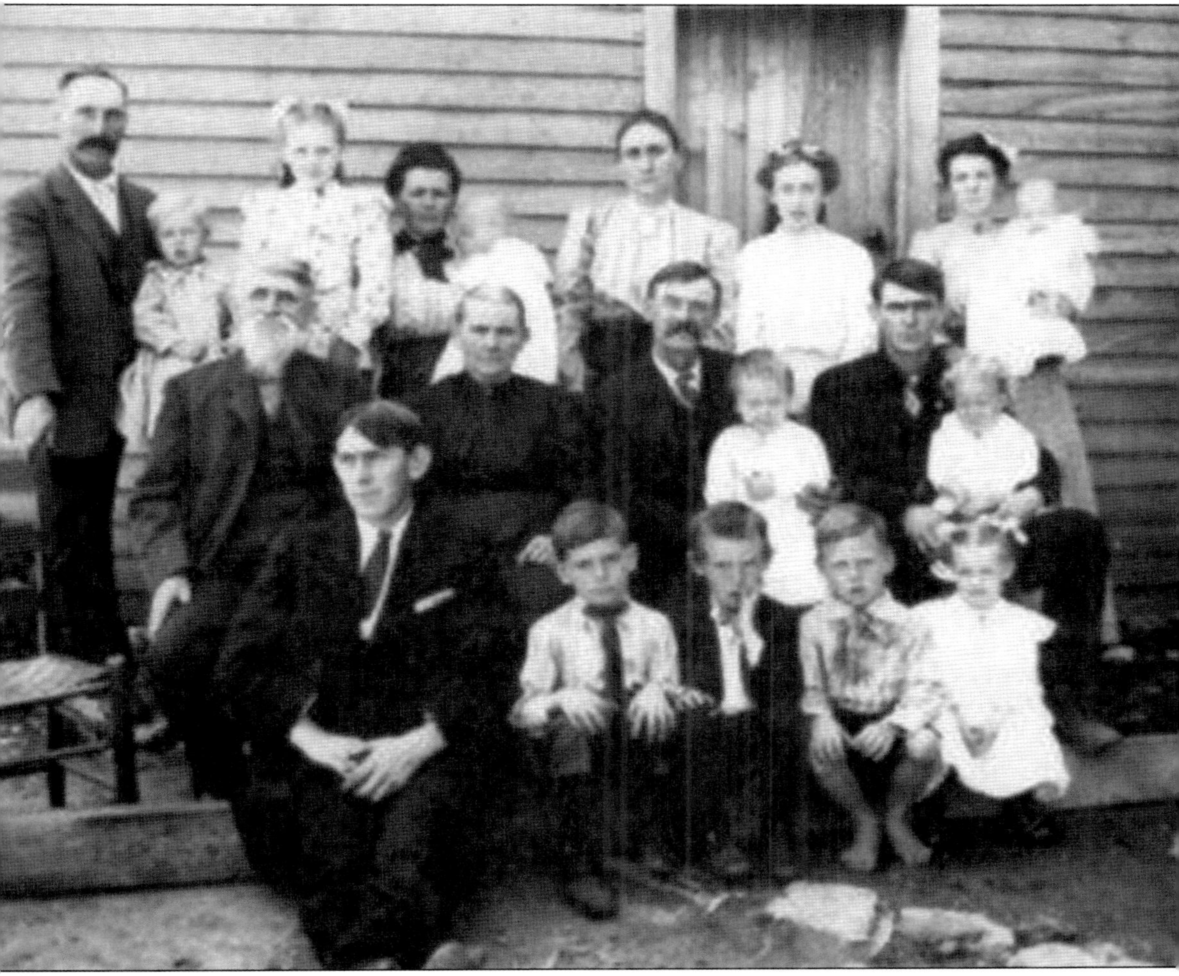

This is the family of John Wesley and Nancy Lavanda (Wilson) Inman. Picture from left to right are: (front row) William D. Inman, Robert Inman, Charles G. Love, George Inman, and Mary Frances Inman; (middle row) John W. Inman, Nancy Inman, Louis F. Inman, John W. Love (the baby), James Inman, and James Homer Inman (the baby); (top row) Finley G. Inman, Lonnie E. Inman (the baby), Grace Inman, Mary Alice (Dewitt) Inman, Fred Inman (the baby), Sara Love, Cora L. Love, Martha Jane Inman, and Florence Inman (the baby).

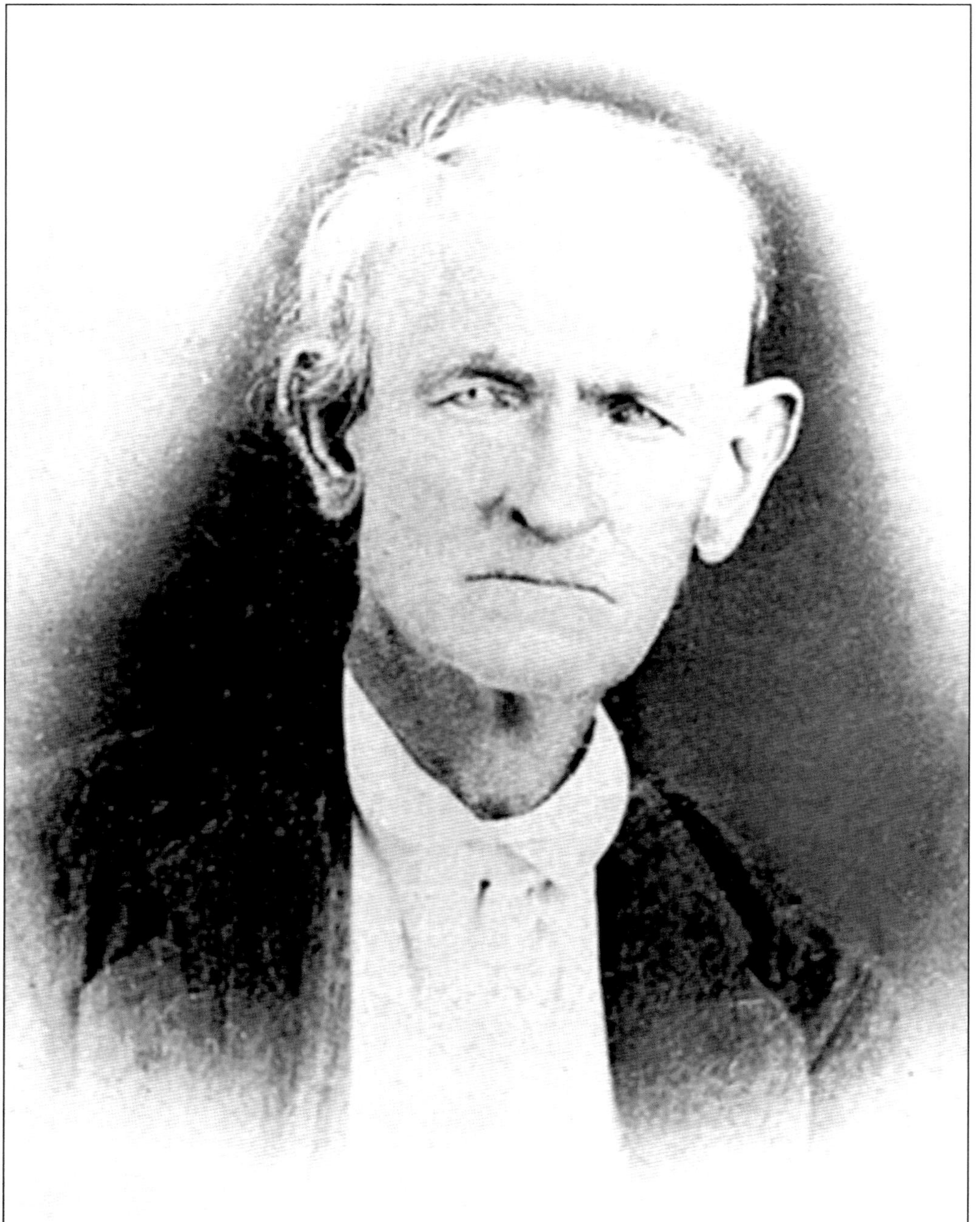

David Alexander Inman was born on September 25, 1796. He married Elizabeth J. Karns around 1828. David and Elizabeth had eleven children. He died on August 6, 1892.

Nicholas Alexander Inman was born on December 17, 1831, in Monroe County, Tennessee. He was the son of David Alexander and Elizabeth J. (Karns) Inman. Nicholas was the second child in a family of eleven children. He came to Nixa and set up a blacksmith shop. In 1860, Nicholas went into the service and served during the Civil War. On March 5, 1863 he married Mary Jane (Roberts) Inman. They had nine children, five girls and four boys. He died on February 5, 1901 in Nixa. This photo was taken *c.* 1865.

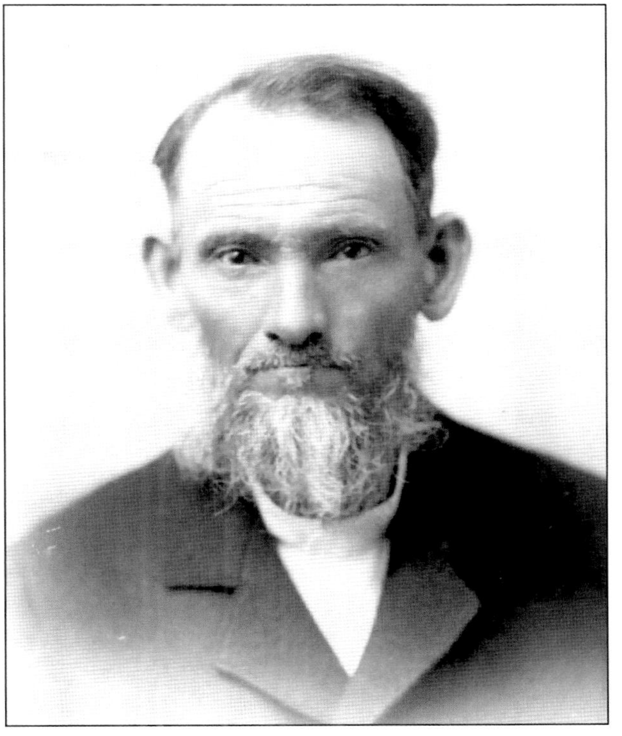

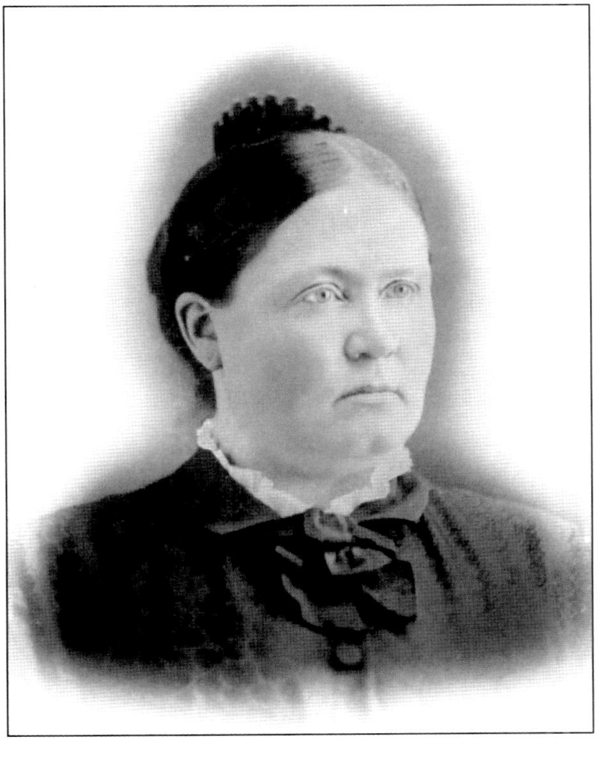

Mary Jane (Roberts) Inman was born on January 21, 1842 in Macon County, Missouri, and was married to Nicholas Alexander Inman on March 5, 1863. She died on February 11, 1893 in Nixa. This photo was taken *c.* 1865.

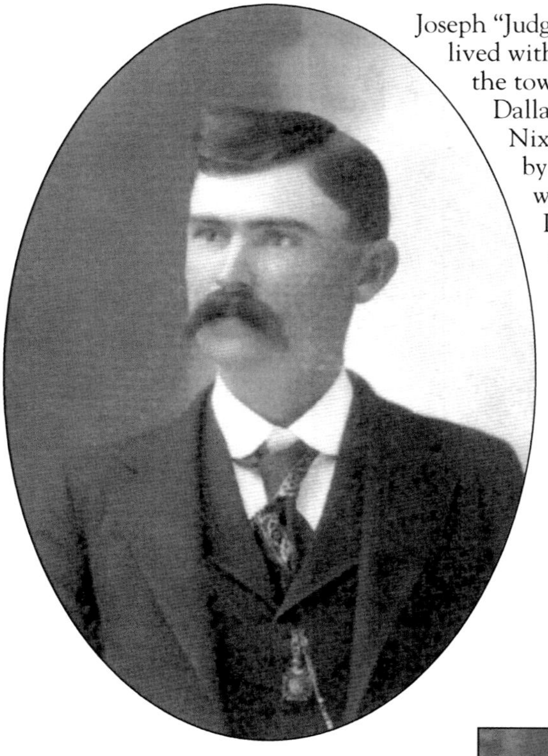

Joseph "Judge J.P." Peter Inman was a judge who lived with his wife, Maggie C. (Ward) Inman, in the town of Texline, Texas, the county seat of Dallam County. He was a former resident of Nixa. He later died due to injuries sustained by a kick to his head by a horse. Judge J.P. was born on December 22, 1864 in Nixa. Later, around 1904, he remarried Catherine (Obrate) Inman. He died on June 10, 1919 in Dalhart, Dallam County, Texas. This photo was taken *c.* 1894.

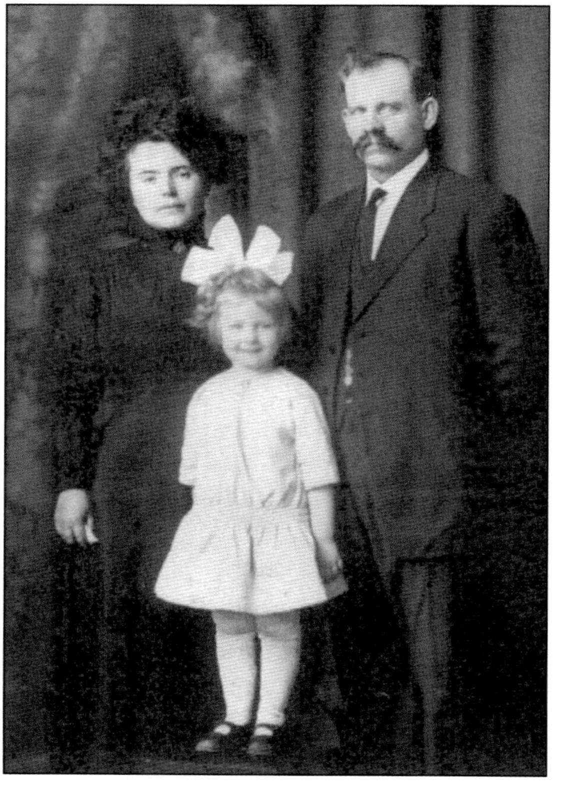

John David Inman was born on September 19, 1907. He married Doris Ethel Rees. According to the "Descendants of Nicholas Alexander Inman," provided by Fred Winston Inman, "The whereabouts of John David in 1910 are unknown at this time. He may have been in Texas since he and Doris were married there. His wife, Doris Ethel, was living at home with her parents. She was listed as being married for two years and having one child. The child was not living with her or her parents. Doris E. Inman was listed as Ethel Inman in the household of her parents." He died in January of 1937, in Nixa. This photo was taken *c.* 1930.

William Neal Inman was born on December 12, 1882 in Nixa. He married Christine Vivian (Wasson) Inman. William was a farmer and his wife was a teacher, who taught school for four years. William and Christine were married on May 1, 1908. William died on October 22, 1981 in Nixa. This photo was taken *c*. 1912.

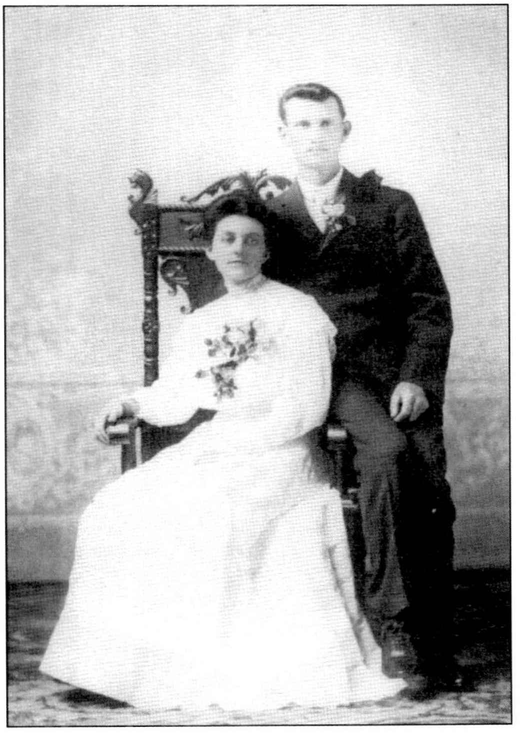

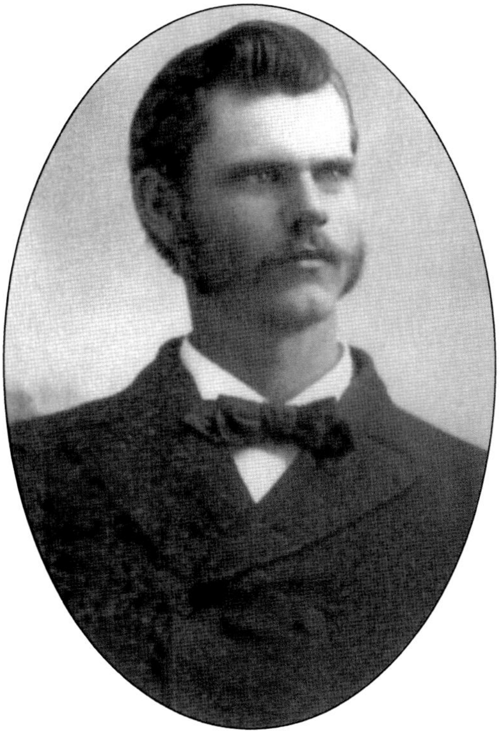

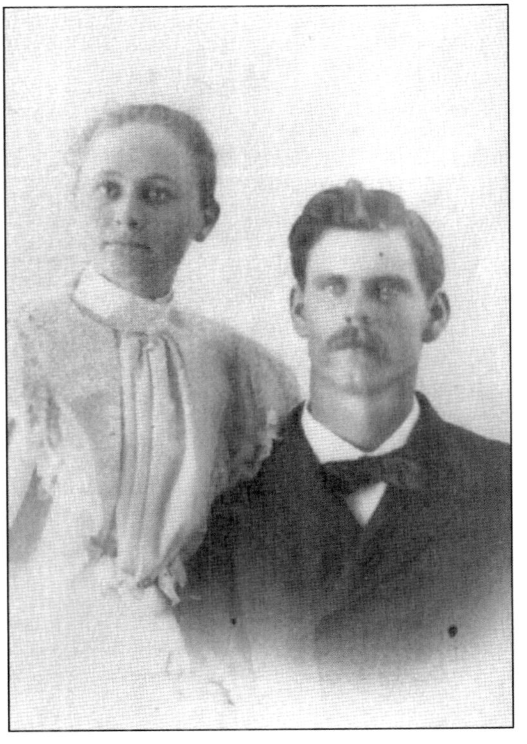

The two photos here show Fredrick Wilson Inman, by himself (top right), and with his wife (top left) Mary E. Nicolas. Mary was a long time schoolteacher who taught at the Berea School in Nixa. Fredrick Wilson Inman, another son of Nicholas Alexander and Mary Jane (Roberts) Inman, was born on September 18, 1873 in Nixa. He married Mary E. Nicholas on December 9, 1896. Fredrick died on August 28, 1902 in Sparta, Christian County, Missouri. This photo was taken *c*. 1898.

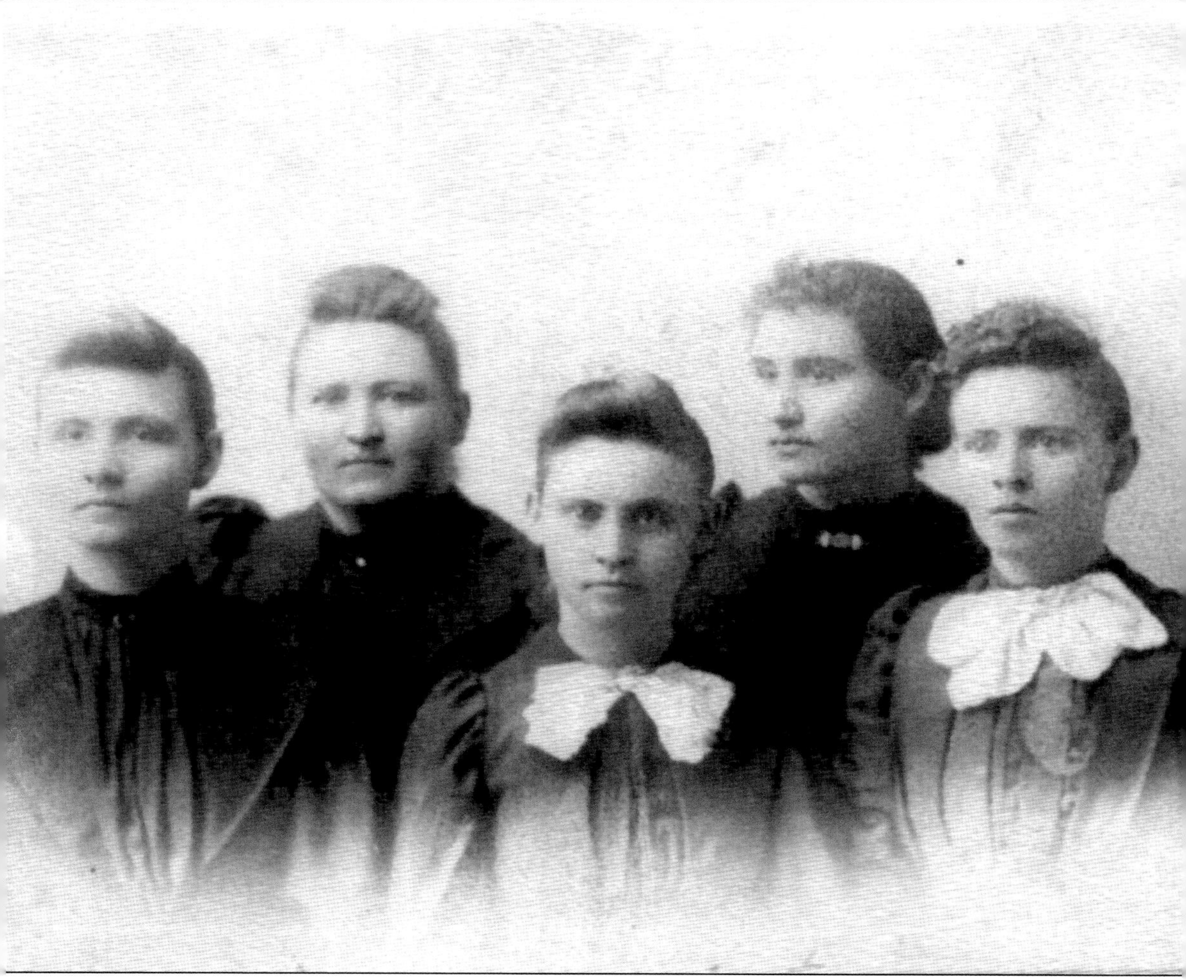

Pictured in this *c.* 1890s photo are the daughters of Nicholas Alexander and Mary Jane (Roberts) Inman. Pictured from left to right are: (front row) Martha Ann (Inman) Huston, Letha Myrtle (Inman) Rees, and Florence Celia (Inman) Parsons; (back row) Mary Frances (Inman) Ward and Nancy Elizabeth (Inman) Crow.

Three

Life in Rural Christian County

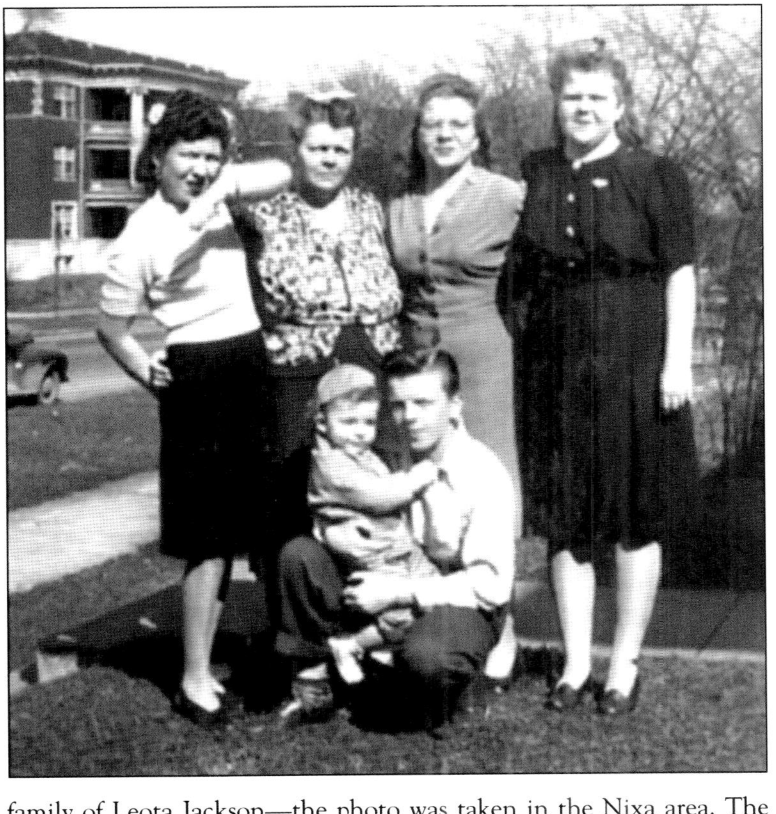

This is the family of Leota Jackson—the photo was taken in the Nixa area. The two people in front are Richard Stine (left) and Orville Jackson. Pictured in the back row, from left to right, are Thelma Jackson, Leota (McCafferty) Jackson, Oleta (Jackson) Hasting, and Olene (Jackson) Couch. Leota Jackson is the daughter of Annahline "Ann" (Carroll) McCafferty. Richard is Olene's son.

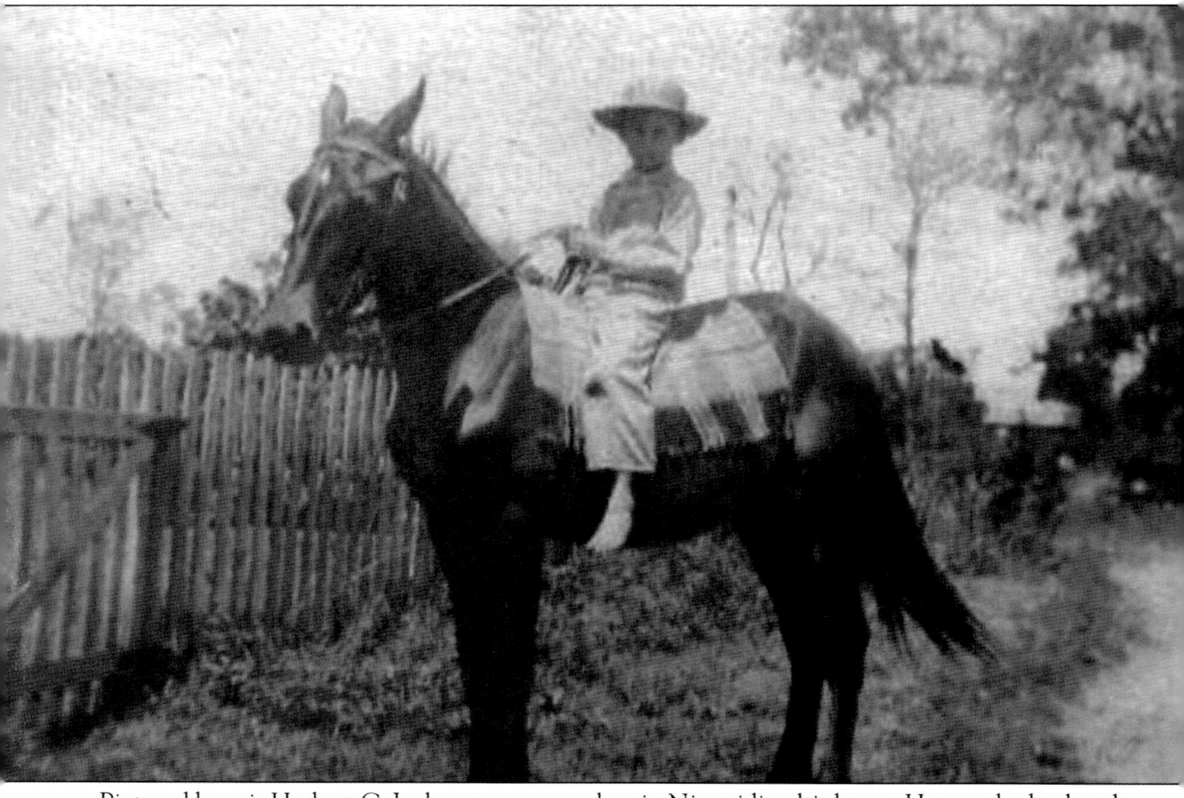

Pictured here is Herbert C. Jackson as a young boy in Nixa riding his horse. He was the husband of Hester Ann (Aven) Jackson and father to Billy "Bill" Gene Fitzpatrick. The date of the photograph is unknown.

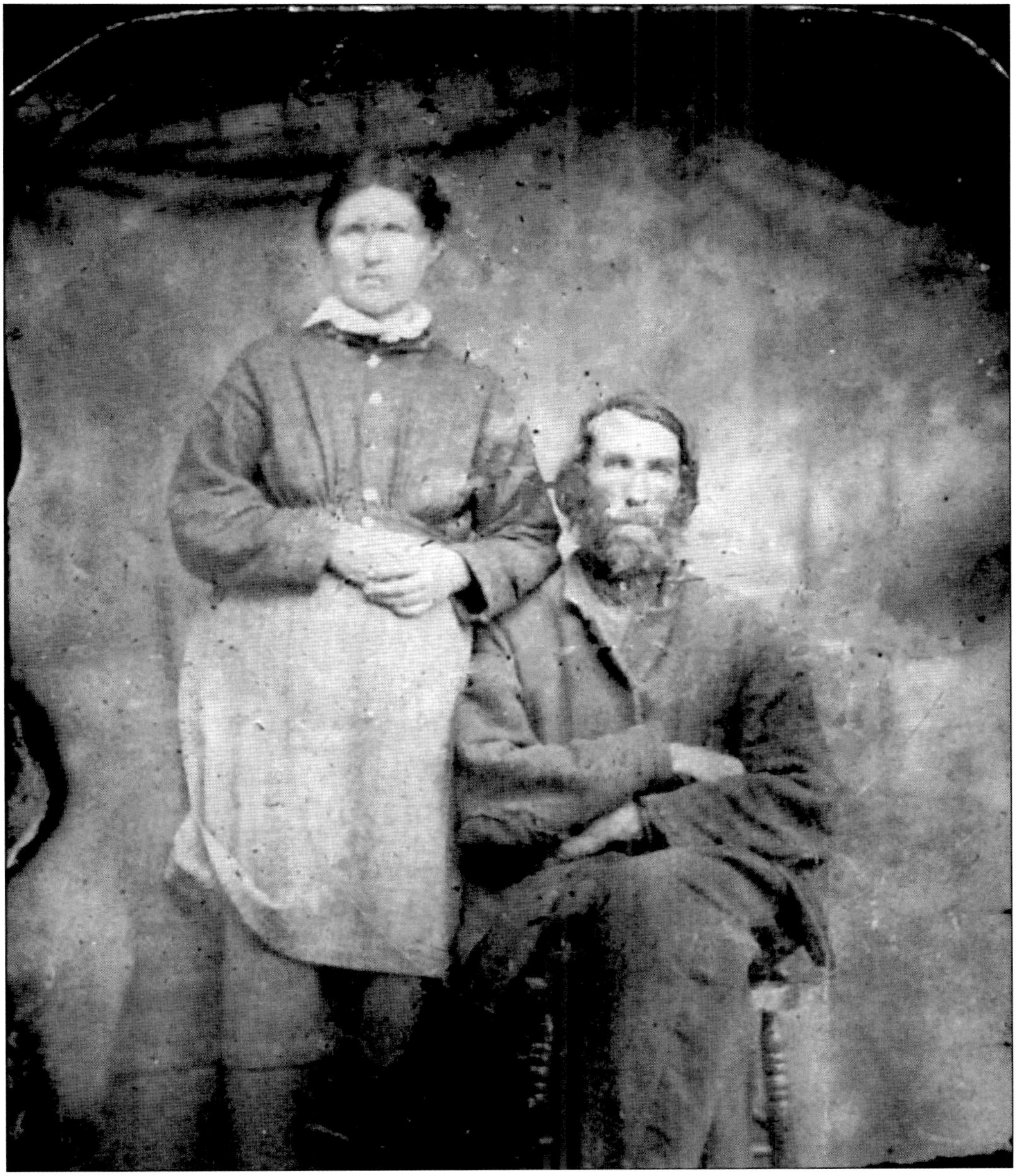

This couple is James "Jim" F. and Minerva (Hedgpeth) Johnson. Jim was born on January 18, 1833 and died on December 30, 1894. Minerva was born on February 11, 1840 and died on January 25, 1903. They both are from Sparta and are buried in the Shipman Cemetery. According to the 1850 census, James was in Greene County, Missouri, living with his parents and was married to Minerva in the 1860. James and his family are early pioneers of Christian County.

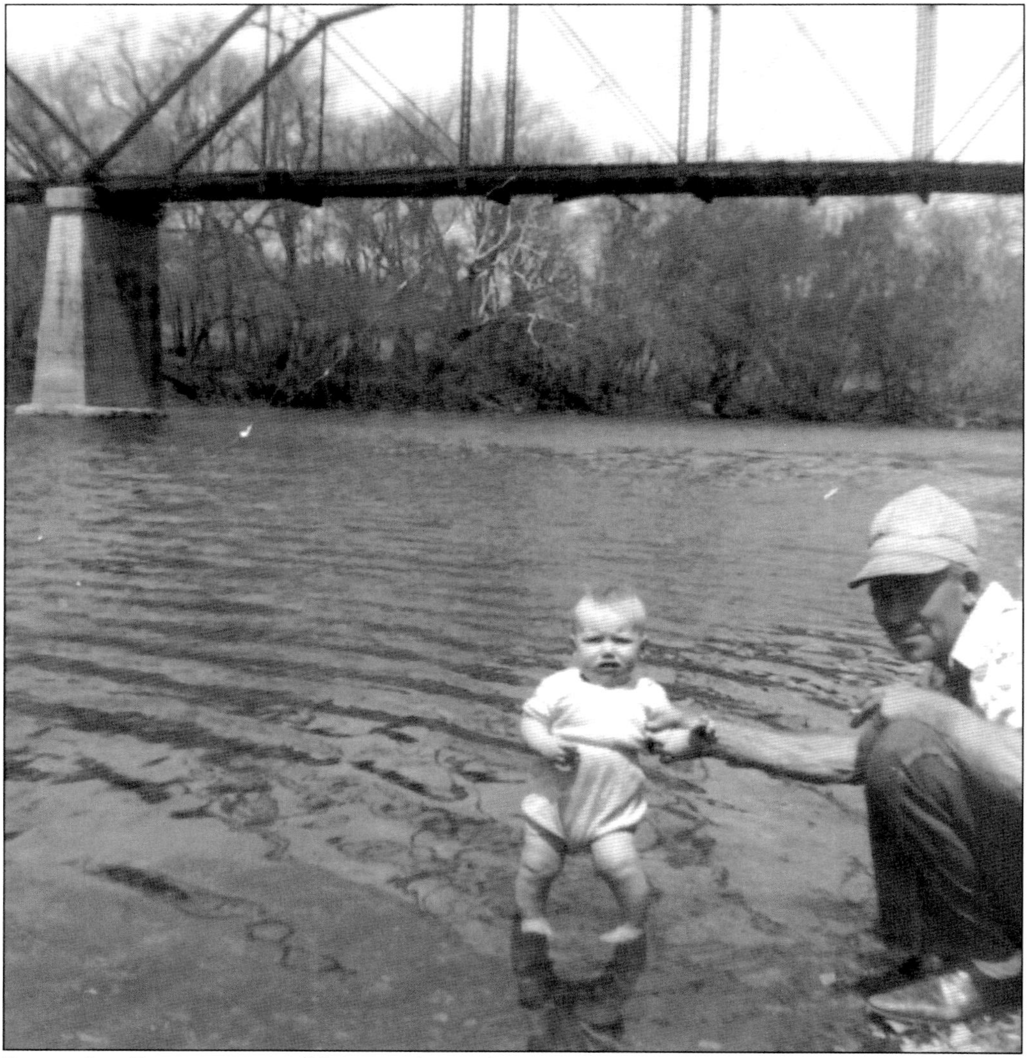

Steven Lee Jones is pictured here at the Finley River with his father James "Homer" Jones of Christian County.

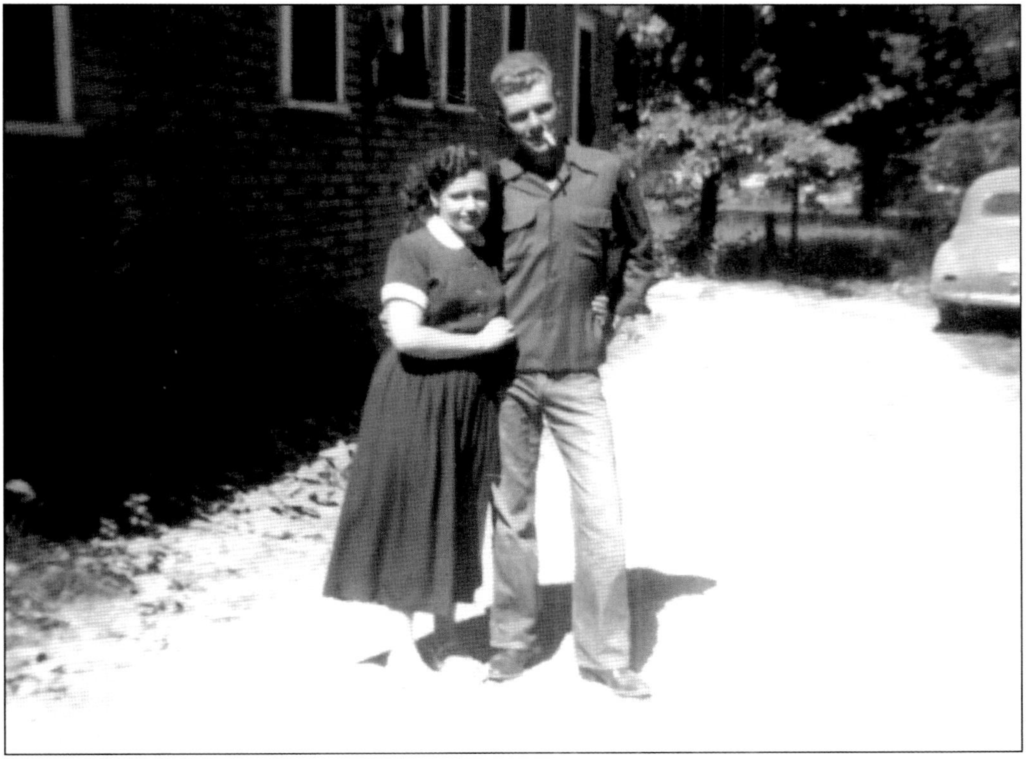

Lester Lee and Alta "Nadine" (Smith) Jones lived in Christian County.

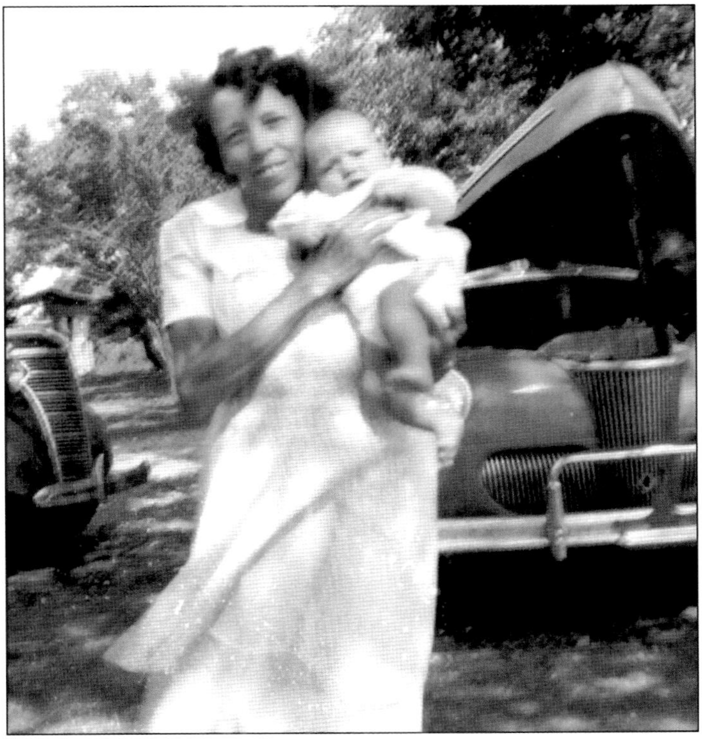

Another Christian County couple was Lorena (Hayes) Jones and Steven Lee Jones.

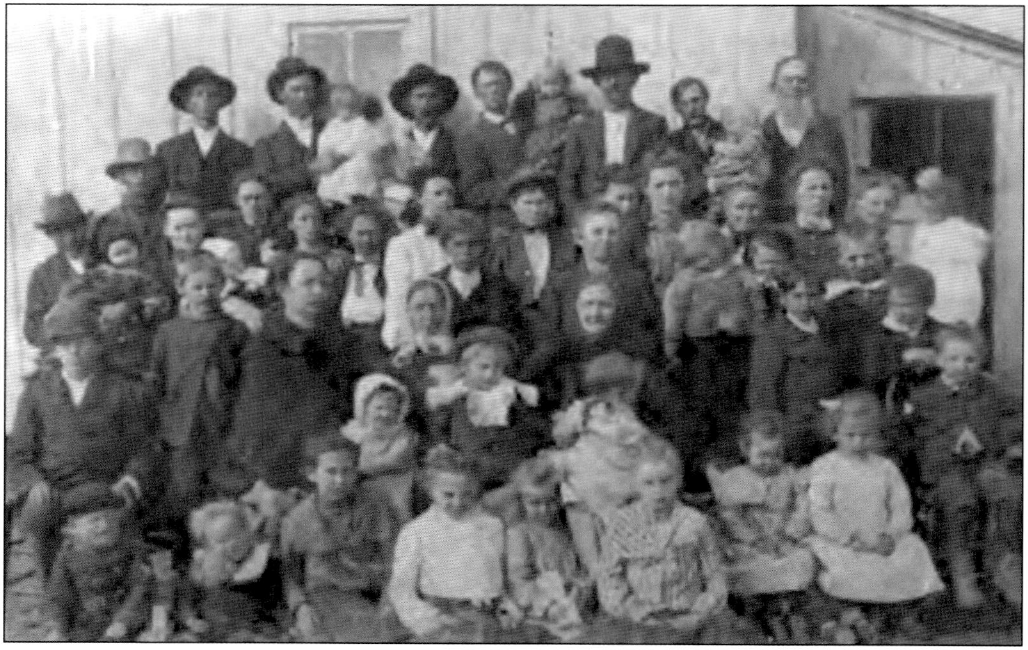

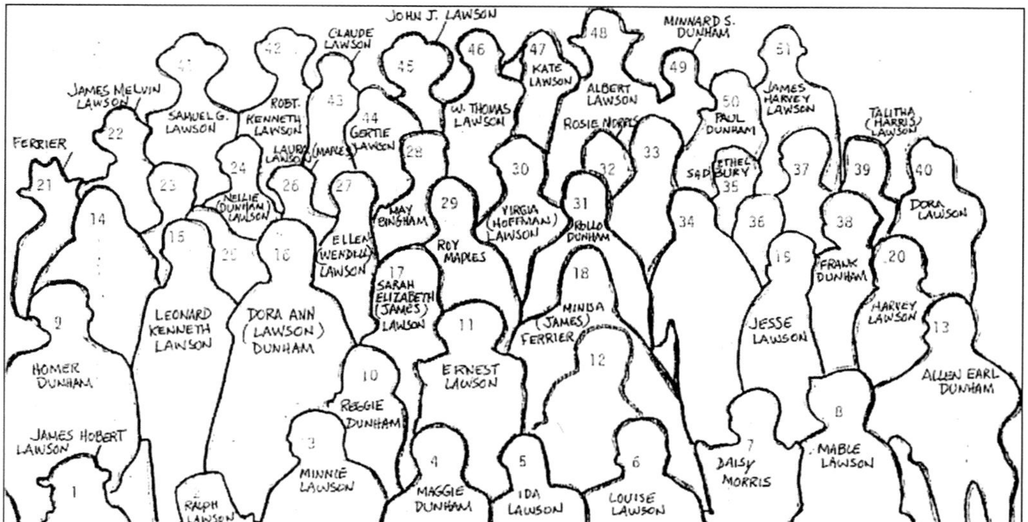

1 James Hobert Lawson
2 Ralph Lawson
3 Minnie Lawson
4 Maggie Edith Dunham(dau/Dora
5 Ida Lawson(dau/Tom)
6 Louise Lawson
7 Daisy Morris
8 Mable Lawson
9 Homer Hubert Dunham
10 Reggie Dunham
Ernest Lawson

Allen Earl Dunham
dau/Ferrier
15 Leonard Kenneth Lawson
16 Dora Ann(Lawson)Dunham
17 Sarah Elizabeth(James)Lawson
18 Minisa(James)Ferrier
19 Jesse Lawson
20 Harvey Lawson
21 Ferrier
22 James Melvin Lawson
23 wife to Ferrier
24 Nellie Grace(Dunham)Lawson
25 child of Ferrier
26 Laura(Maples)Lawson
27 Ellen Lawson
28 May Bingham(dau/Maggie)
29 Roy Maples(bro/Laura)
30 Virgia(Hoffman)Lawson
31 Rollo Rupert Dunham
32 Rosie Morris
33 (nieghbor)
34
35 Ethel Sadbury
36
37 (neighbop)
38 Frank Dunham
39 Talitha Lawson
40 Dora Lawson
41 Samuel G. Lawson
42 Robert Kenneth Lawson
43 Claude Lawson
44 Gertie Lawson
45 John J. Lawson
46 W. Thomas Lawson
47 Kate Lawson
48 Albert Lawson
49 MInard Dunham
50 Paul Dunham
51 James Harvey Lawson

Opposite: This is the family reunion of James Harvey Lawson in about 1903. The individuals who are known can be identified by the numbers in the outline. You can read the names and match them to the numbers listed to the outlined photo.

01 James Hobert Lawson
02 Ralph Lawson
03 Minnie Lawson
04 Maggie Edith Dunham (daughter of Dora)
05 Ida Lawson
06 Louise Lawson
07 Daisy Morris
08 Mable Lawson
09 Homer Hubert Dunham
10 Reggie Dunham
11 Ernest Lawson
12 ?
13 Allen Earl Dunham
14 ? (daughter of Ferrier)
15 Leonard Kenneth Lawson
16 Dora Ann (Lawson) Dunham
17 Sarah Elizabeth (James) Lawson
18 ? (James) Ferrier
19 Jesse Lawson
20 Harvey Lawson
21 ? Ferrier
22 James Melvin Lawson
23 ? (wife of Ferrier)
24 Nellie Grace (Dunham) Lawson
25 ? (child of Ferrier)
26 Laura (Maples) Lawson
27 Ellen Lawson
28 May Bingham (daughter of Maggie)
29 Roy Maples (brother of Laura)
30 Virgia (Hoffman) Lawson
31 Rollo Rupert Dunham
32 Rosie Morris
33 ? (neighbor)
34 ?
35 Ethel Sadbury
36 ?
37 ? (neighbor)
38 Frank Dunham
39 Talitha Lawson
40 Dora Lawson
41 Samuel G. Lawson
42 Robert Kenneth Lawson
43 Claude Lawson
44 Certie Lawson
45 John J. Lawson
46 W. Thomas Lawson
47 Kate Lawson
48 Albert Lawson
49 ? Dunham
50 Paul Dunham
51 James Harvey Lawson

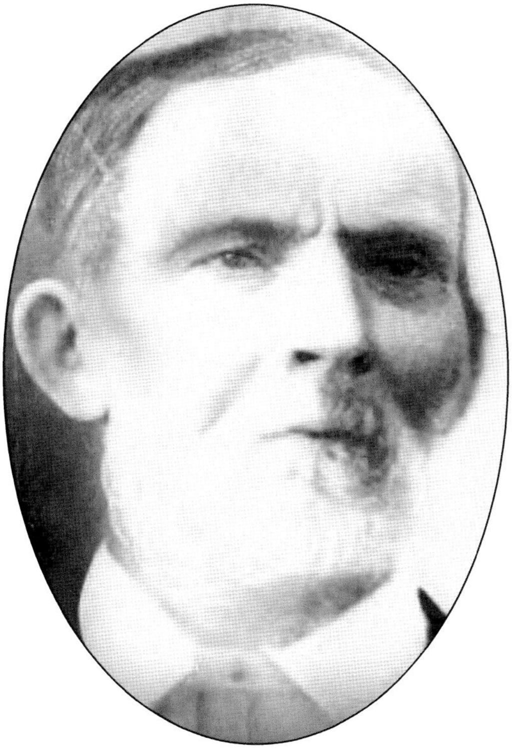

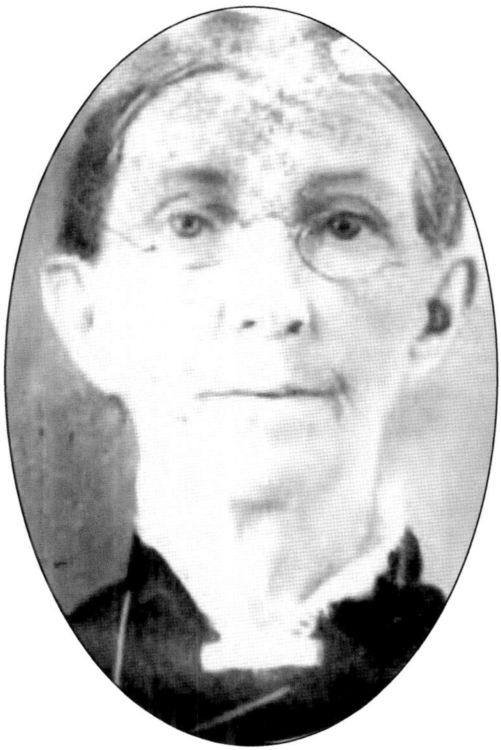

These photos are of James Harvey and Sarah Elizabeth Lawson. They had eleven children all together. One of their children, Edgar Willard Lawson, lived his entire life in the Highlandville area. Edgar married Rachael Sidney (White) Lawson and they had four children together. Their youngest was born in 1910. Edgar was born on December 23, 1878 and died on May 20, 1960 in Highlandville.

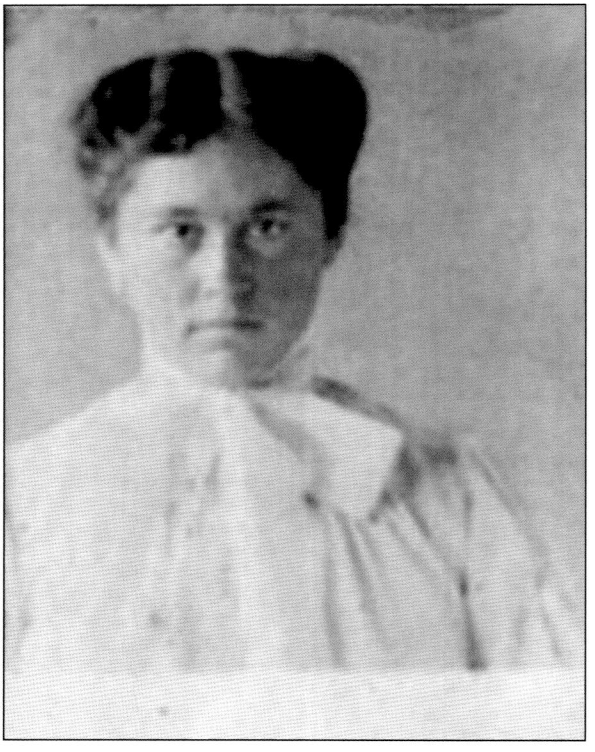

Nellie (Winslow) Lee who was born on March 24, 1883 and died on March 17, 1956; she lived in Chadwick, Missouri.

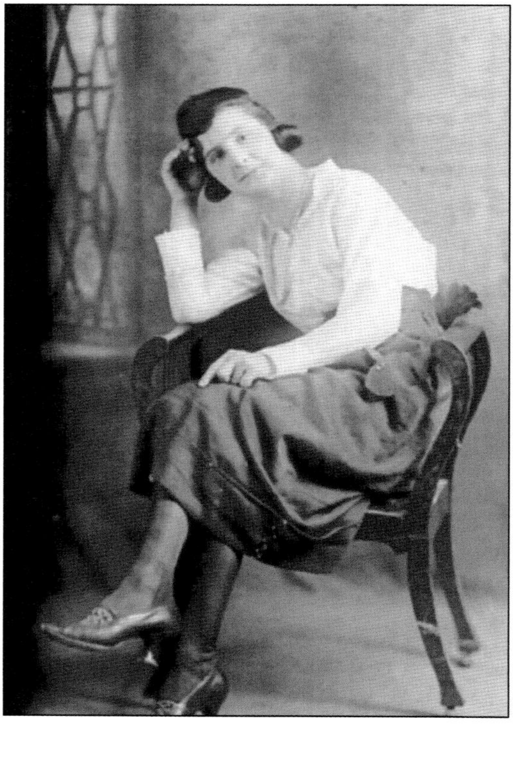

This 1920 photograph shows Iva Lewis of Sparta.

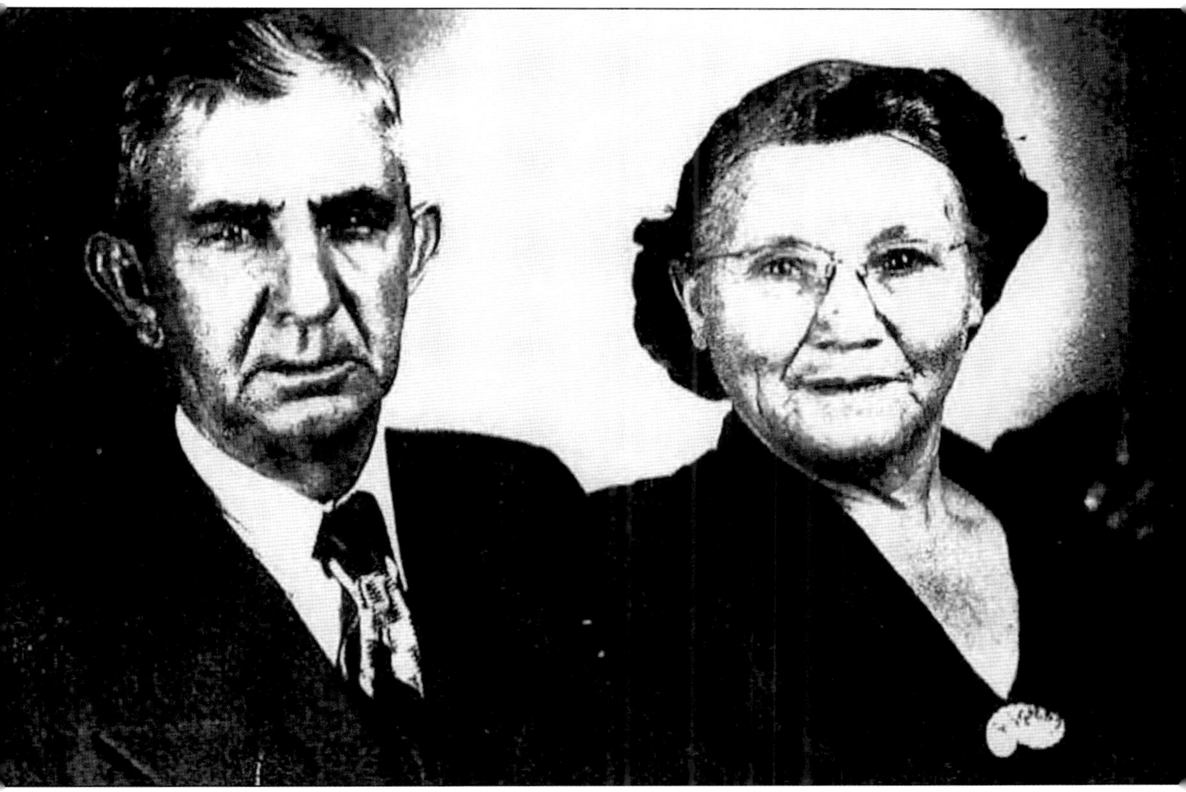

Jack Andrew and Hattie (Hodges) Lewis are pictured here. They lived in Sparta, but later moved to Wagoner, Oklahoma.

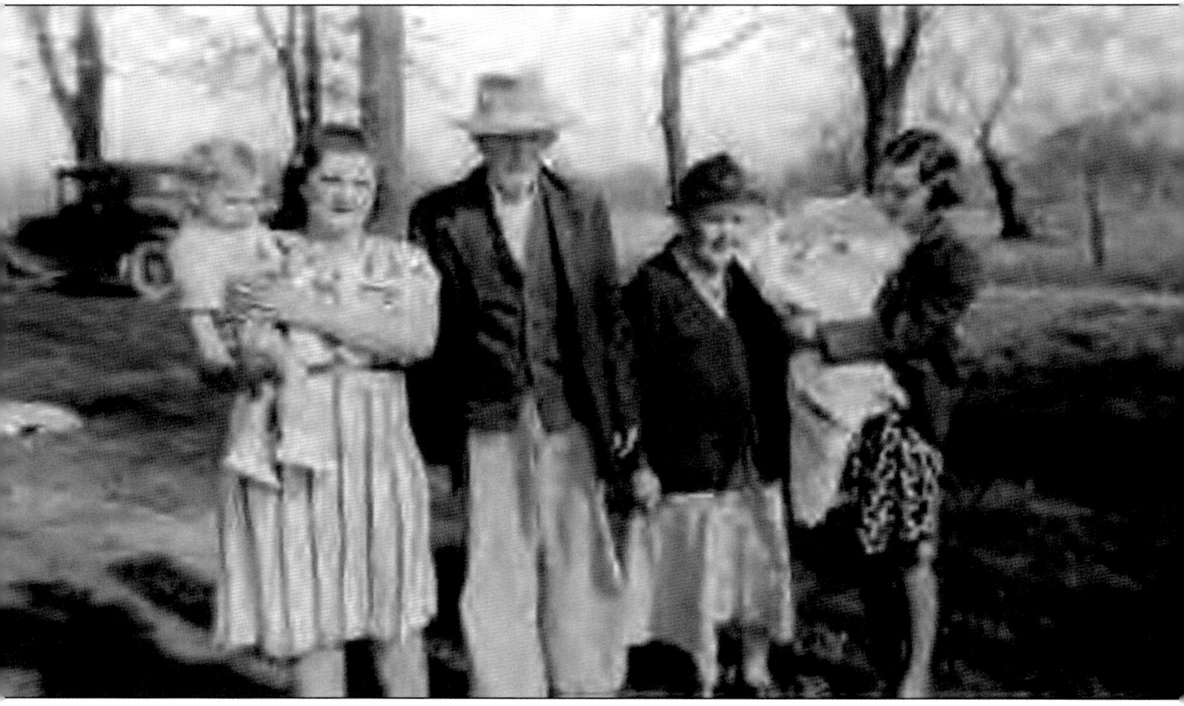

Pictured from left to right are the baby Woodford LeRoy Owsley, Lydia (Newberry) Lewis, Charles Lewis, Nancy Lewis, Jimmy Dale Owsley (the second baby), and Juanita "Bobbie" Owsley. Charles and Nancy Lewis lived in Sparta.

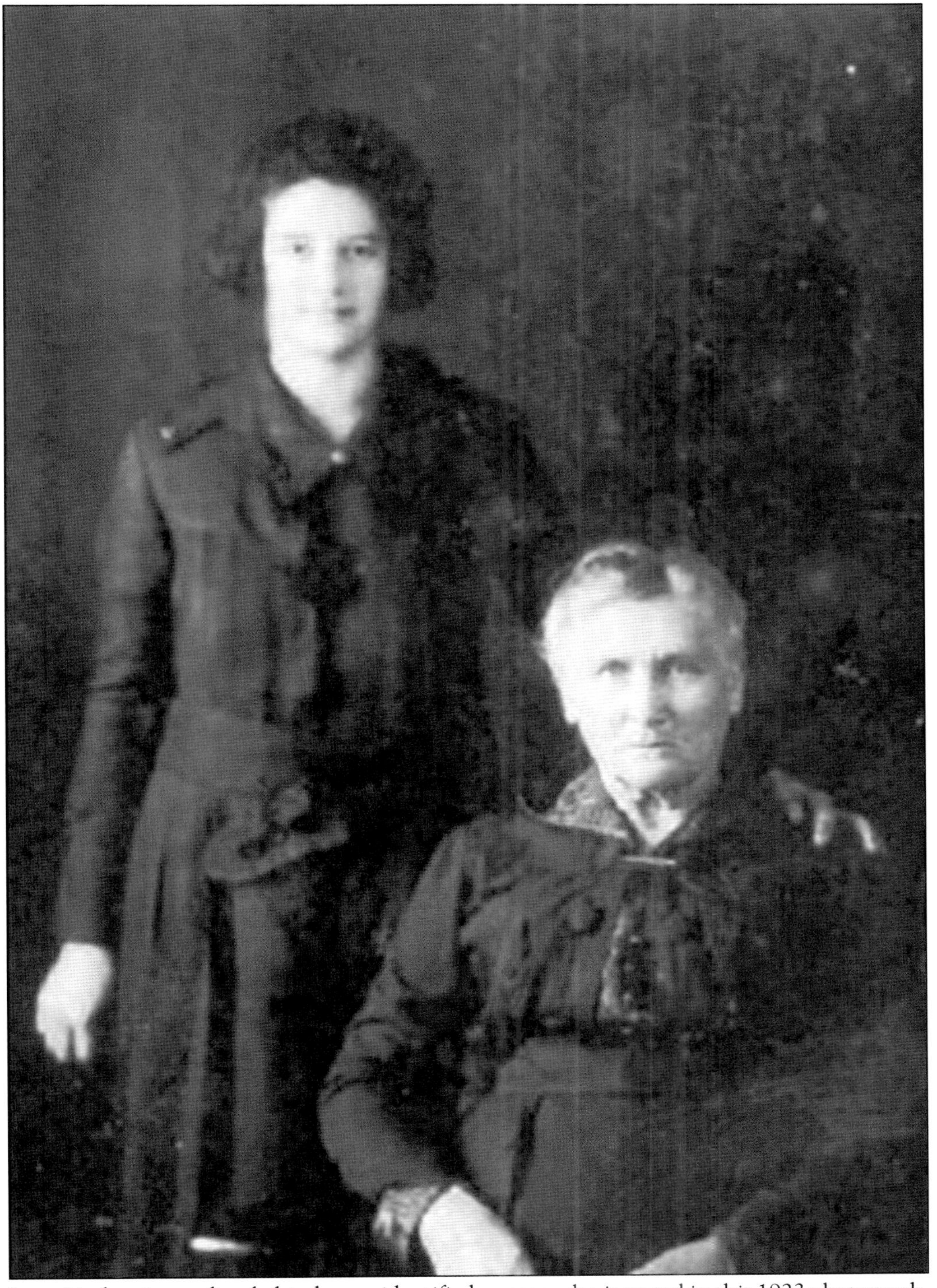

Lena Lindsey is standing behind an unidentified woman who is seated in this 1923 photograph. On the back of the photograph are written the words, "Uncle Jim's girl."

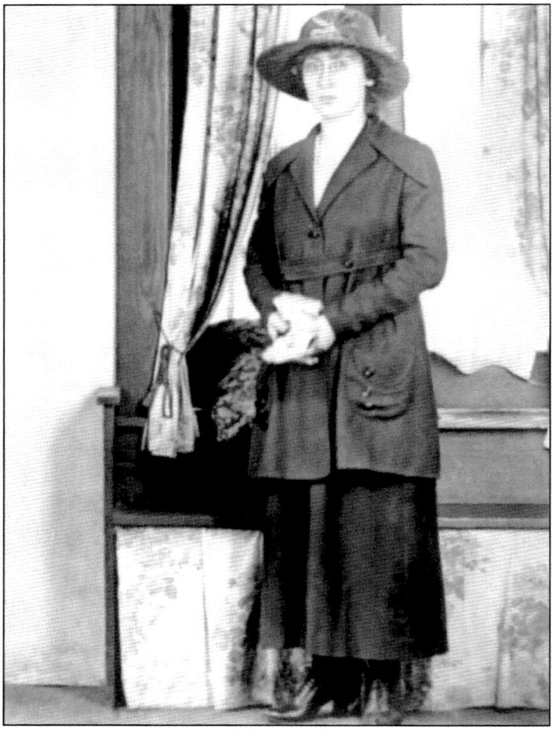

Nixa resident Cora L. Love is pictured in this undated photograph.

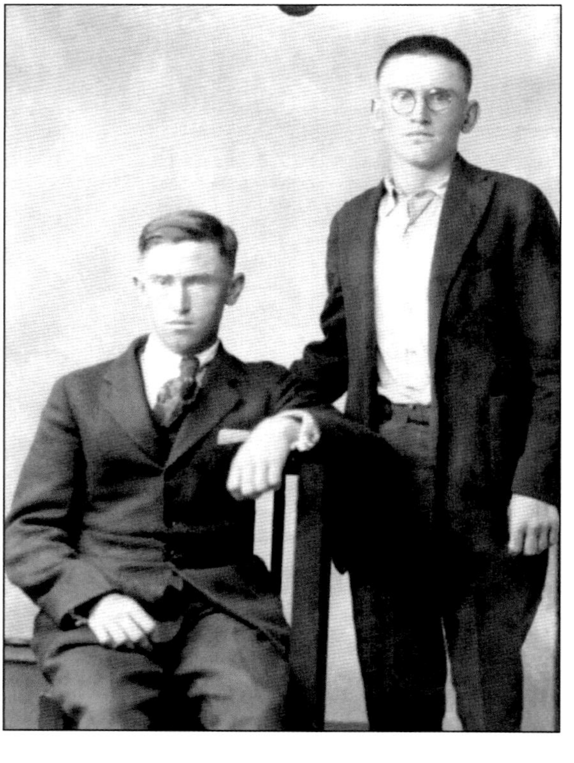

These two men are Charley Love (sitting in the chair), and John W. Love (standing). They are the sons of Lewis F. and Sarah Jane (Inman) Love. Sarah was the daughter of John Wesley and Nancy Lavanda (Wilson) Inman. Sarah was the mother of Cora L. Love. Charley, John, and Cora were all siblings and all three were born in the Christian County area. However, they all moved to Florida and died there, but were brought back to Springfield, Missouri to be buried in the Greene Lawn Cemetery with their parents.

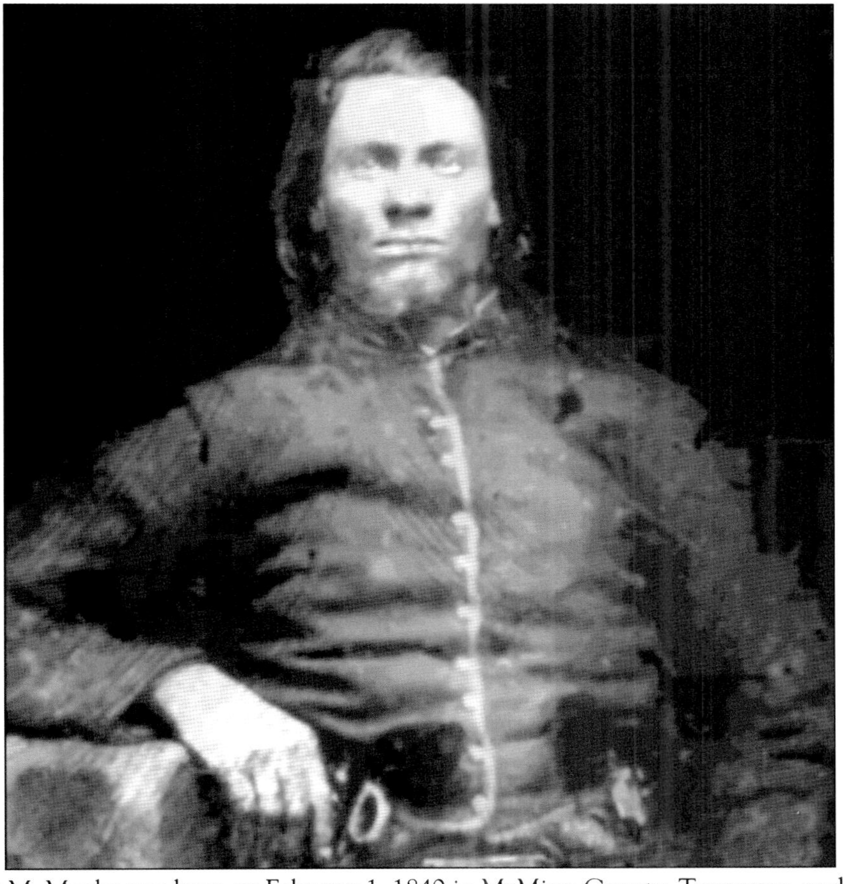

Pleasant M. Maples was born on February 1, 1840 in McMinn County, Tennessee, and died on February 10, 1911 in Stone County, Missouri. He is buried at the Frazier Cemetery in Christian County. Pleasant was the oldest child of Simeon Perry Maples of Christian County and Elizabeth "Betsy" (Webb) Maples, who was from Tennessee. Simeon and Elizabeth are both also buried in the Frazier Cemetery in Christian County. Pleasant was married on June 19, 1857 in Greene County, Missouri, to a Kiziah Frazier who was born in McMinn County, Tennessee. She was born on January 18, 1842 and died on December 2, 1909 in Stone County, Missouri. She was the daughter of a Dr. Lorenzo Lowe Frazier and Hannah Bryant Frazier, who are also buried at the Frazier Cemetery. Pleasant was a farmer just as his father and grandfather were before him. He was a part-time minister, as were many of the male members of the Maples family. In 1860, he was living in Porter Township—Nixa, Missouri—and in 1880 he lived in the Lincoln Township, which is in the Clever, Missouri, area. By 1900, he was living in Cass Township, Stone County, also near Clever, and remained there until his death. During the Civil War era, Pleasant served in Co F. 14th MO Volunteer Cavalry, which later became Co L 8th MO Regiment State Militia Cavalry. He was discharged on April 19, 1865. His grandfather, Josiah Maples Jr., along with many of his children and grandchildren migrated from Tennessee to Greene County(now Christian County, MO), in 1854. According to family legend, Pleasant and his parents where unable to make the trip with the rest of the family due to his mother Elizabeth's pregnancy, so they made their journey to Missouri the following year. June Wilson Weaver is a descendant of Josiah Maples Jr.'s oldest son, Ephraim Maples, and has researched the family for many years. Still, she is sure there is a lot she doesn't know.

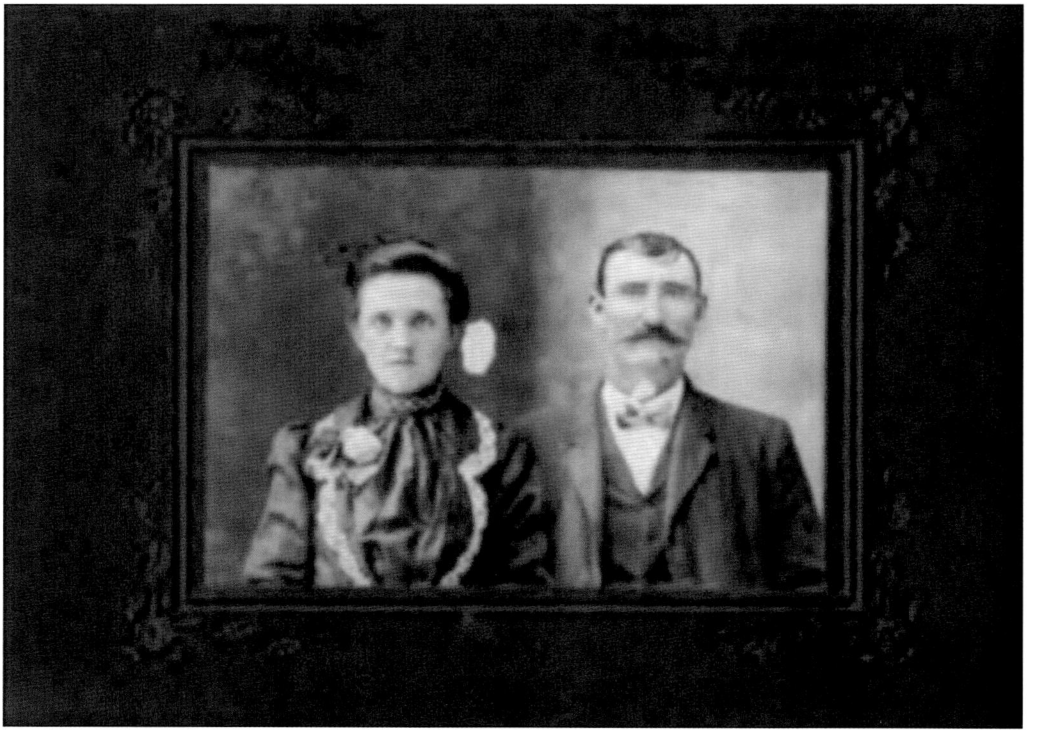

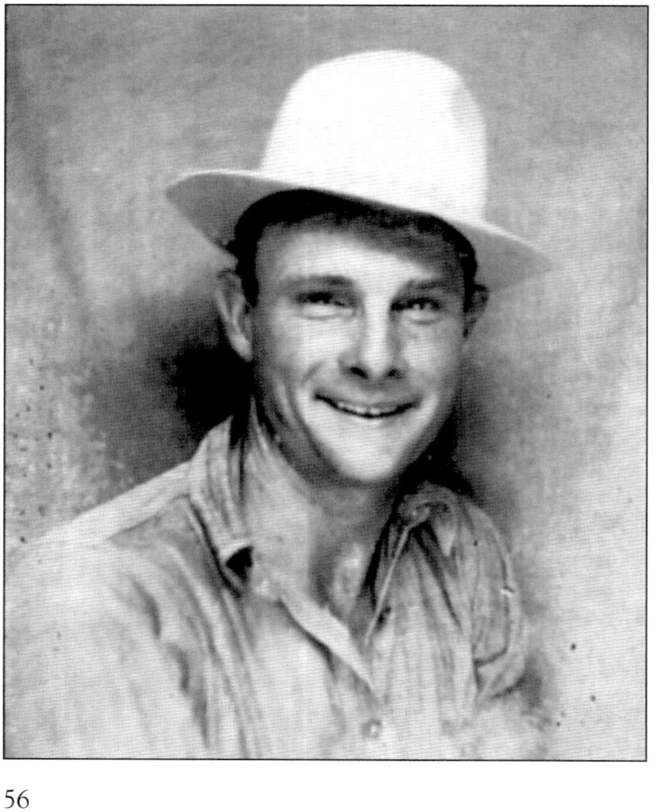

Nancy Alzy Gooch and William Edward Mayabb were married on March 31, 1894 in Nixa.

This man's name is believed to have been John Q. McCafferty, but he went by the name of Que. It is believed he is the son of James F. and Annahtina (Carroll) McCafferty from the Nixa area. He married Calidona D. Faught, who was the daughter of John W. and Mary Ann (McConnell) Faught. Calidona was also the niece of James Jasper Faught. Later, Que moved to Decatur, Texas.

Elesa McCafferty is to be believed the daughter of James F. and Annahlina (Carroll) McCafferty, who are from Christian County.

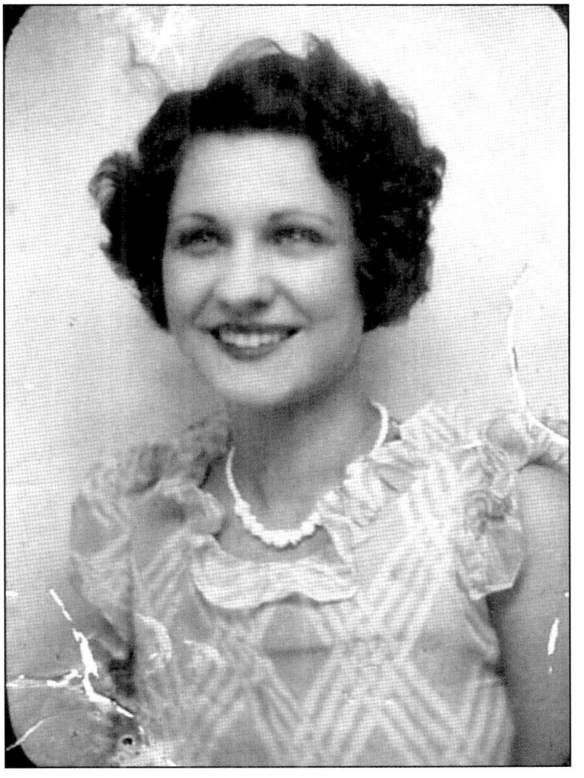

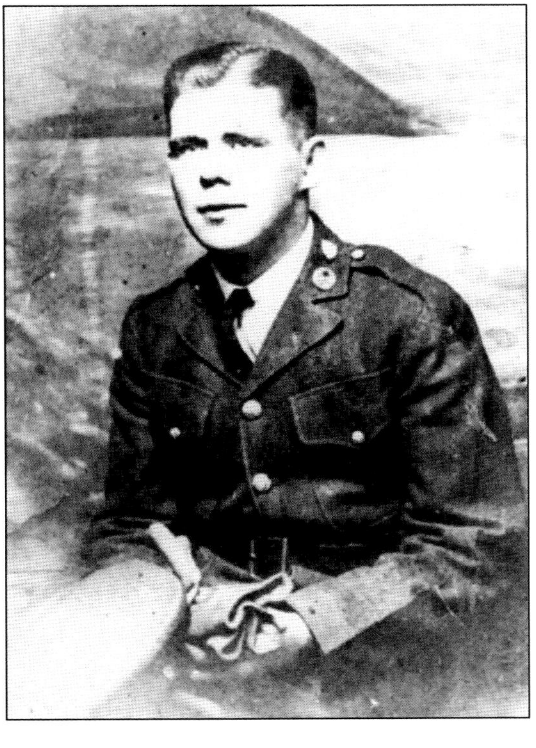

This is Sparta's Lewis McMillan in his Army uniform about 1927 or '28.

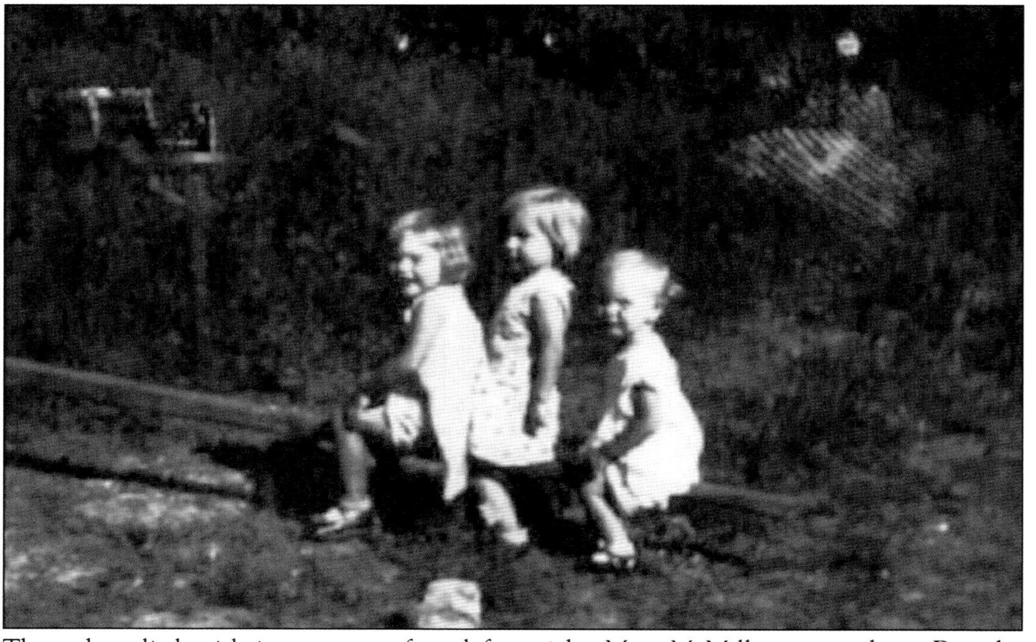

These three little girls in a row are, from left to right, Mary McMillan at age three, Dorothy Winslow at age two, and Louise McMillan at age one. The photo was taken during the summer of 1932 in Sparta.

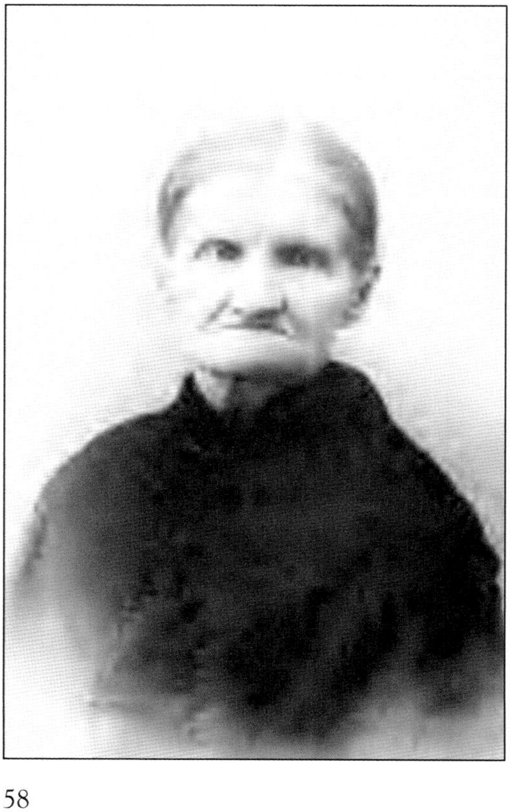

Peggy Ann (Bilyeu) Melton, from Nixa, was the wife of Martin Fisher Melton. Both are buried in the McCoy Cemetery.

Pictured here is Rhoda Jane Mooney, who was the wife of Elisha P. Stillings.

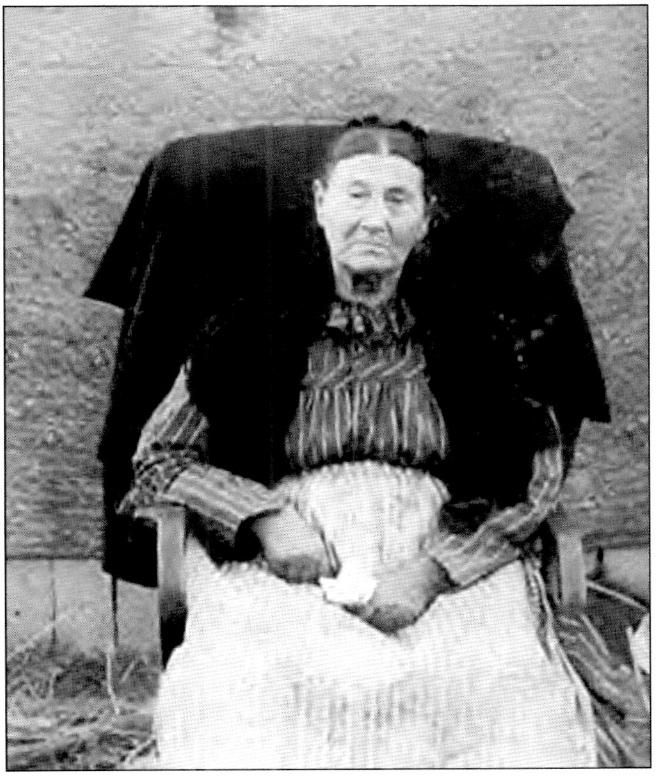

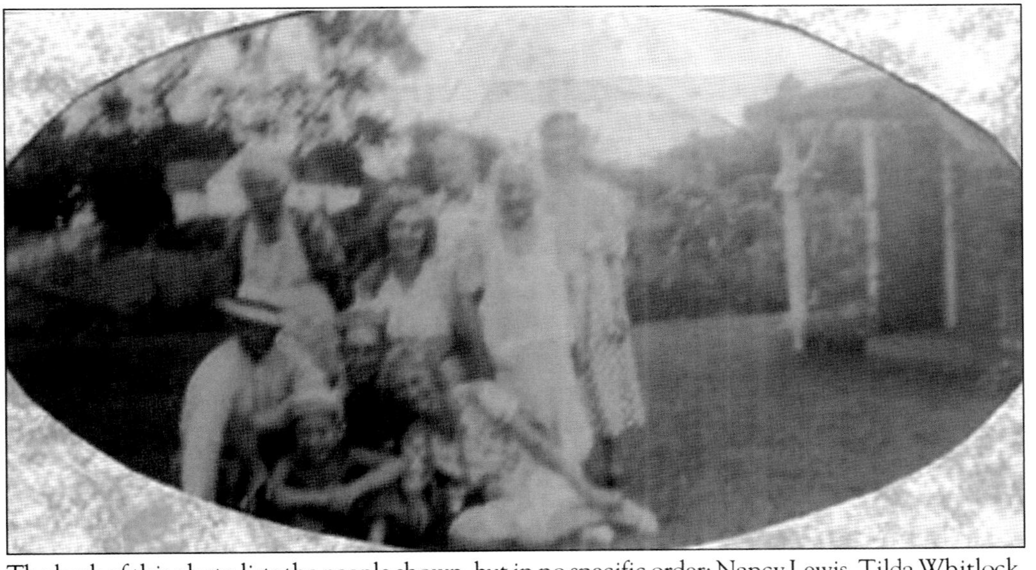

The back of this photo lists the people shown, but in no specific order; Nancy Lewis, Tilda Whitlock, Iva Mooney, Myrtle Newberry, Maude Lewis, Tom Vaughn, Everett Mooney, Charles Newberry, and Lydia Alsup. Maude is a daughter-in-law, Tom is a son-in-law as well as Everett, Charles is a grandson, and Lydia is a neighbor. This photo was taken on July 16, 1948 in Sparta.

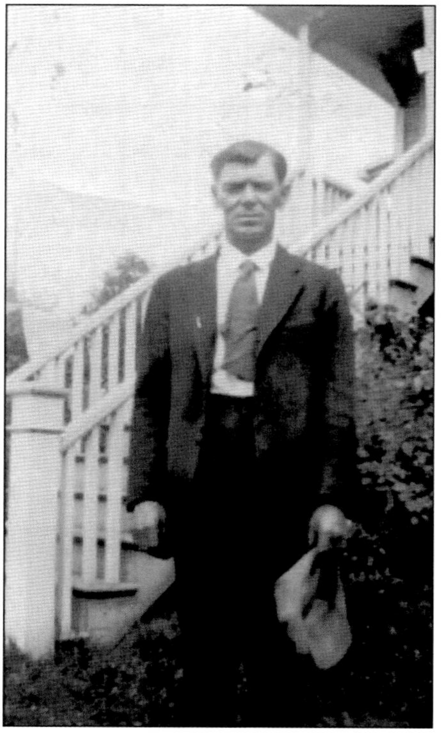

All that is known about this 1929 photo is that it was taken in Sparta, the man is 49 years old, and is named either Sam or Sammy.

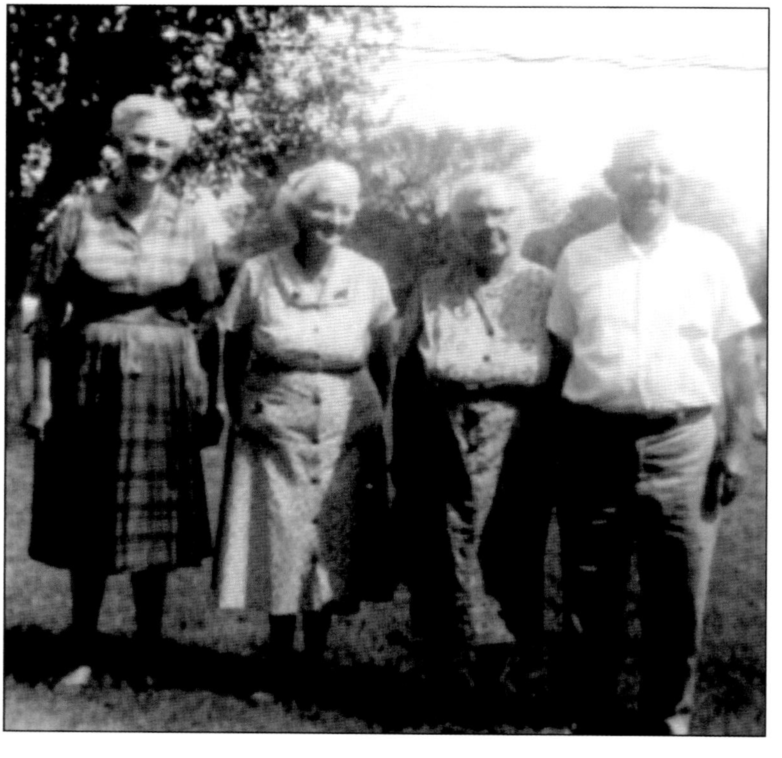

This photo was taken in the 1950s in Sparta. Some of those pictured are Newberrys and some are Whitlocks.

This is believed to be Abigail Frazier, the mother of Minerva Frazier Danner and wife of Edmond Pearce.

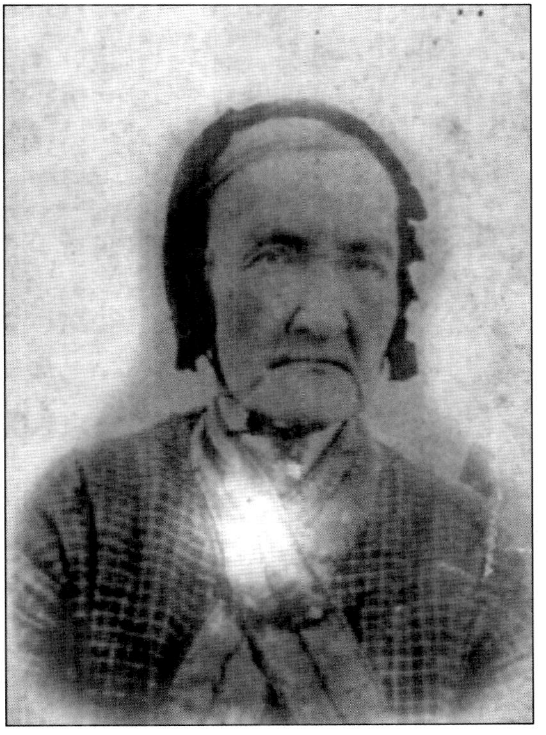

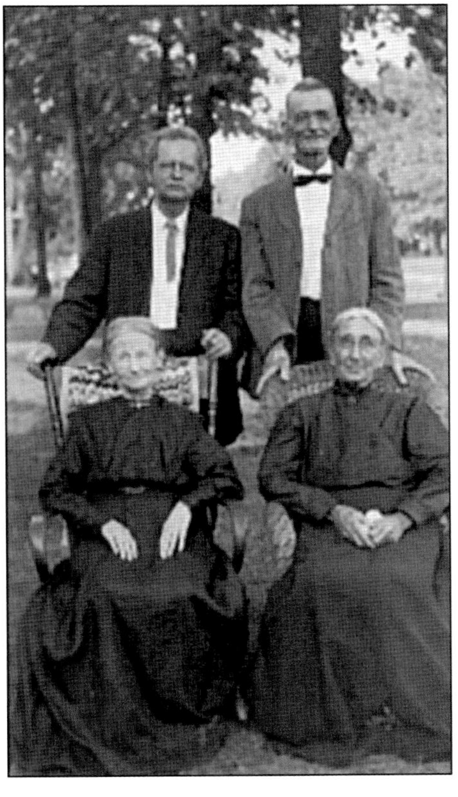

Pictured from left to right are: (front row) Dianna Pearce and Rosanna Pearce; (back row) Thomas Noblitt and Leroy Skaggs. Rosanna and Dianna are the daughters of Edmond and Abigail Frazier.

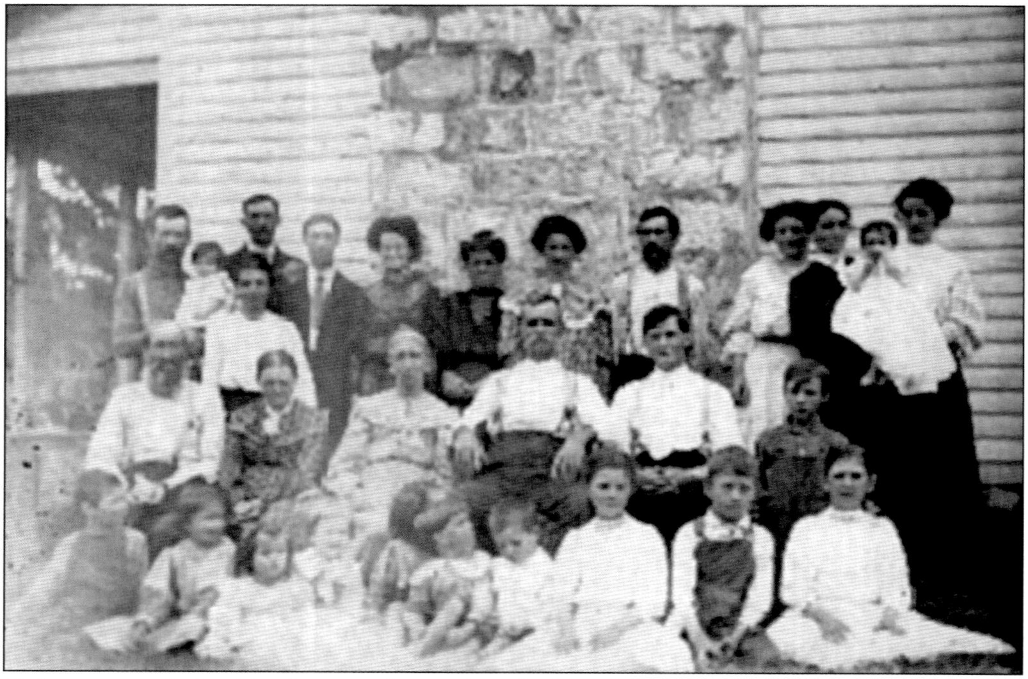

Only two people in this photograph are identified. In the second row, sitting on the left are John Pearce and Nancy Kerr.

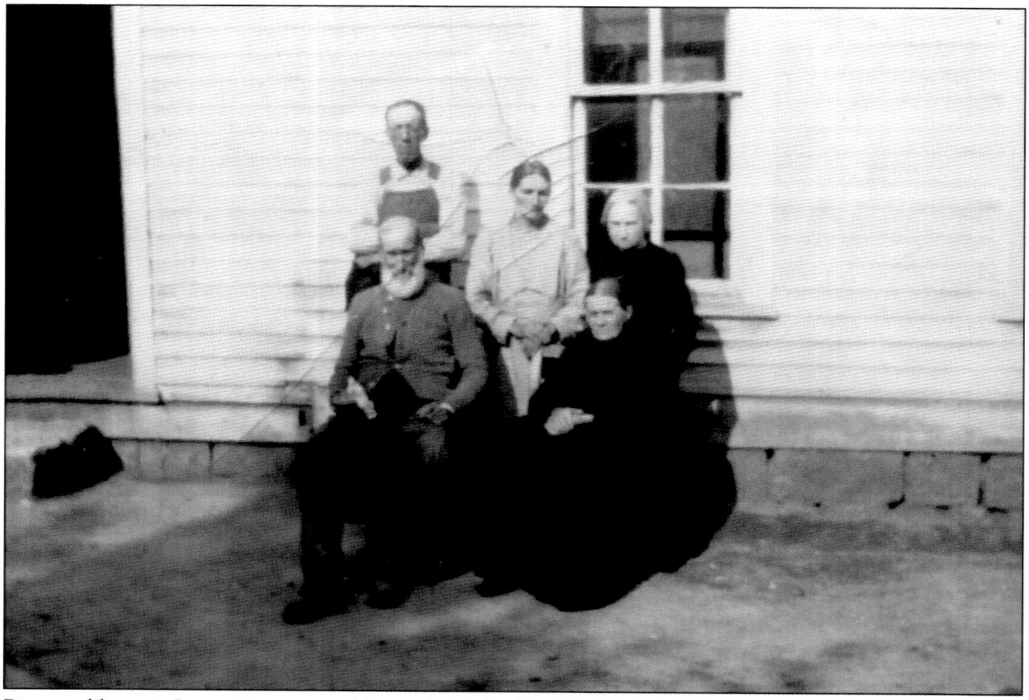

Pictured here is James Pearce and his wife Nola (Peebles) Pearce along with Nola's mother, who is in the back row.

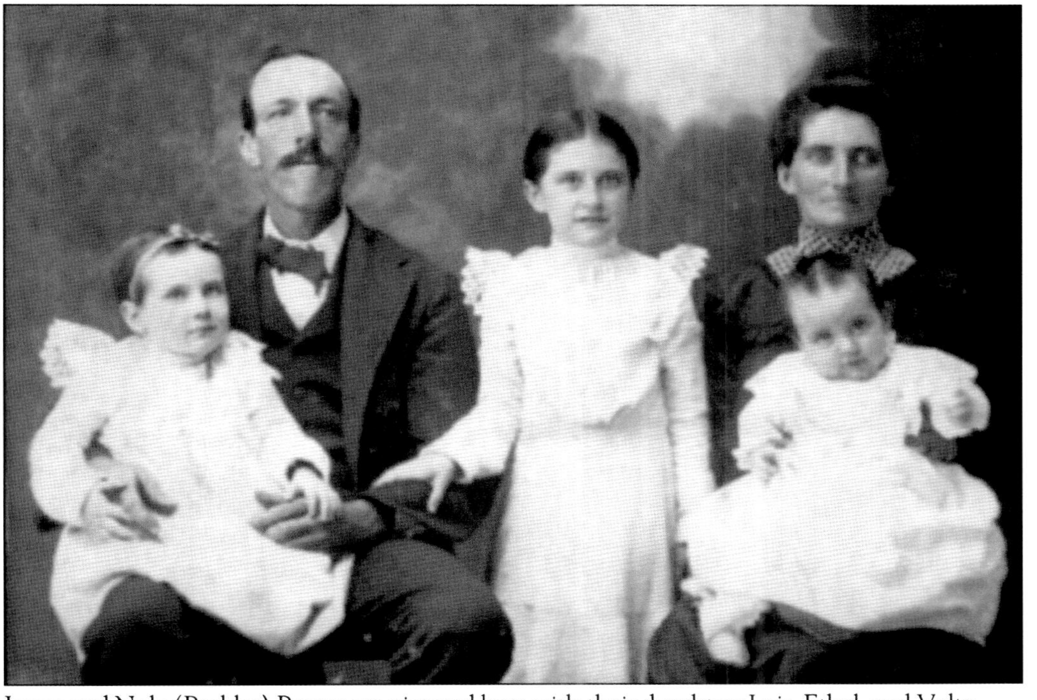

James and Nola (Peebles) Pearce are pictured here with their daughters Lois, Ethel, and Velta.

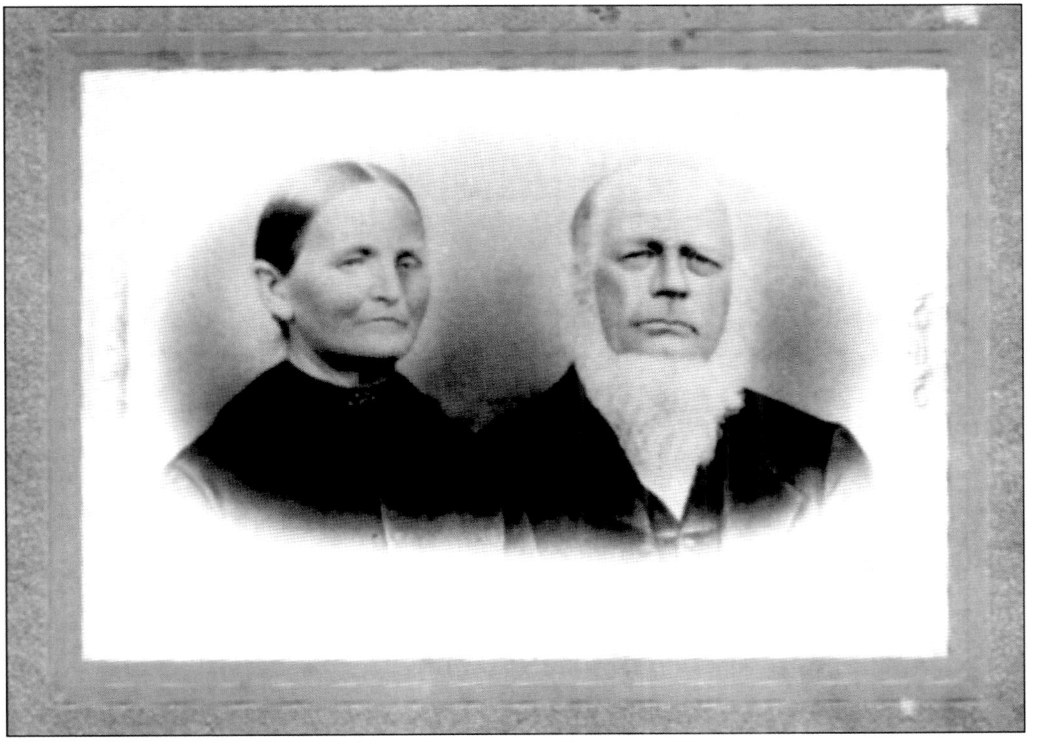

These are the parents of Nancy Kerr, who is pictured on page 62.

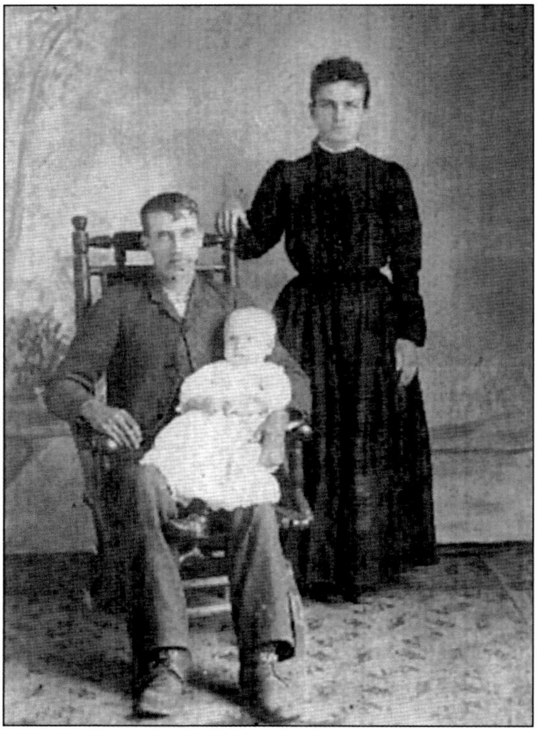

Ted Burlison and Mary Ellen Pearce—Mary Ellen is the daughter of Samual Pearce, who is the son of Edmond and Abigal Frazier.

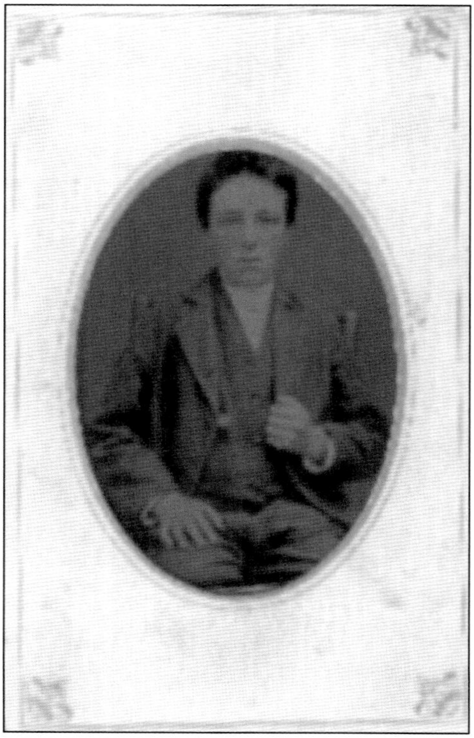

James Pearce was the son of John and Nancy Pearce.

This photo is of Minerva Danner, the daughter of Edmond and Abigail Frazier. It is believed she was married to a man named Nathan Danner.

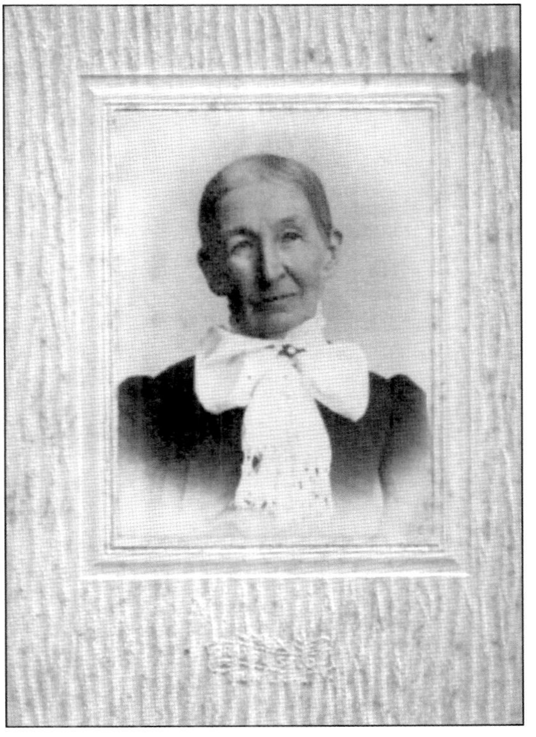

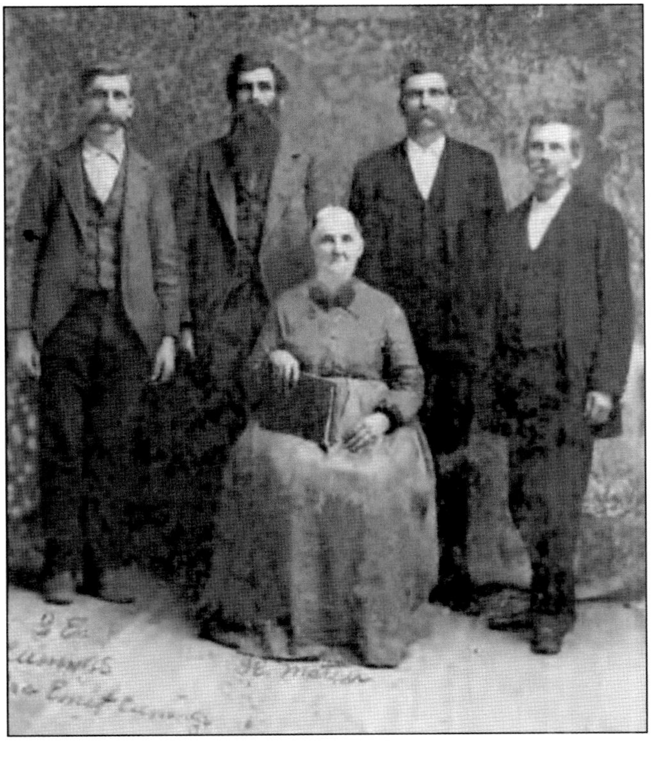

Three of the men standing are believed to be Noah, Edwin, and David Jr., the sons of David and Matilda Huskey Peebles of Christian County. Seated is their mother, Matilda Huskey Peebles Cummins. The fourth man is unidentified.

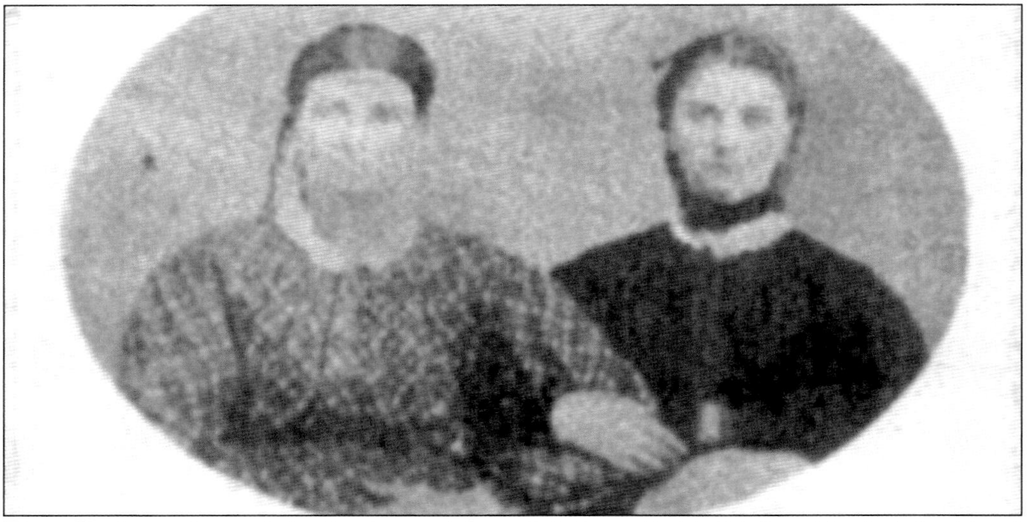

This is a photo of two of the daughters of Caswell Roberts (1817-1891) and Rachel (Burkhart) Roberts (1817-1883) of the Garrison area. Caswell and Rachel were part of the large group, including Garrisons, Hartwells, Roberts, Burkharts, etc. that traveled from Tennessee to Taney and Christian Cos., MO. Caswell was from Hamilton Co., TN. There was also another Caswell Roberts in the area. On the left is Catherine (Roberts) Mitchell and on the right, Mary Ann Roberts. Catherine was the wife of Thomas J. Mitchell, who was also from Garrison. The photo was taken c. 1880. Catherine was born about 1840, near Garrison, Christian Co., MO (Taney Co., MO); she died of tuberculosis October 13, 1894. She was the first wife of Thomas Josephus Nathaniel Thilo Benton Mitchell, whom she married on January 21 1869. Thomas (1848 to 1920) and Catherine were the parents of four children; Amelia Jane Mitchell (Frank, then Nichols), William Marion Mitchell, Patterson Monroe "Pat" Mitchell, and Martha Elvira Mitchell (Reece). Mary Ann Roberts was born about 1863, also near Garrison. She married William P. Martin. Thomas, Catherine, Rachel and Caswell are all buried at Old Boston Cemetery.

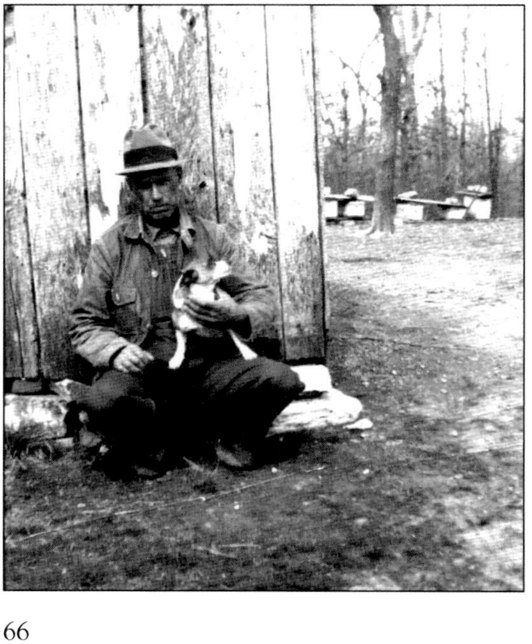

Jim Robertson built a grist mill, which later was sold and moved to the world-famous Silver Dollar City in Branson, Missouri. Pictured here with his dog, Jim was from Sparta.

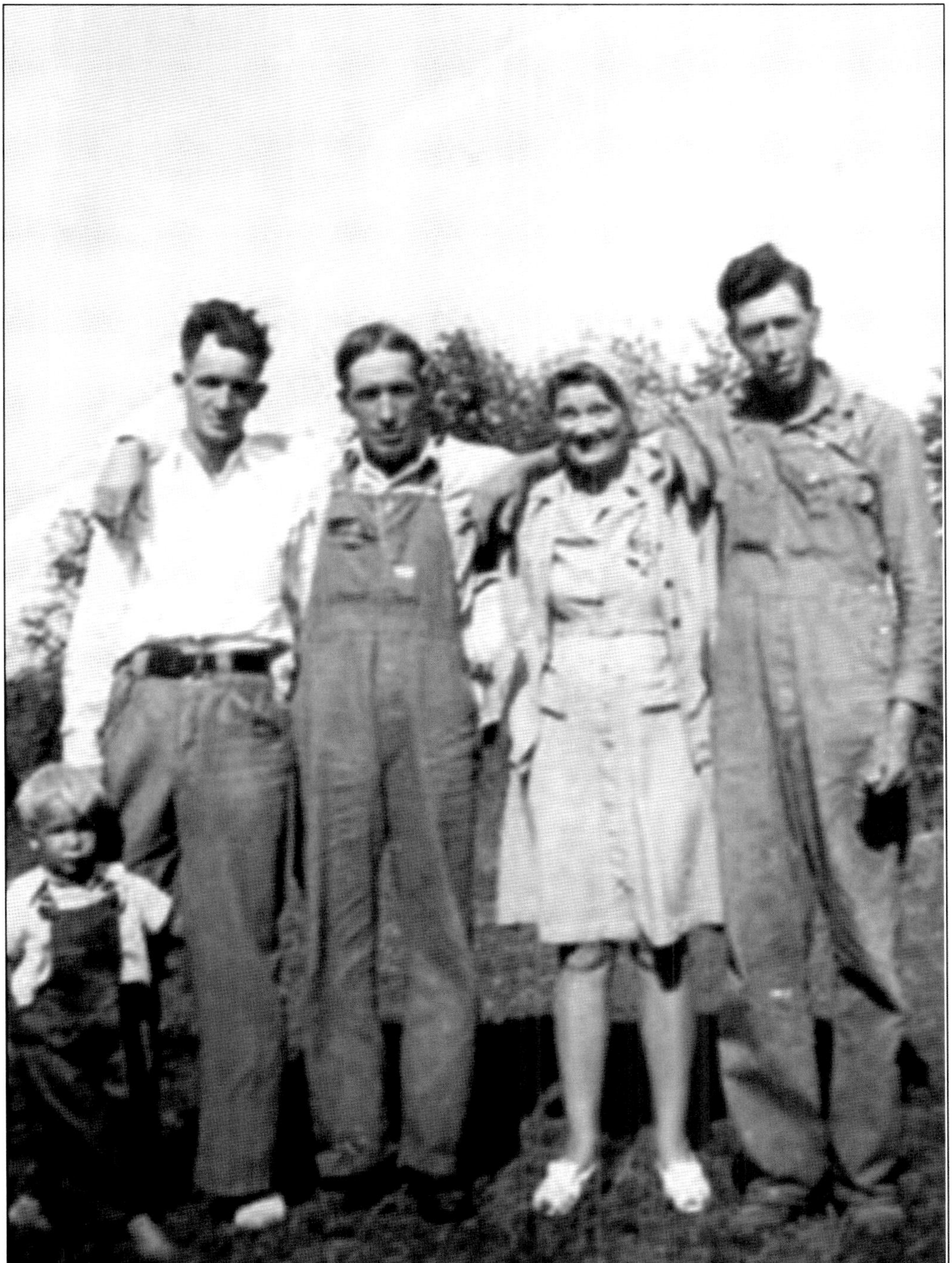

This photo was taken of Nixa residents c. 1942. Pictured from left to right are: Jerry Gene Inman, Ira Porter Inman, Aubry T. Seaton, Sarah (Burns) Seaton, and Orville H. Bolin. Aubry T. and Sarah (Burns) Seaton were husband and wife; Aubry was the son of Felix and Martha (Day) Seaton.

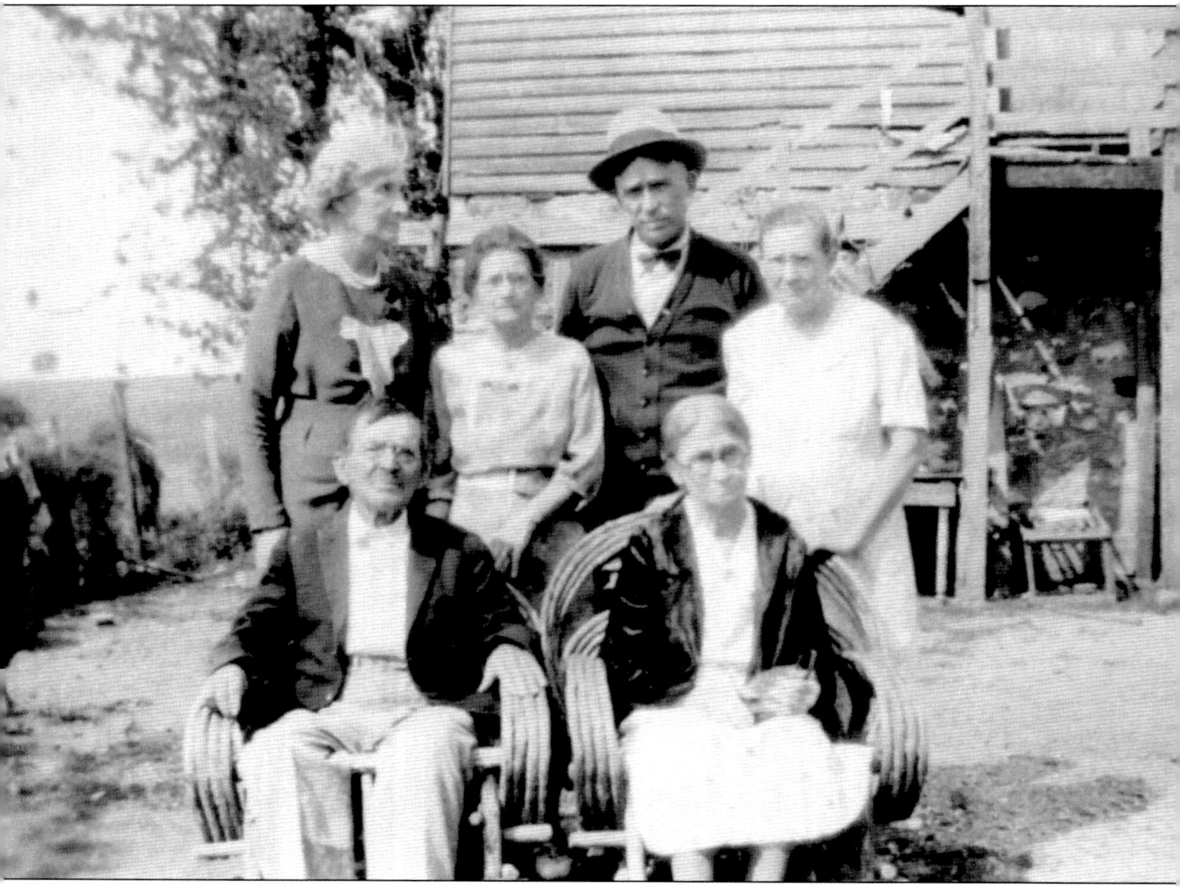

Pictured from left to right are: (front row) Felix H. Seaton and Martha L. (Day) Seaton; (back row) unidentified, Nancy W. (Day) Farrell, Everett L. Seaton, and Addie E. (Seaton) Bolin. Nancy is the sister of Felix's wife, Martha, and they are the daughters of Stephen L. and Sarah F. (Hatfield) Day. Everett and Addie are two of Felix H. and Martha L. (Day) Seaton's children. Felix is the son of Caleb B. and Mary Ann (Allen) Seaton of Nixa.

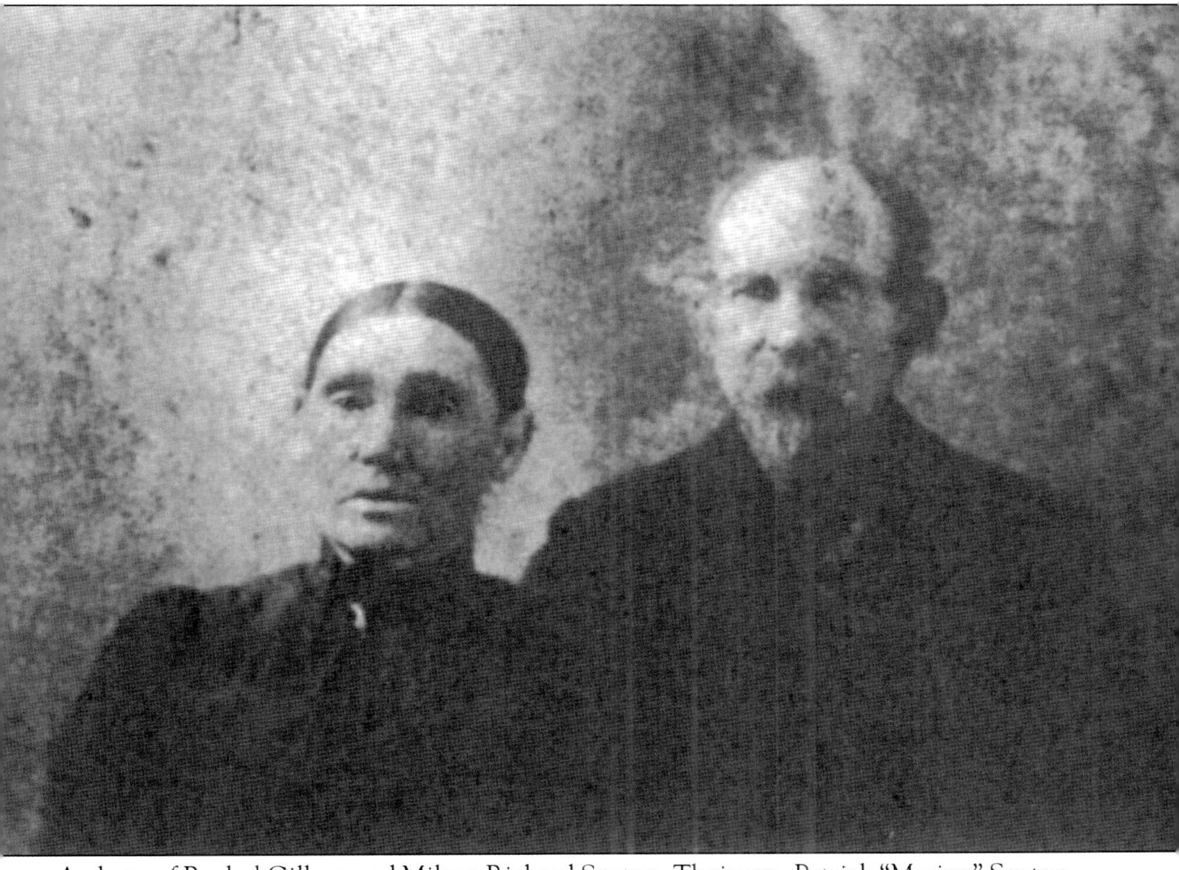

A photo of Rachel Gilbert and Milton Richard Sexton. Their son, Patrick "Marion" Sexton, from Christian County, married Anna Turner. Their son, James (Russ) Sexton, married Winnie Atterberry.

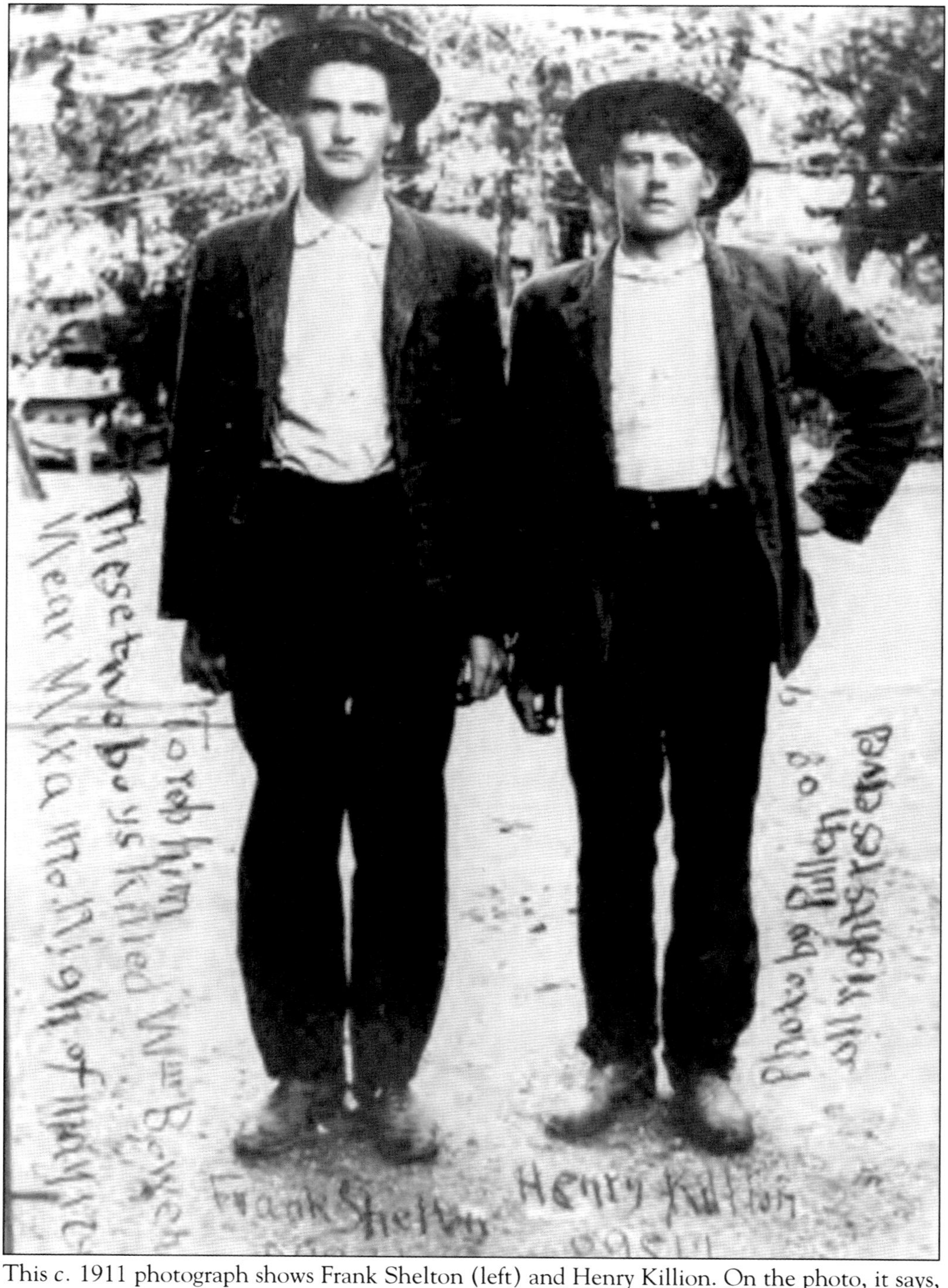

This *c.* 1911 photograph shows Frank Shelton (left) and Henry Killion. On the photo, it says, "Frank and Henry both robbed and murdered a Nixa resident named William "Wm." Bowen on the night of May 12th. Year is unknown.

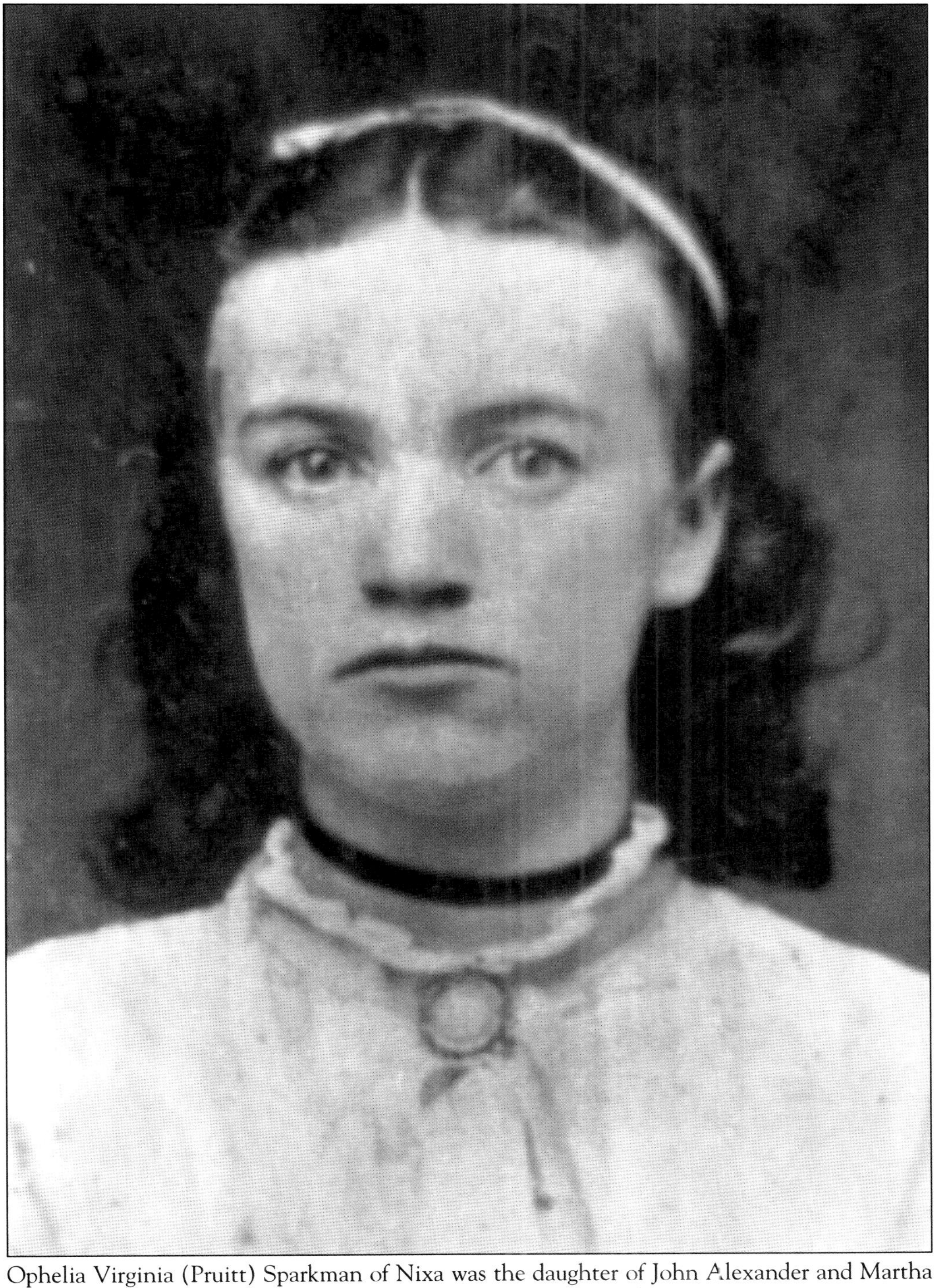

Ophelia Virginia (Pruitt) Sparkman of Nixa was the daughter of John Alexander and Martha Ann (Perkins) Pruitt. Her daughter was Martha Jane (Sparkman) Inman.

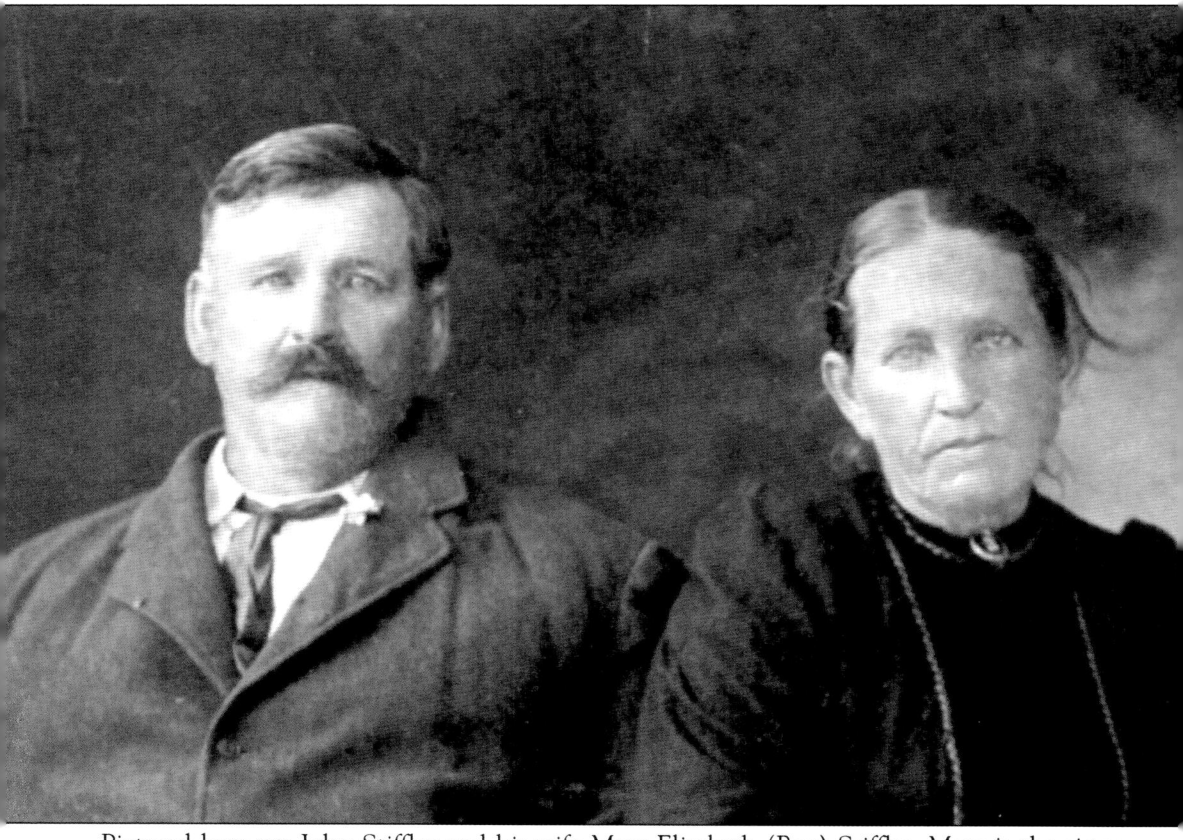

Pictured here are John Stiffler and his wife Mary Elizabeth (Ray) Stiffler. Mary is the sister of Margaret M. (Ray) Bolin. Mary and Margaret are the daughters of James and Margaret N. (Maze) Ray. John Stiffler is the son of John Bardell and Martha Ann (Brumbelow) Stiffler. He is also the brother to Albert J. Stiffler who was married to Leah Melissa Nokes.

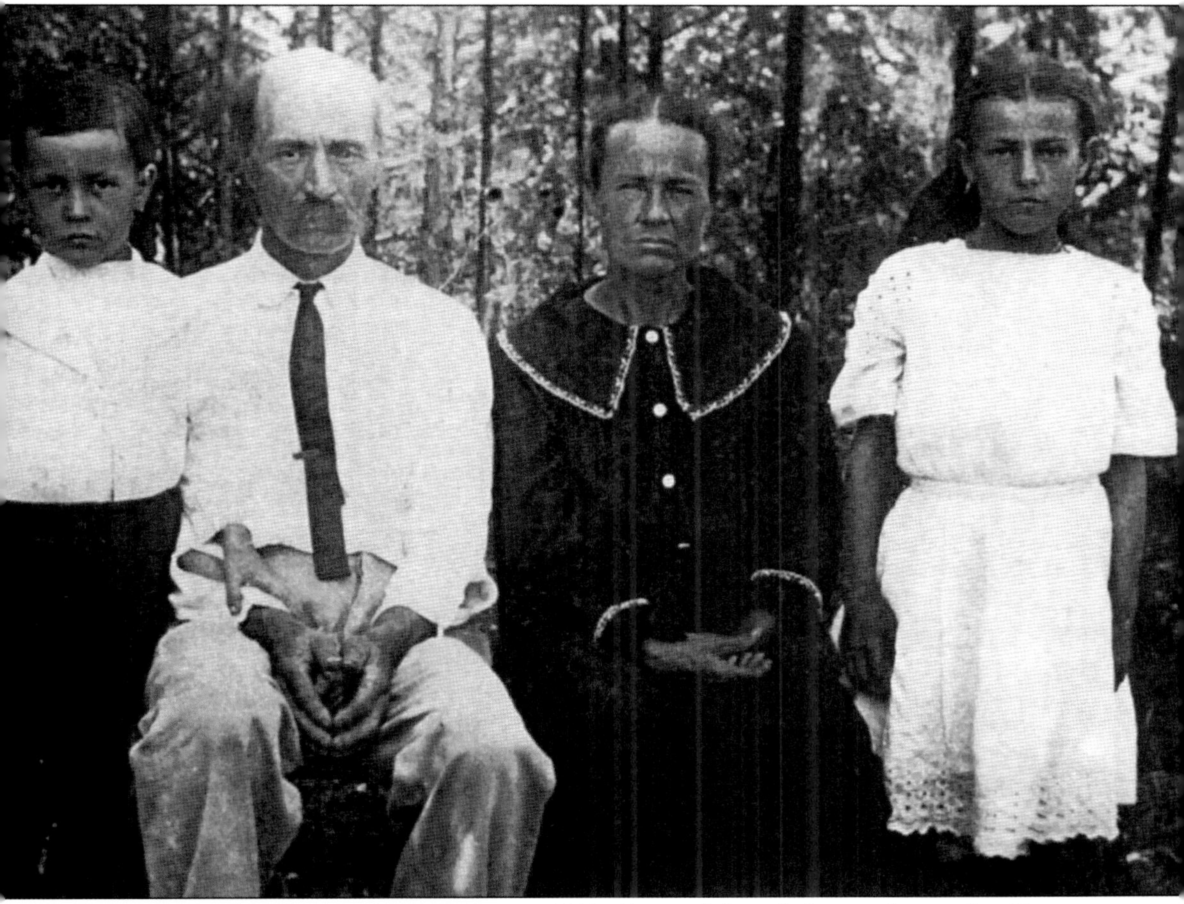

This Terry family photograph was taken c. 1912. Pictured from left to right are Joe Terry, Napoleon Bonaparte "Bone" Terry, Sarah Arminta (Moulder) Terry, and Desi Terry. Arminta and Bone Terry are both buried in Meadow's Cemetery. It is not known where Joe and Desi Terry are buried. Bone was born in 1864 and died January 6, 1939. Arminta was born in 1866 and died October 20, 1935. They lived by Bull Creek. Its not known precisely how many children they had, but they had at least one other daughter, Effie Terry, who is not shown in this family photograph.

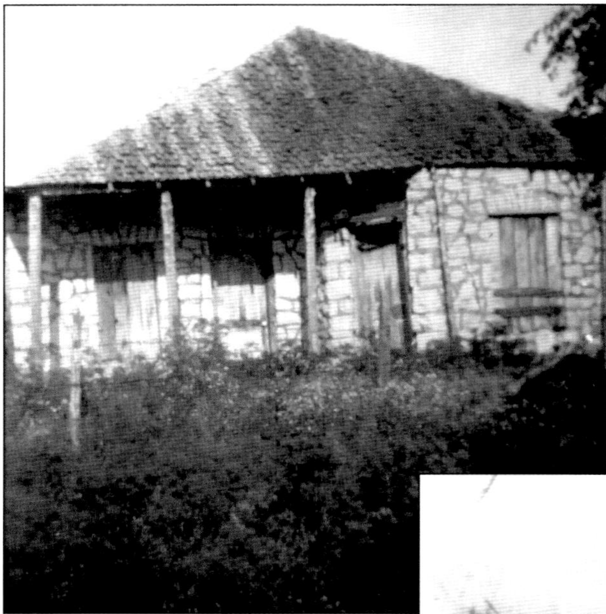

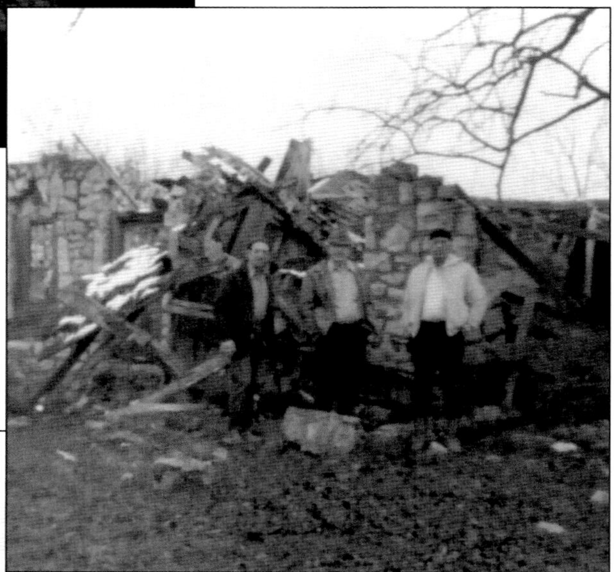

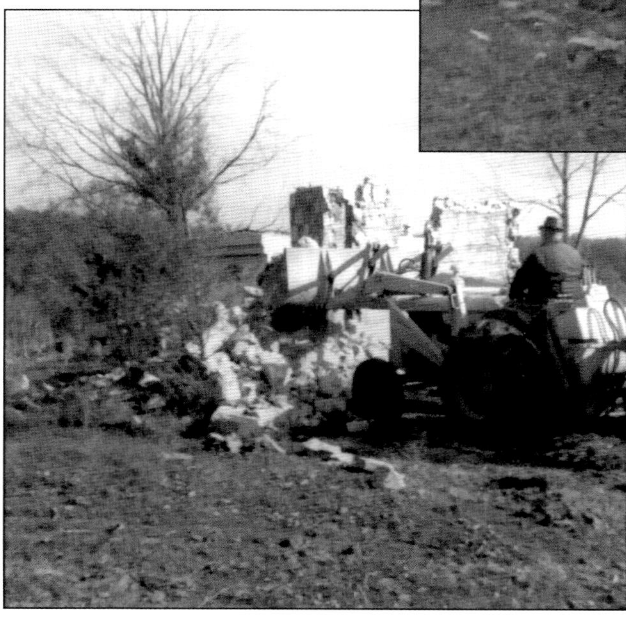

These photographs show the site of Napoleon Bonaparte "Bone" Terry's homestead. They top left photo is what Bone's house originally looked like. The top right photo shows his home as it was being torn down. The bottom left photo is Bone's house at bull Creek after it had been torn down. The men in these photos are all unknown.

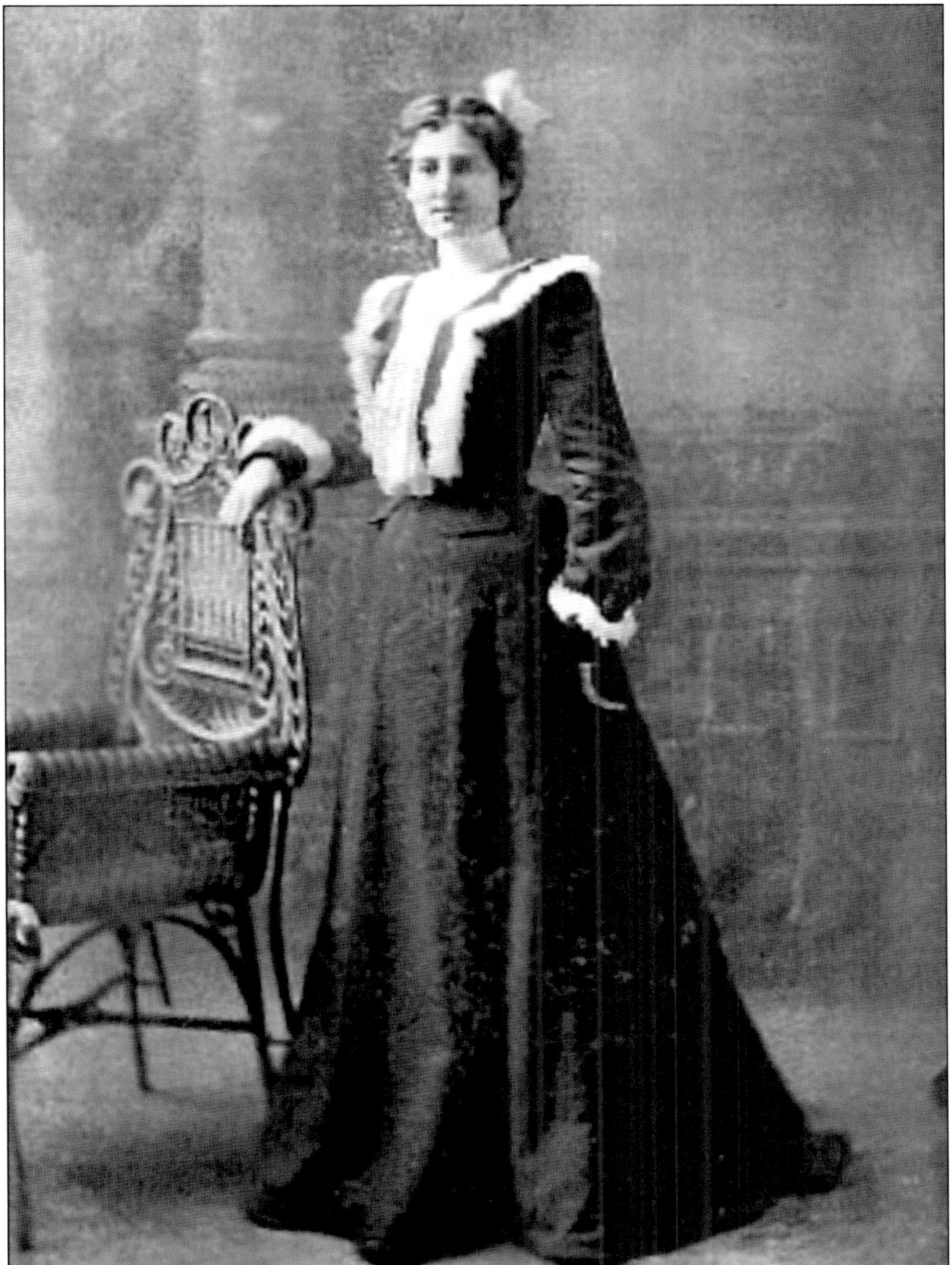

Kate L. (Perkins) Thacker was the daughter of James H. and Margaret A. (Keltner) Perkins. Kate was married to Joseph H. Thacker, who was the son of James L. and Sarah E. (Inman) Thacker of Nixa.

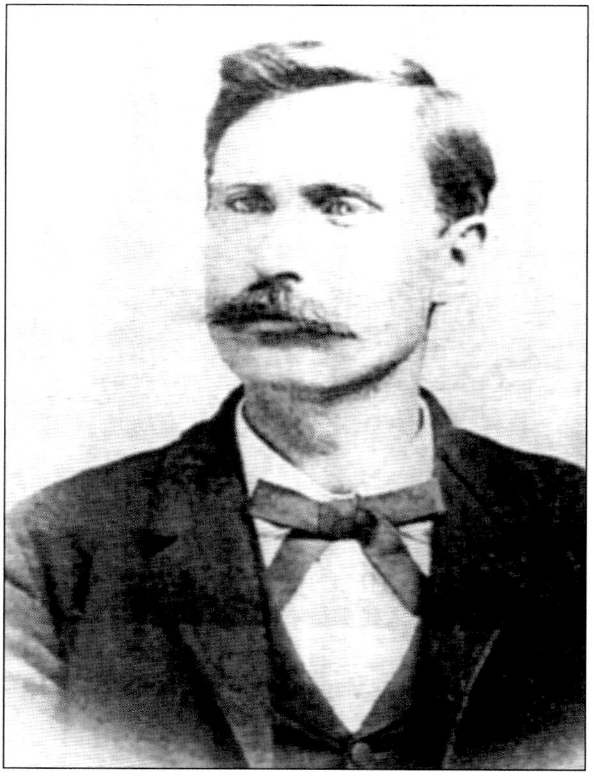

David Lyda Thacker of the Nixa area was the son of James L. and Sarah E. (Inman) Thacker.

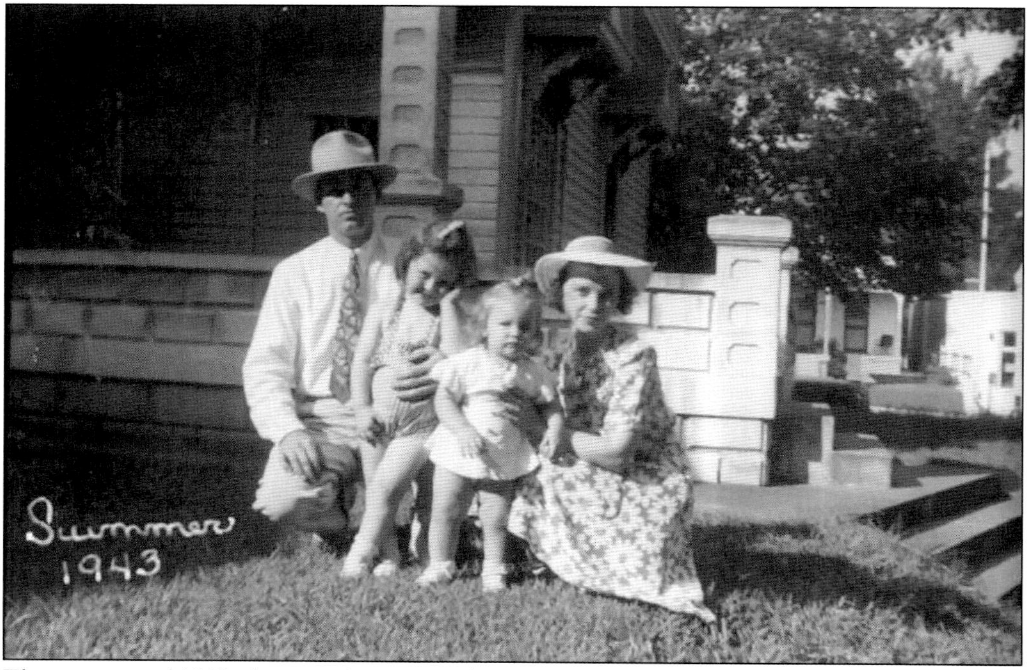

This summer of 1943 photograph portrays the Truex family.

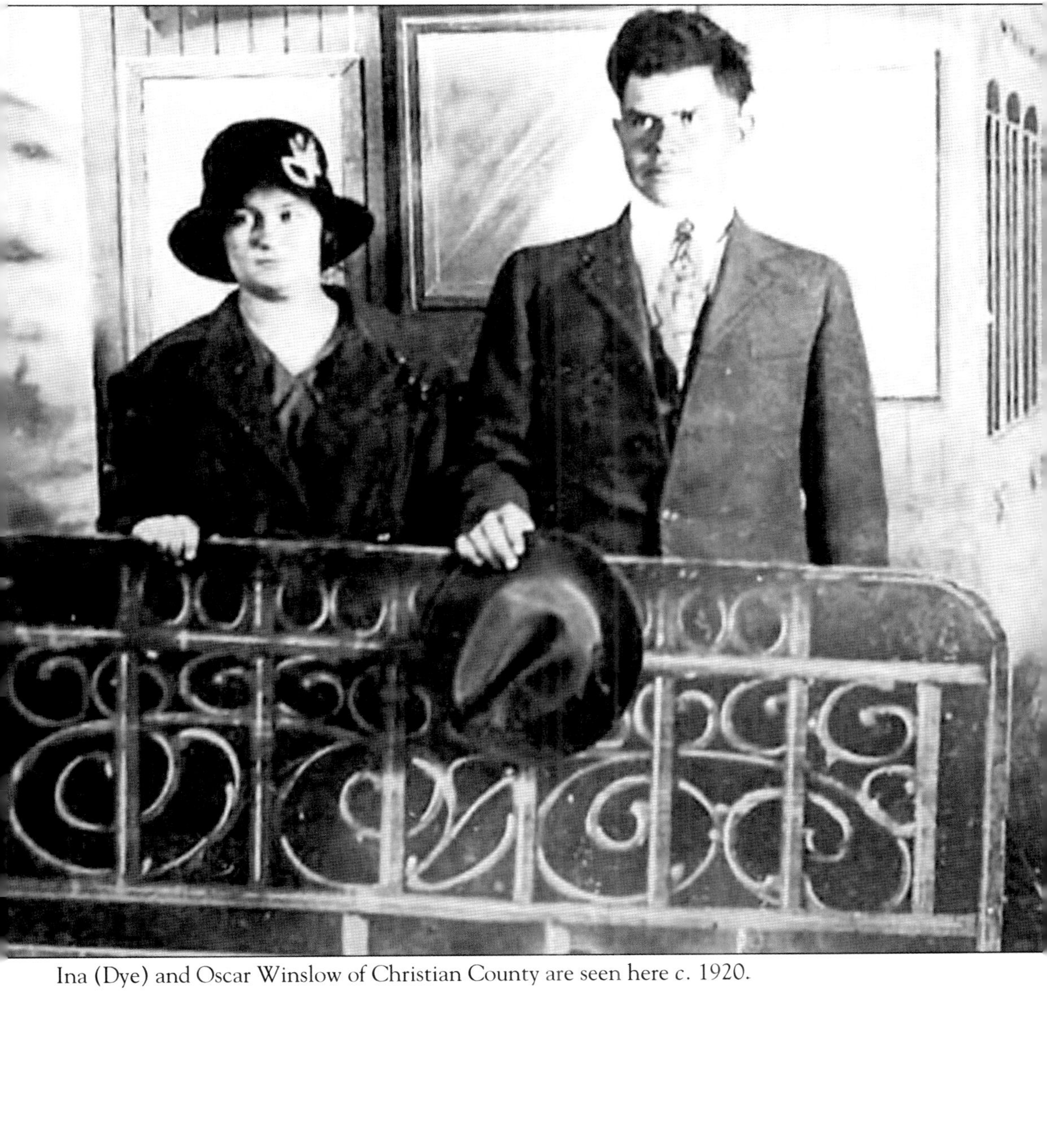

Ina (Dye) and Oscar Winslow of Christian County are seen here *c.* 1920.

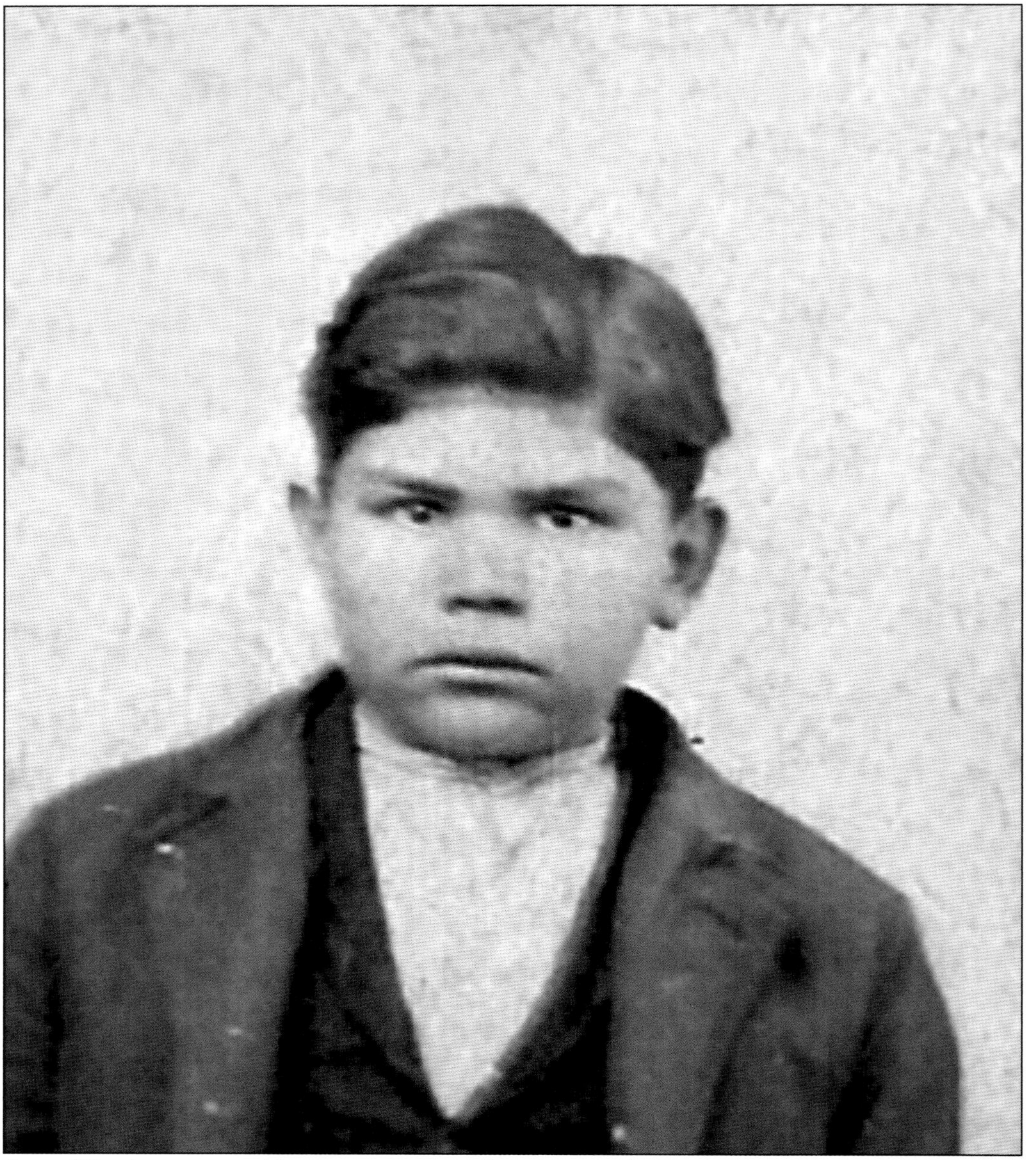

Oscar Winslow, pictured here at age 10, was born September 21, 1893 in Willow Hills, Illinois and died on September 28, 1973 in Christian County. This photo was taken in 1903.

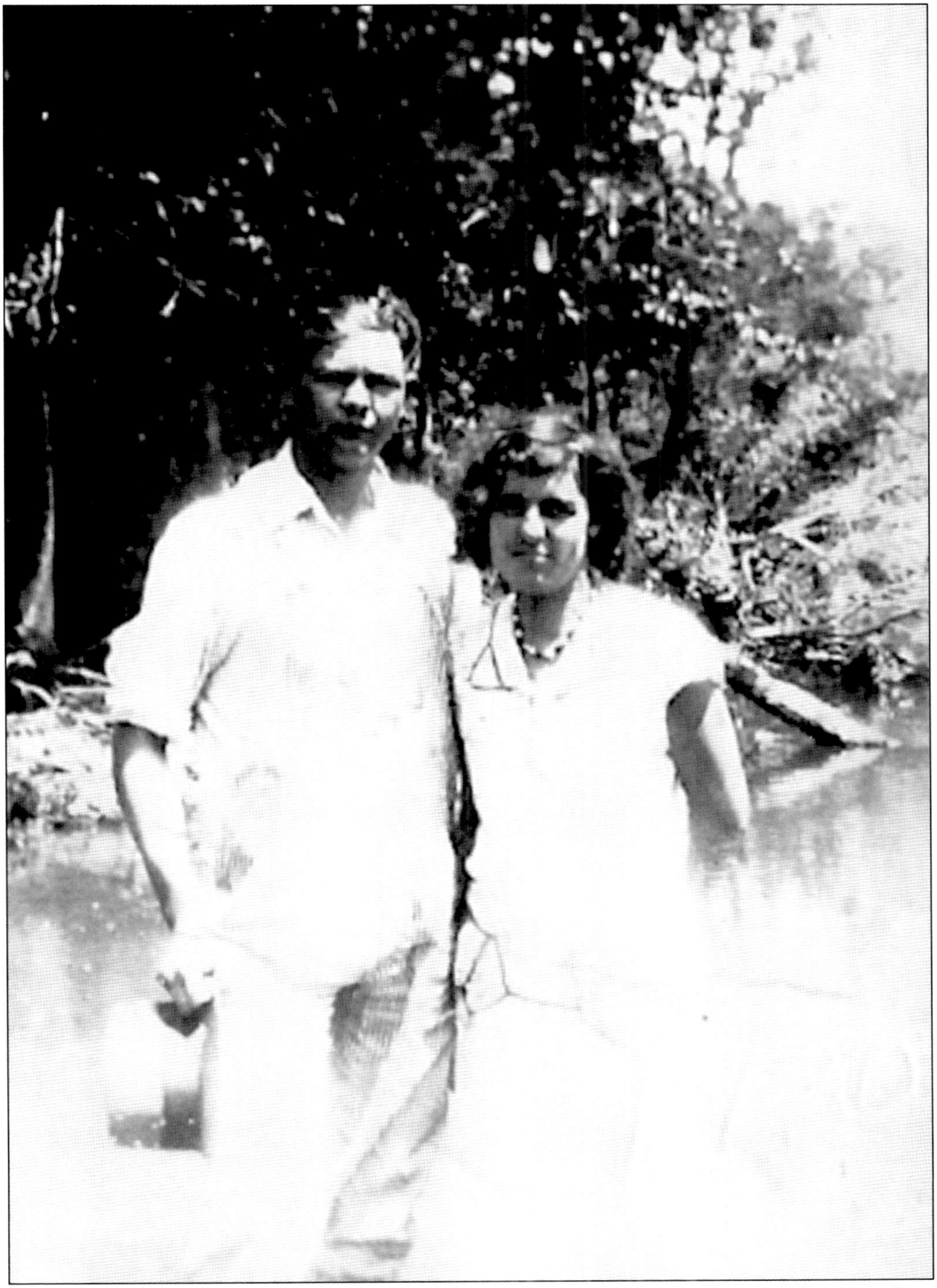

Thomas Basil Winslow and Della Williams, pictured in this 1930 photograph, were from Christian County. Thomas, born on November 15, 1912, was the son of Henry and Rosa (Pettit) Winslow.

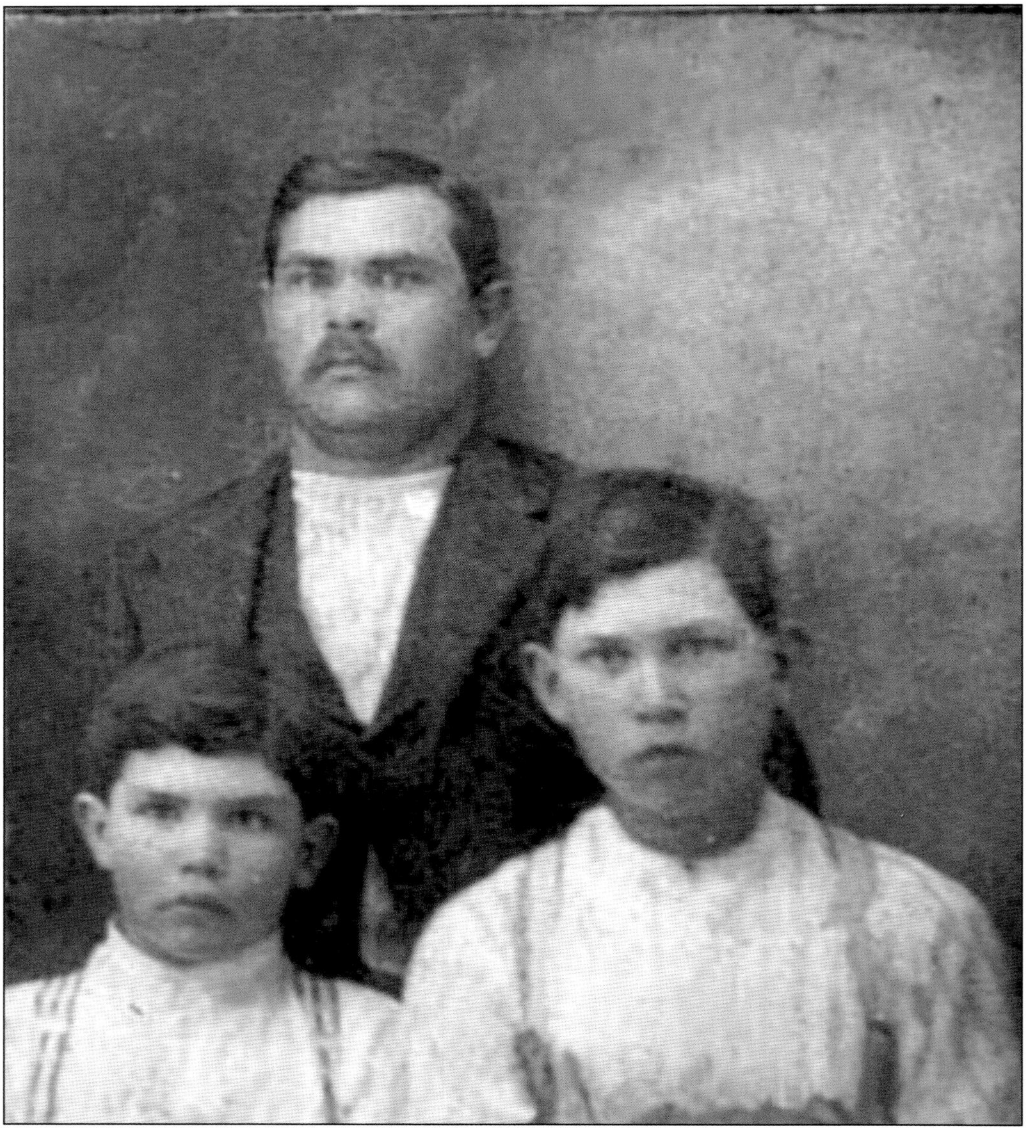

Charles C. Winslow is pictured here with his sons Oscar and Harve. Oscar was born on September 21, 1893 and Harve was born on September 2, 1890. They were all born in Illinois and lived there until they moved to Christian County around 1899. Charles' parents were Albert and Mary Winslow.

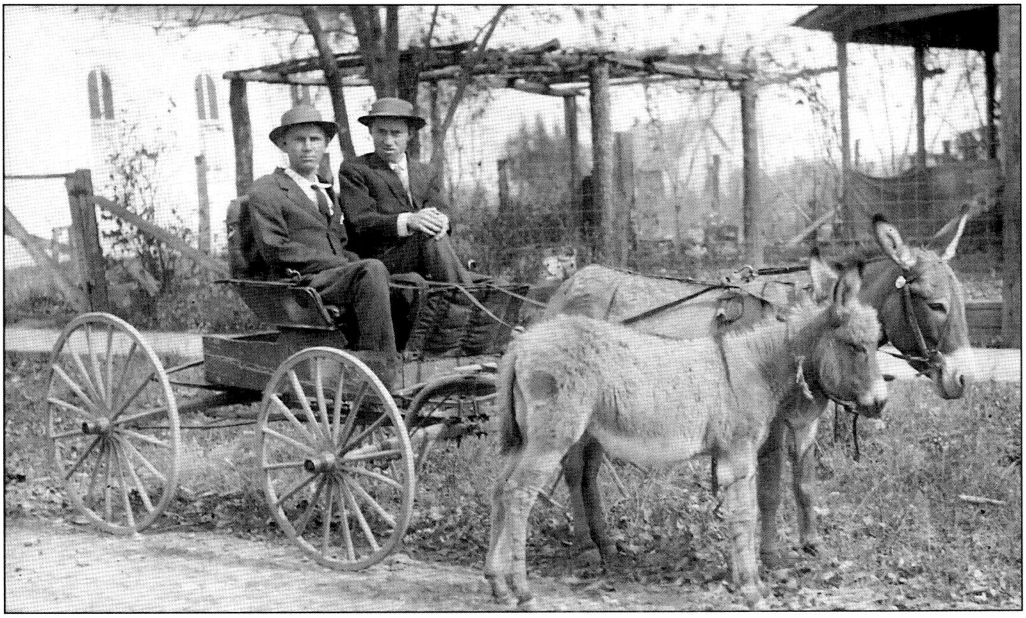

Earnest Winslow and Allen Winslow were the sons of Jerome and Julie Winslow. This photograph was taken in October 1917 in Christian County.

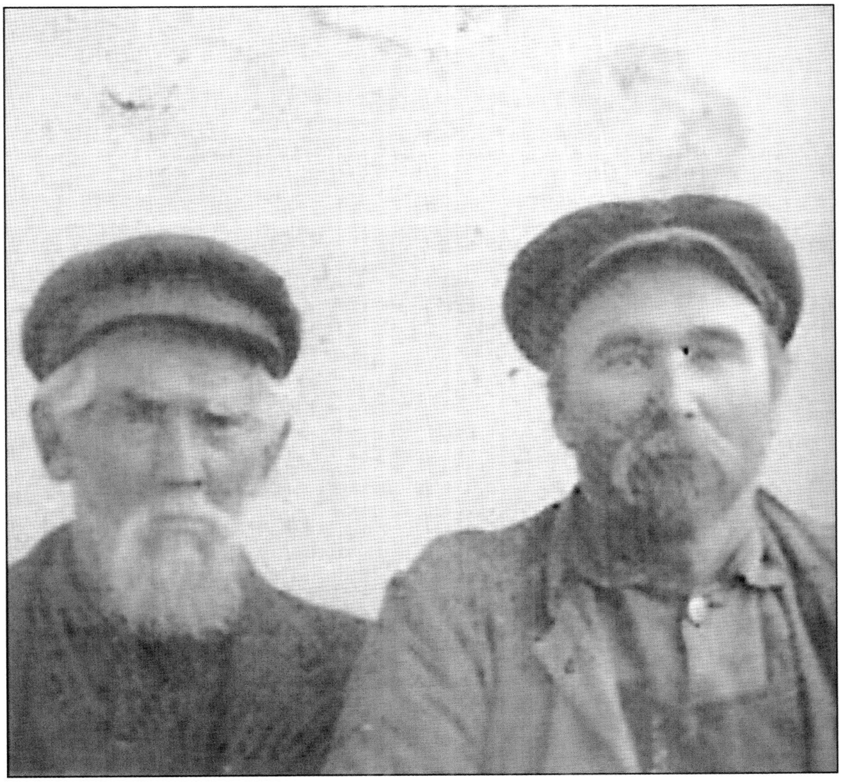

Albert Winslow (left) and Sigel Davis of Christian County are pictured here in 1920.

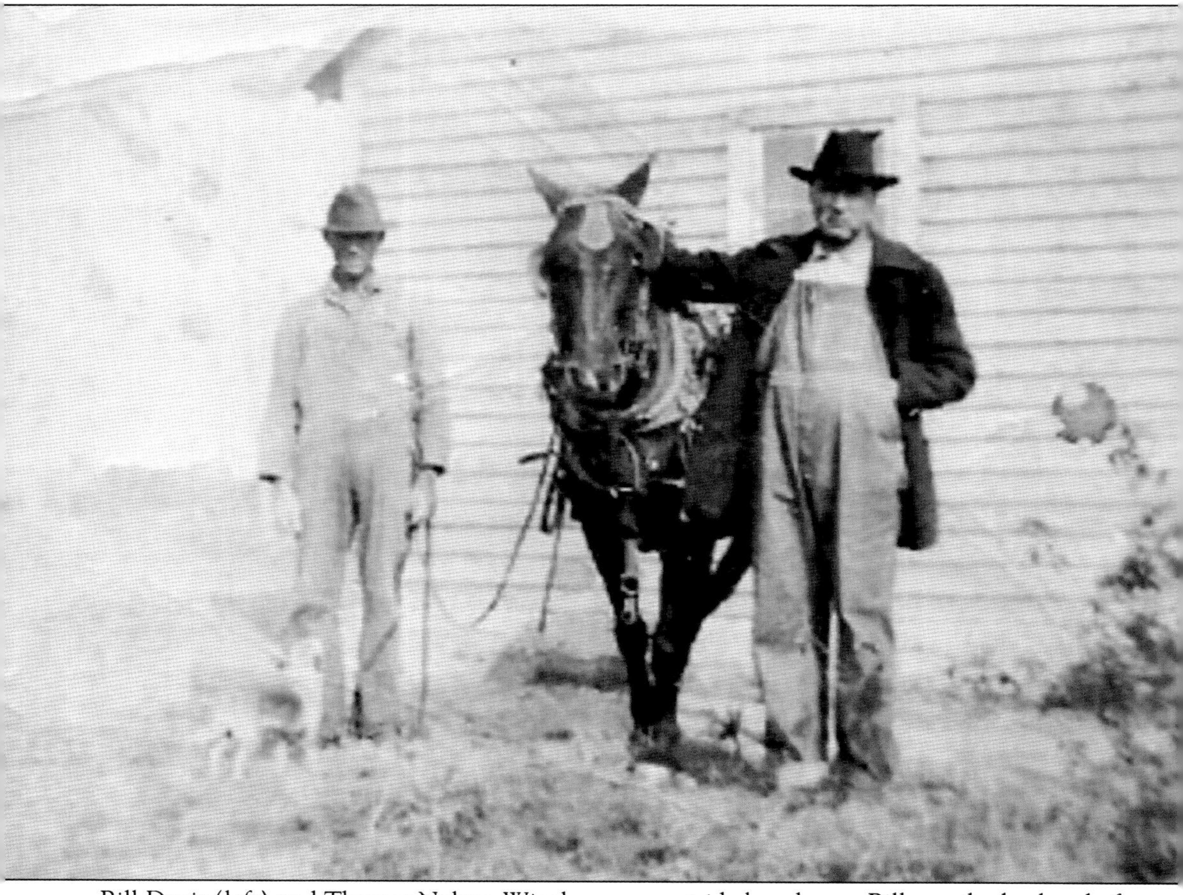

Bill Davis (left) and Thomas Nelson Winslow pose outside by a horse. Bill was the husband of Minnie Davis and Thomas was the husband of Harriet McDaniel. Thomas and Harriet were the parents of Minnie Davis.

Thomas Nelson Winslow is pictured here at his home in Willow Hill, Illinois on November 19, 1880. He later moved to Christian County, Missouri.

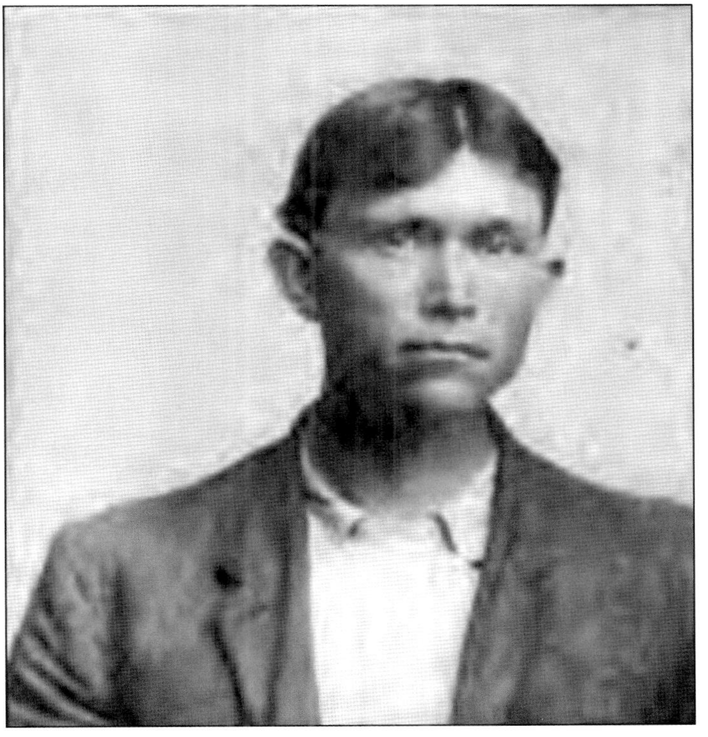

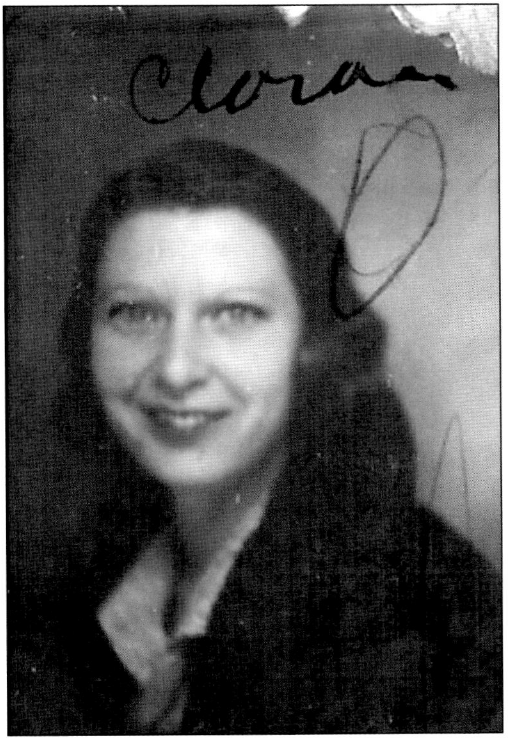

Clara Winslow of Christian County was born on March 31, 1915.

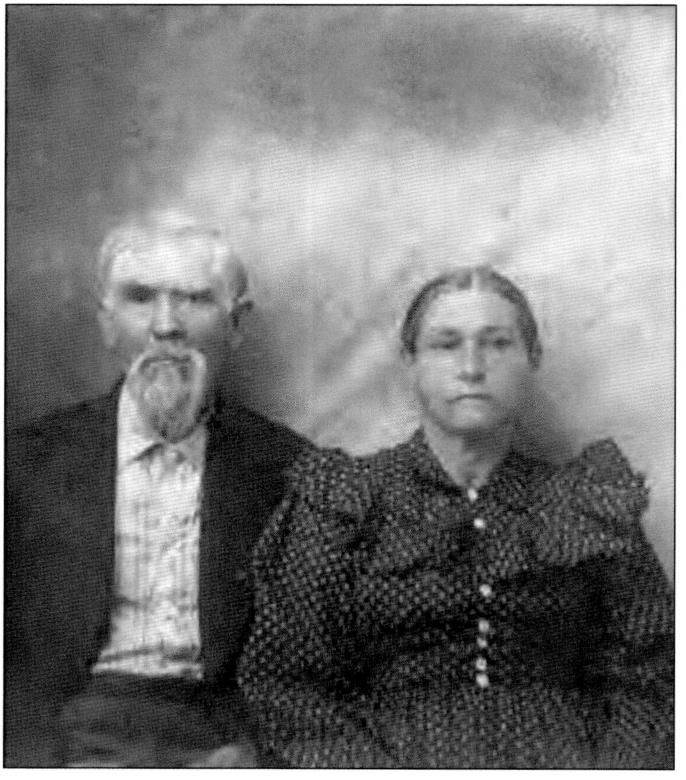

Albert Winslow and his wife Mary F. (Cooley) Winslow, seen here in 1918, lived in Sparta. Albert was a farmer who moved his family to Sparta from Illinois some time between 1895 and 1900.

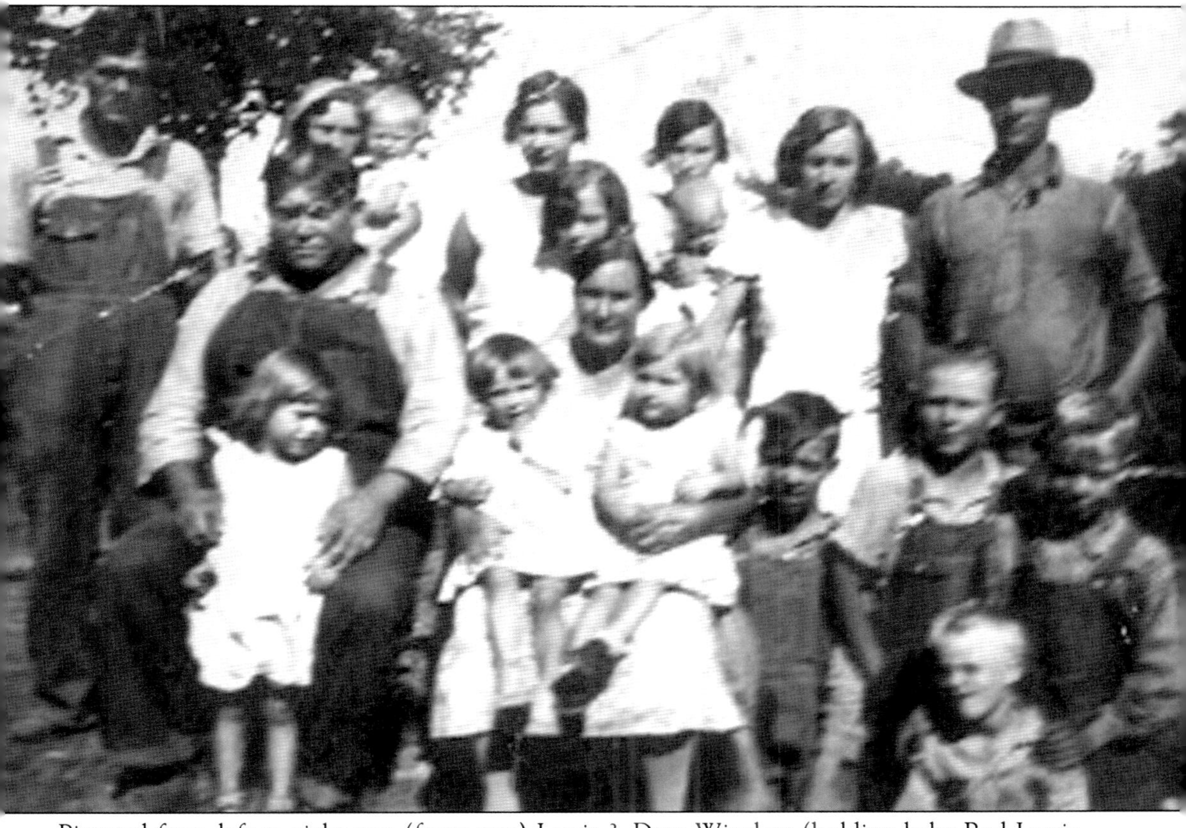

Pictured from left to right are: (front row) Lewis ?, Dora Winslow (holding baby Bud Lewis McMillan), Clara Winslow, Florence Winslow (holding Milbern Winslow), Estle Robison, and Walter Winslow; (second row) Harvey Winslow, Grace Lewis, and Aubery ? (standing behind Grace), and Fred Winslow; (last row) Mary Elizabeth McMillian, Louise McMillan, Dorothy Winslow, and two unknown boys. At the very front on the right side is another unknown boy. John Winslow's sons were Norman Winslow, Harold Winslow, and James Winslow.

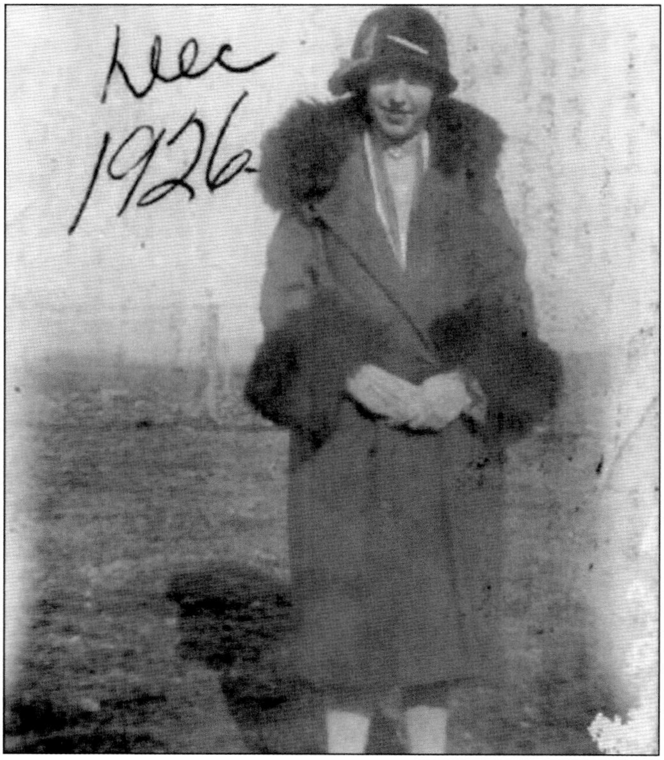

Dora Winslow is pictured here in the winter of December 1926 in front of her home in Sparta.

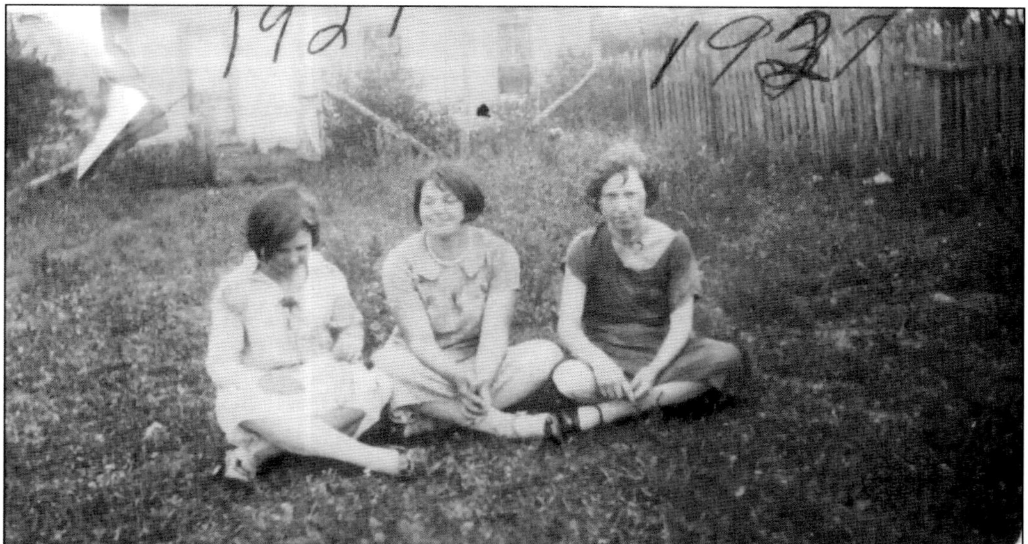

Pictured from left to right, on May 27, 1927, in Sparta, are Dora Winslow McMillan, Clara Winslow, and Olive.

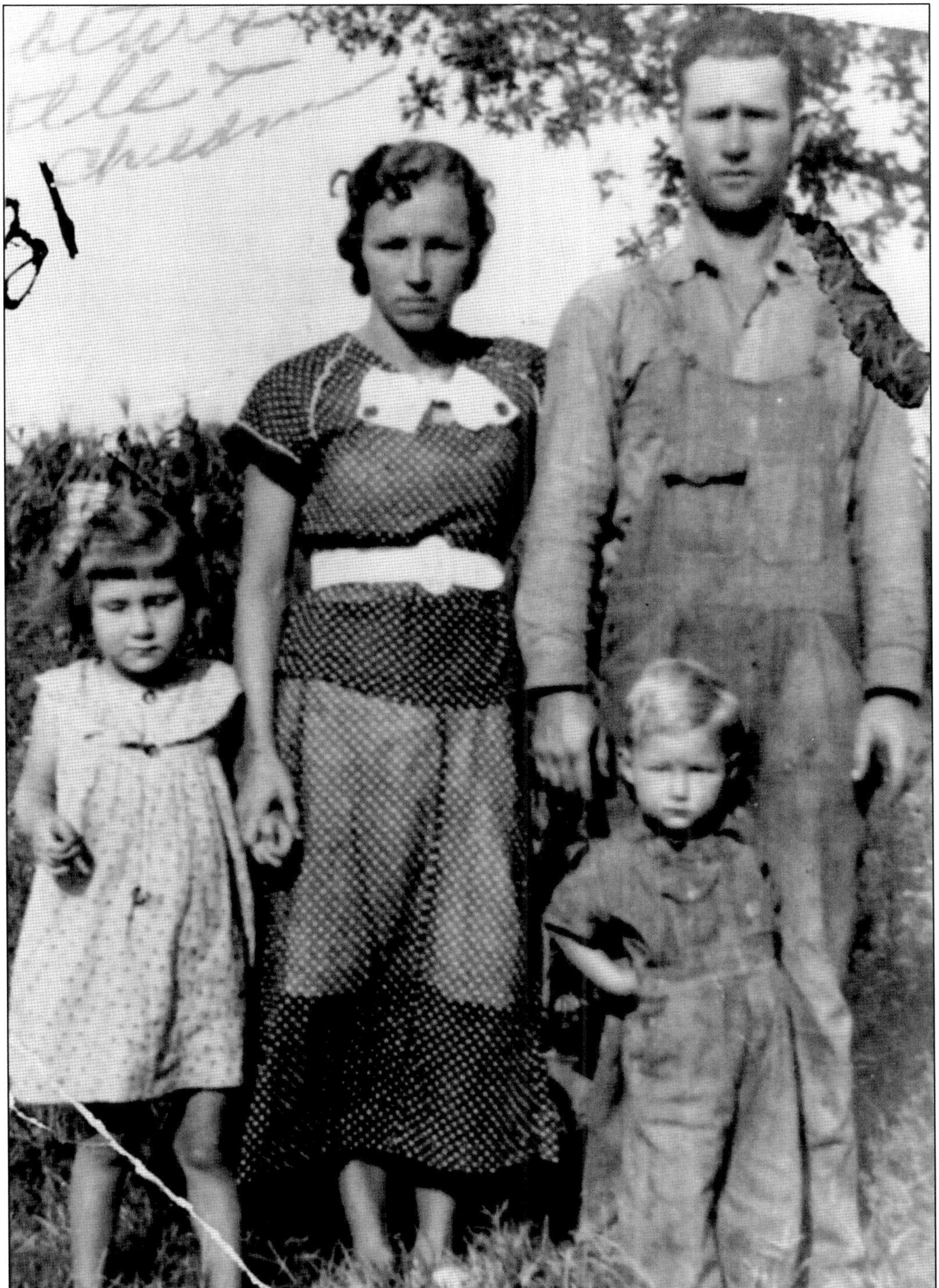

Dorothy Winslow, Estle Winslow, Walter Winslow, and Dinver Winslow (the little boy) pose for this photograph in 1934 in Sparta.

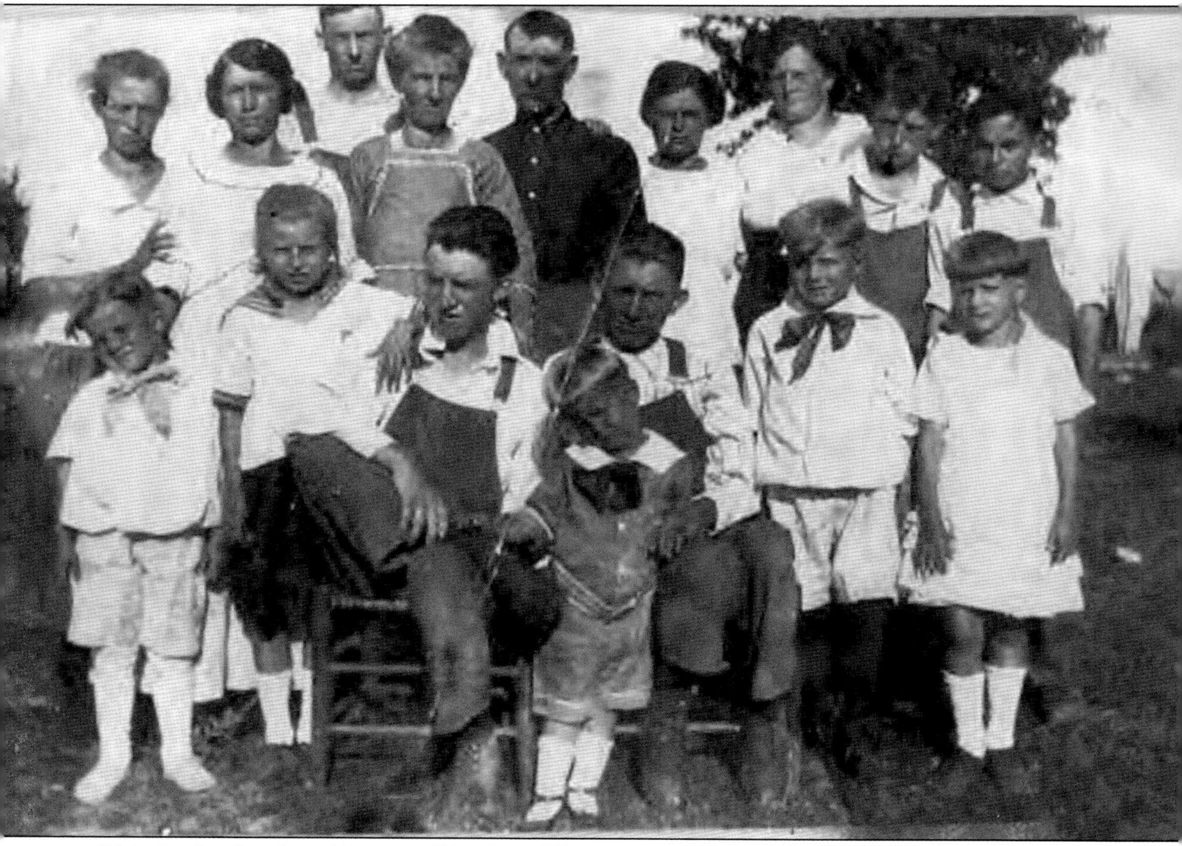

This is the family of Jerome Winslow. These names are listed on the back of the original photo as Annie (Winslow) Gilley, Nora (Winslow) Johnson, Ada (Winslow) Williams, Allen Winslow, and Roy Winslow. The grandchildren are Julie Ann (Adamson) Winslow, born on December 12, 1871, in Sparta, and Jerome Winslow, born in 1861. Some of his grandchildren were Chester, Charles, and J.W. No last names were specified for the children listed. This photo was taken in 1920.

Dora Winslow and Lewis McMillian pose with Walter Winslow and Estle Robinson of Sparta on August 8, 1928.

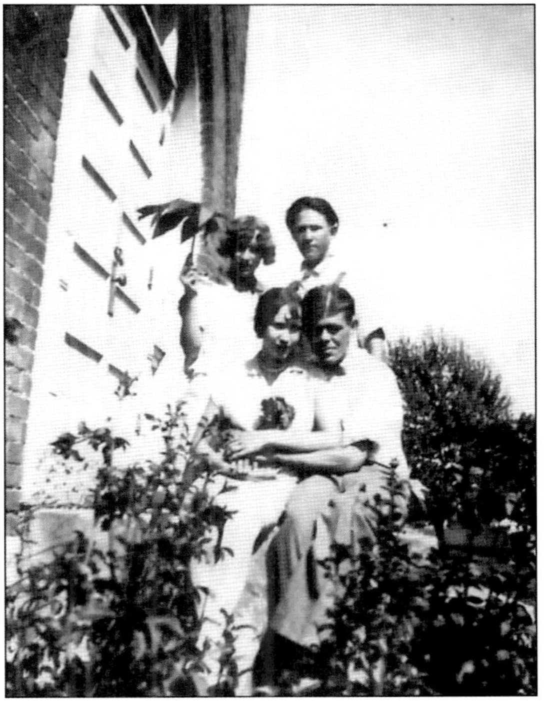

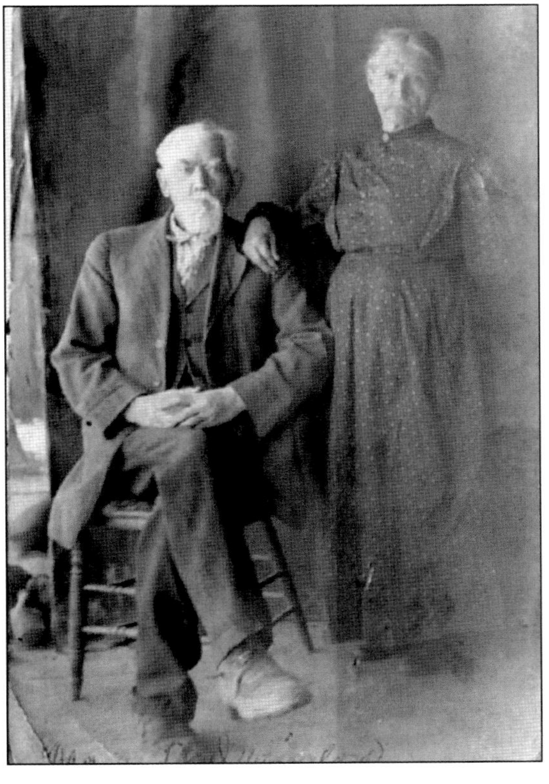

Albert Alvin and Mary Francis (Cooley) Winslow are pictured here in Sparta in 1918 or 1819.

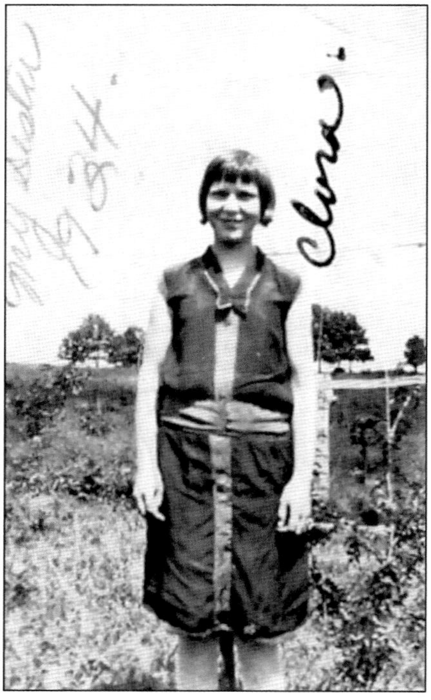

Clara Winslow of Sparta, the aunt of Clara Jaramillo, is seen here in 1934.

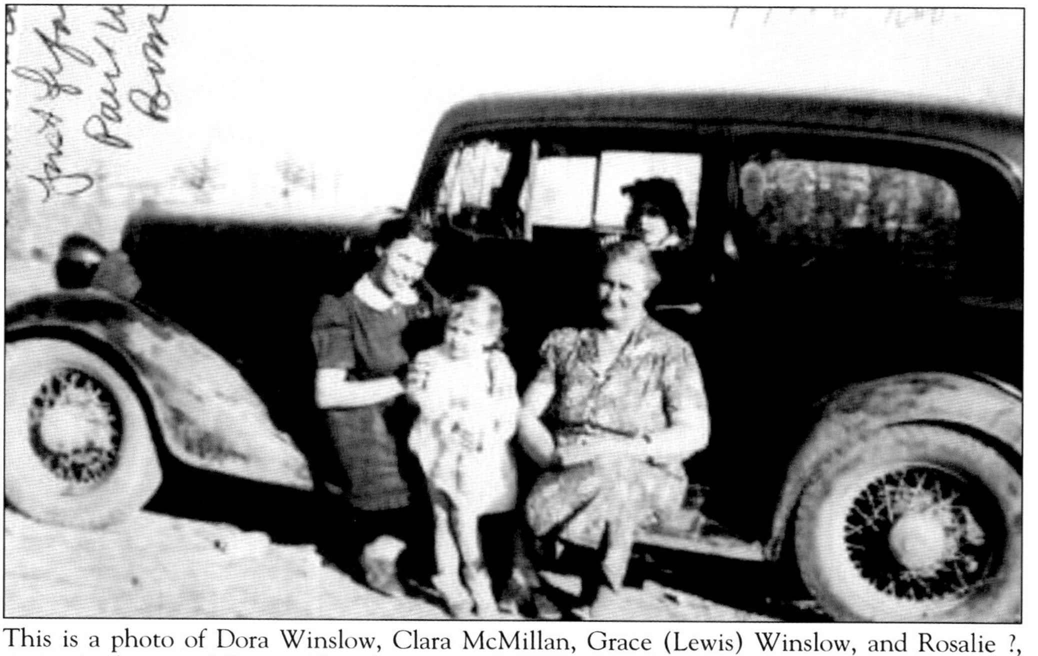

This is a photo of Dora Winslow, Clara McMillan, Grace (Lewis) Winslow, and Rosalie ?, sitting in the car, of Sparta. This photo was taken in November, 1942.

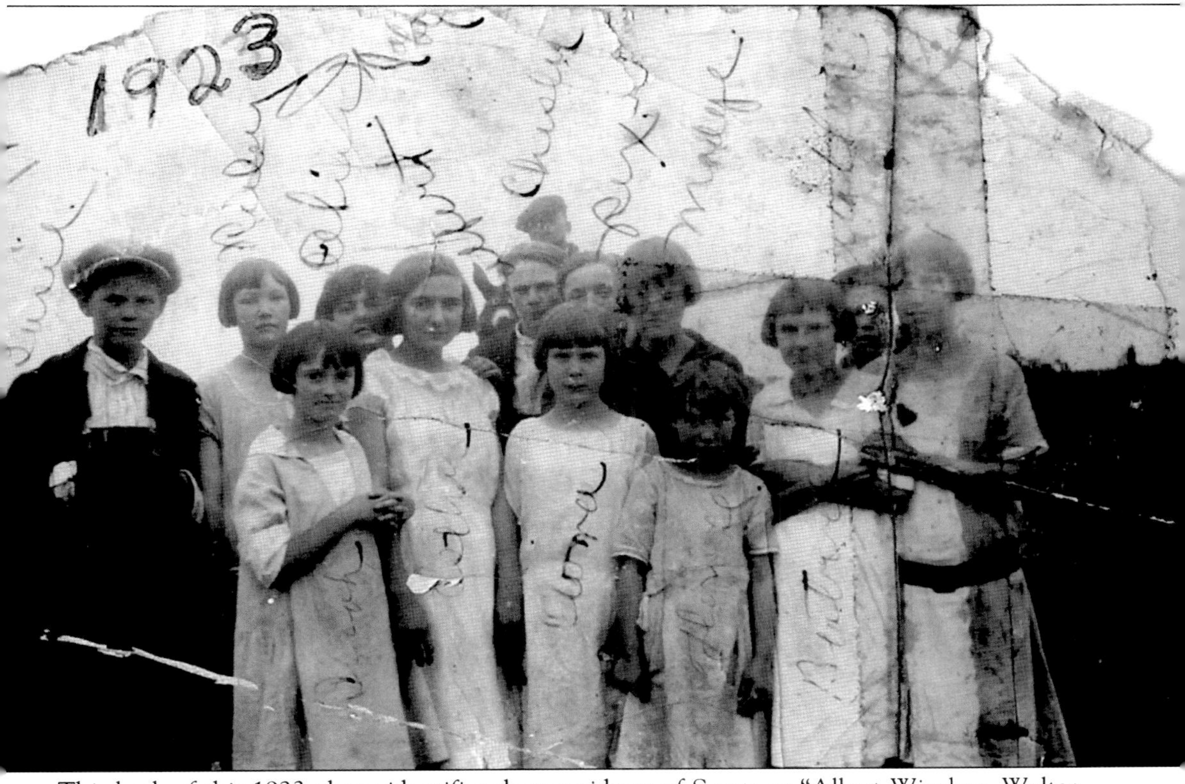

This back of this 1923 photo identifies these residents of Sparta as "Albert Winslow, Walter Winslow, Rex Robertson, Esther Johnson, Ol ?, Beatrice ?, Dora Winslow, and Mack ?"

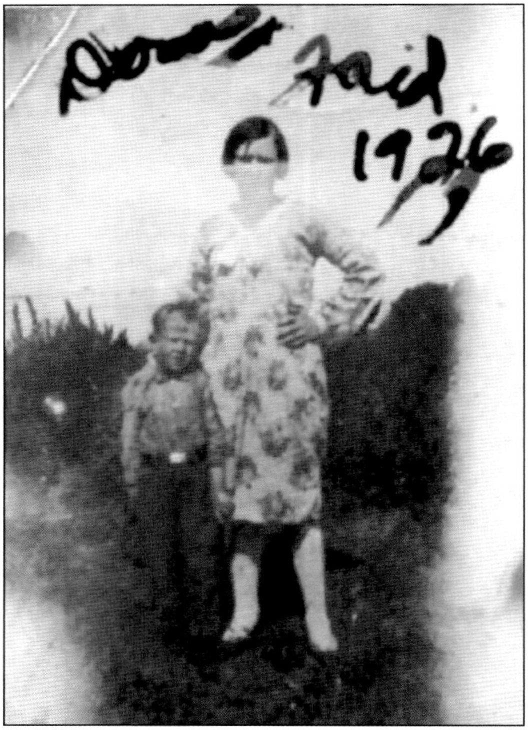

Dora and Fred Winslow of Sparta are pictured here in 1926.

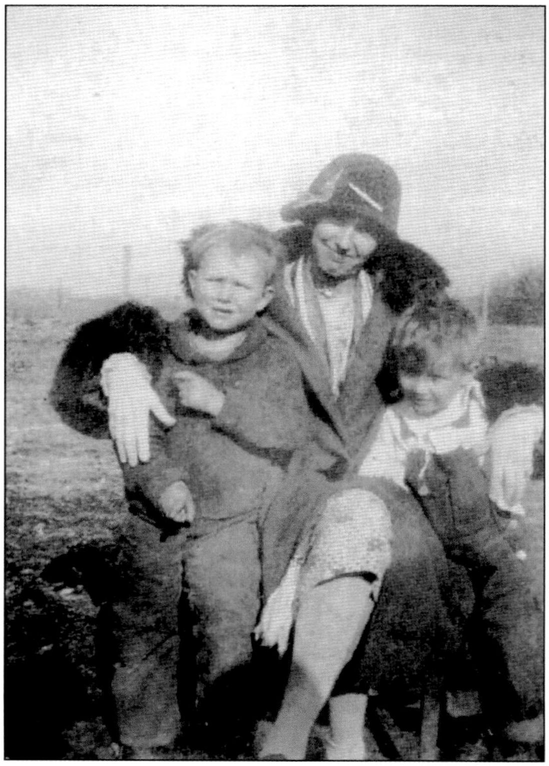

Dora and Fred Winslow are pictured here with Everett Lewis, who was also from Sparta. This photograph was also taken in 1926.

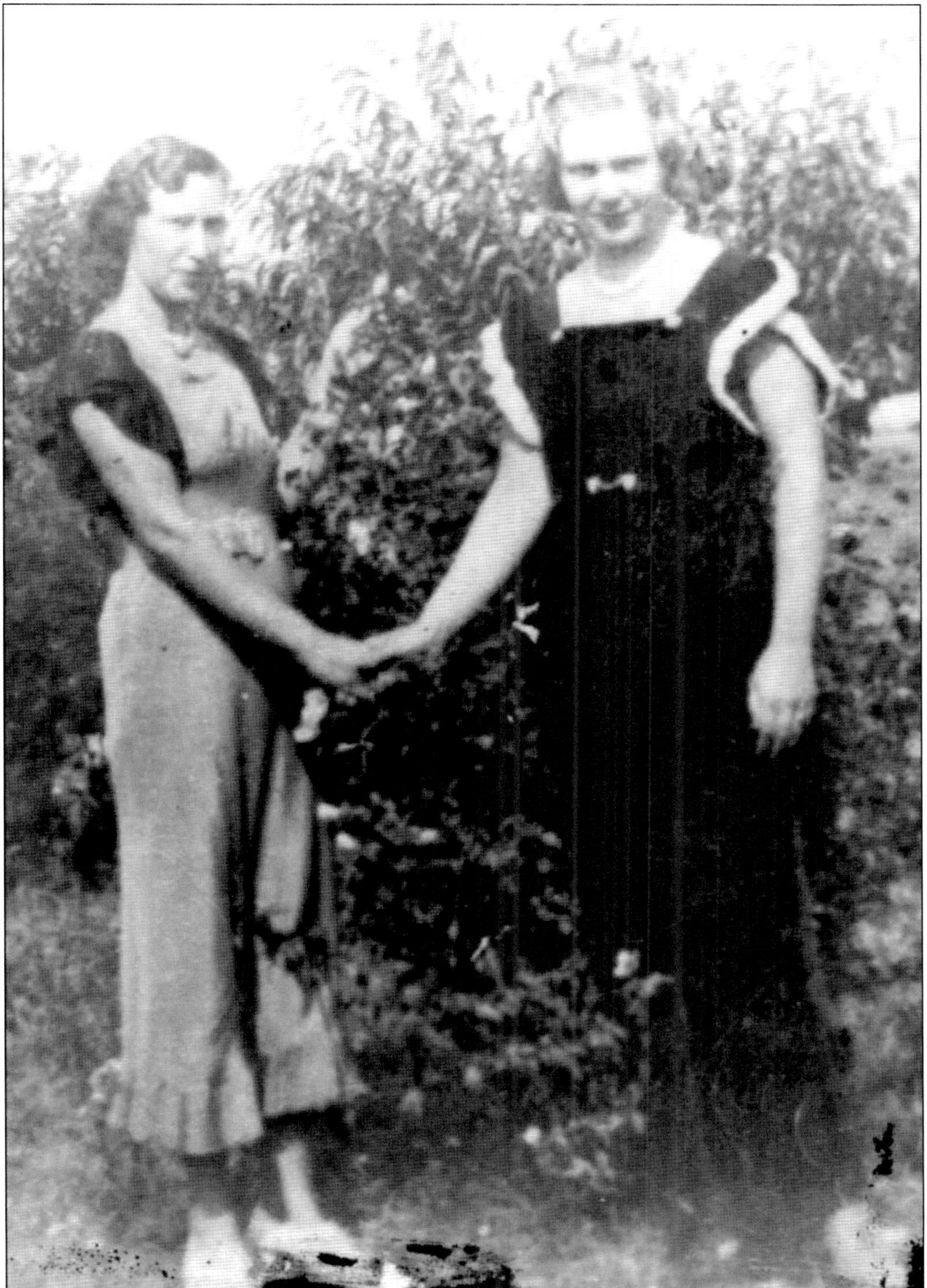

This is Dora (Winslow) McMillan (left) and Clara Winslow of Sparta in the spring of 1934. This photo was taken at their parents' home. Dora was 24 years old and Clara was 19 years old.

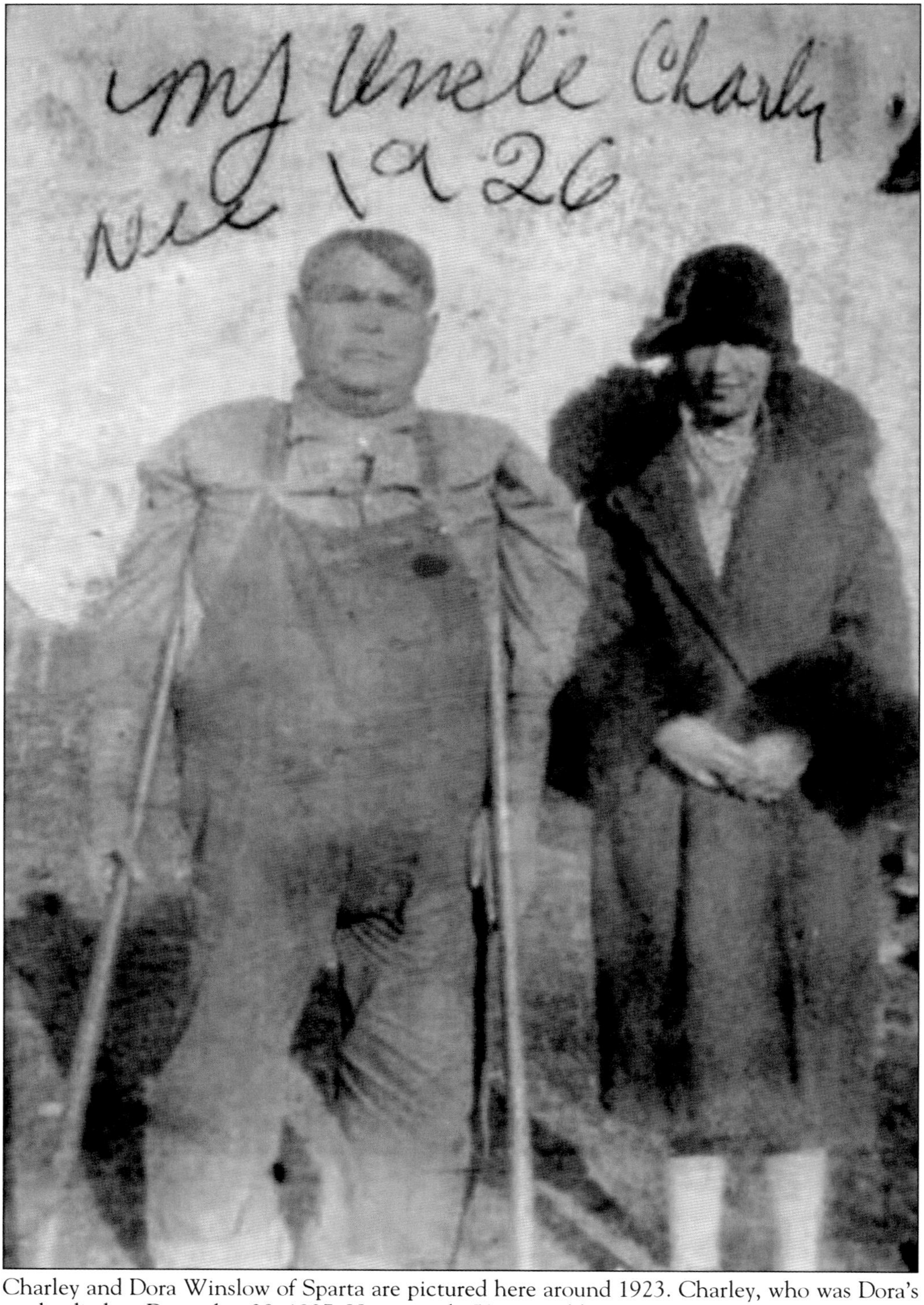

Charley and Dora Winslow of Sparta are pictured here around 1923. Charley, who was Dora's uncle, died on December 28, 1927. He was only 50 years old.

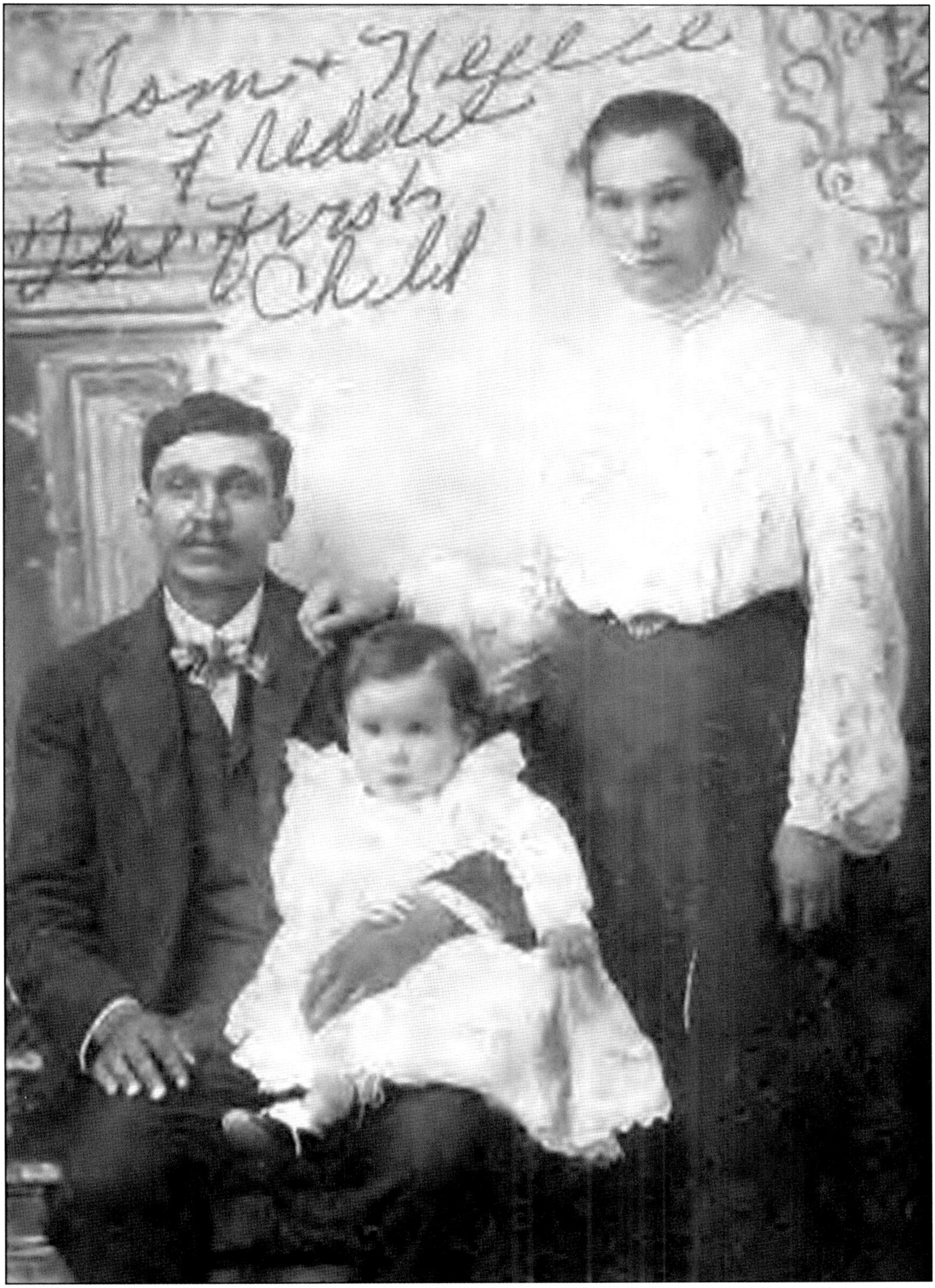

Pictured here are Thomas Lee, Nellie (Winslow) Lee, and their baby, Freddie Lee. Thomas was born on January 30, 1871, Nellie on March 24, 1883, and Freddie in 1903. This family was from Sparta and they had this photo taken in either 1904 or 1905.

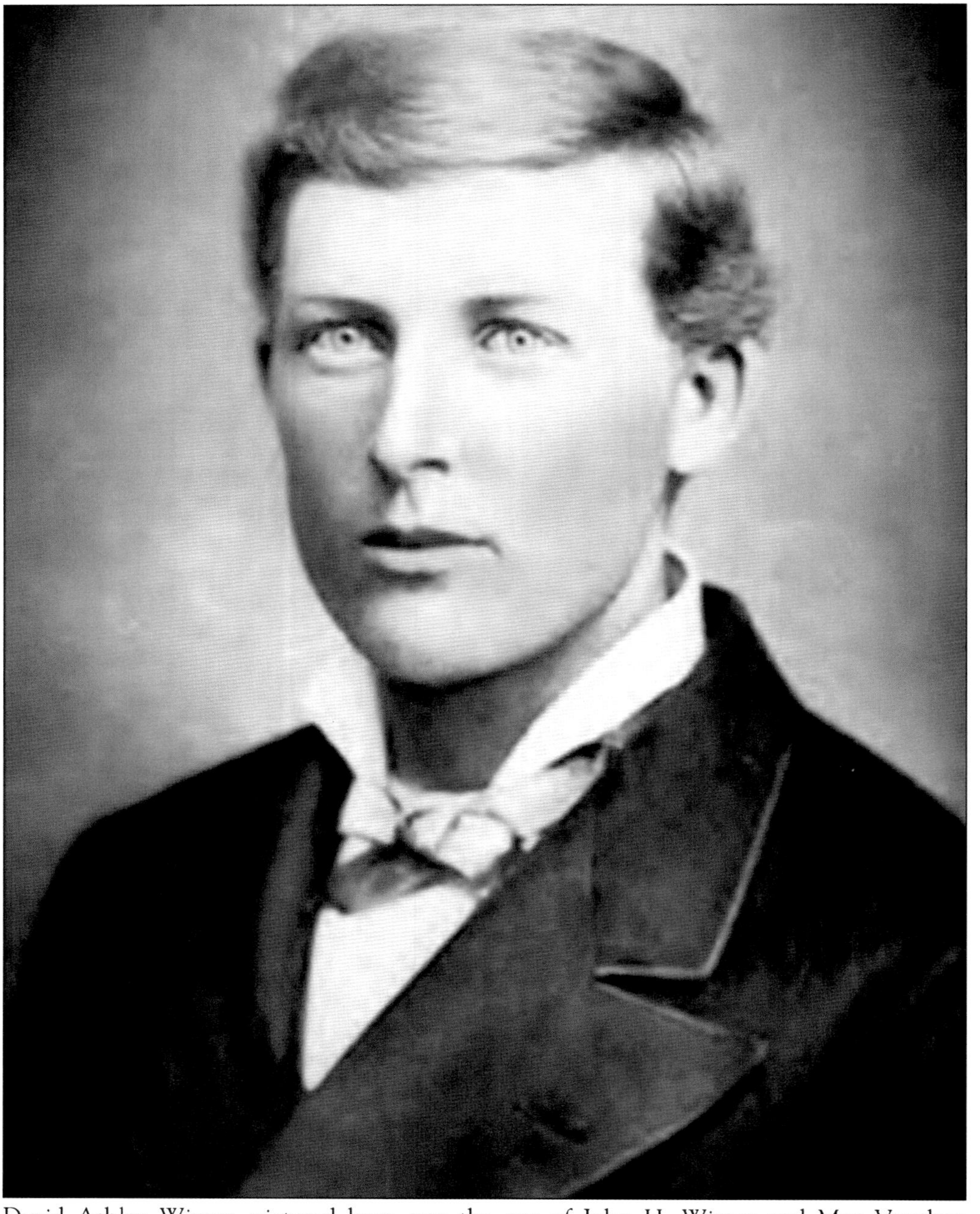

David Ashley Wisner, pictured here, was the son of John H. Wisner and May Vaughan Wisner.

Four

NIXA BUSINESSES

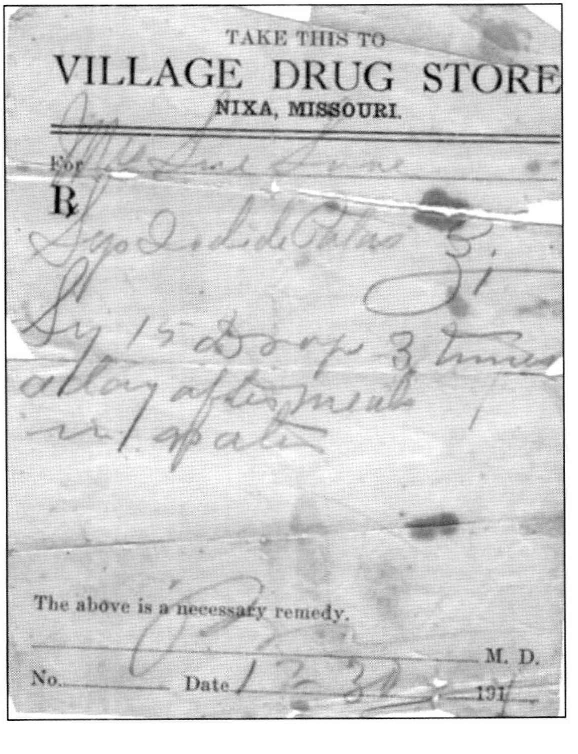

TAKE THIS TO
VILLAGE DRUG STORE
NIXA, MISSOURI.

For

℞

The above is a necessary remedy.

M. D.

No. Date 12 30 1911

This prescription form dated December 30, 1911, was made out for the Village Drug Store in Nixa.

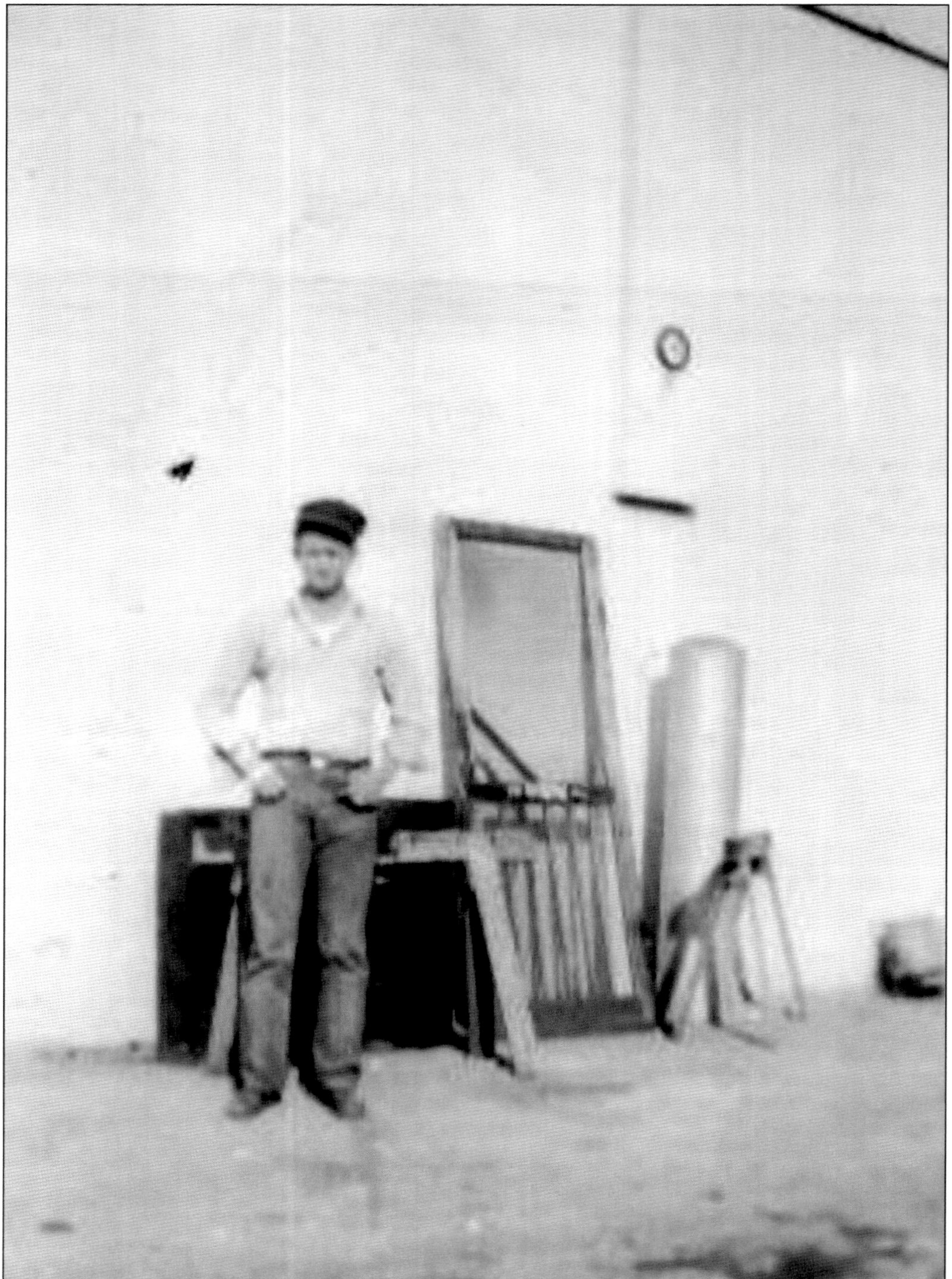

The man in this photo is unknown. However, he appears to be standing in front of a warehouse in Nixa.

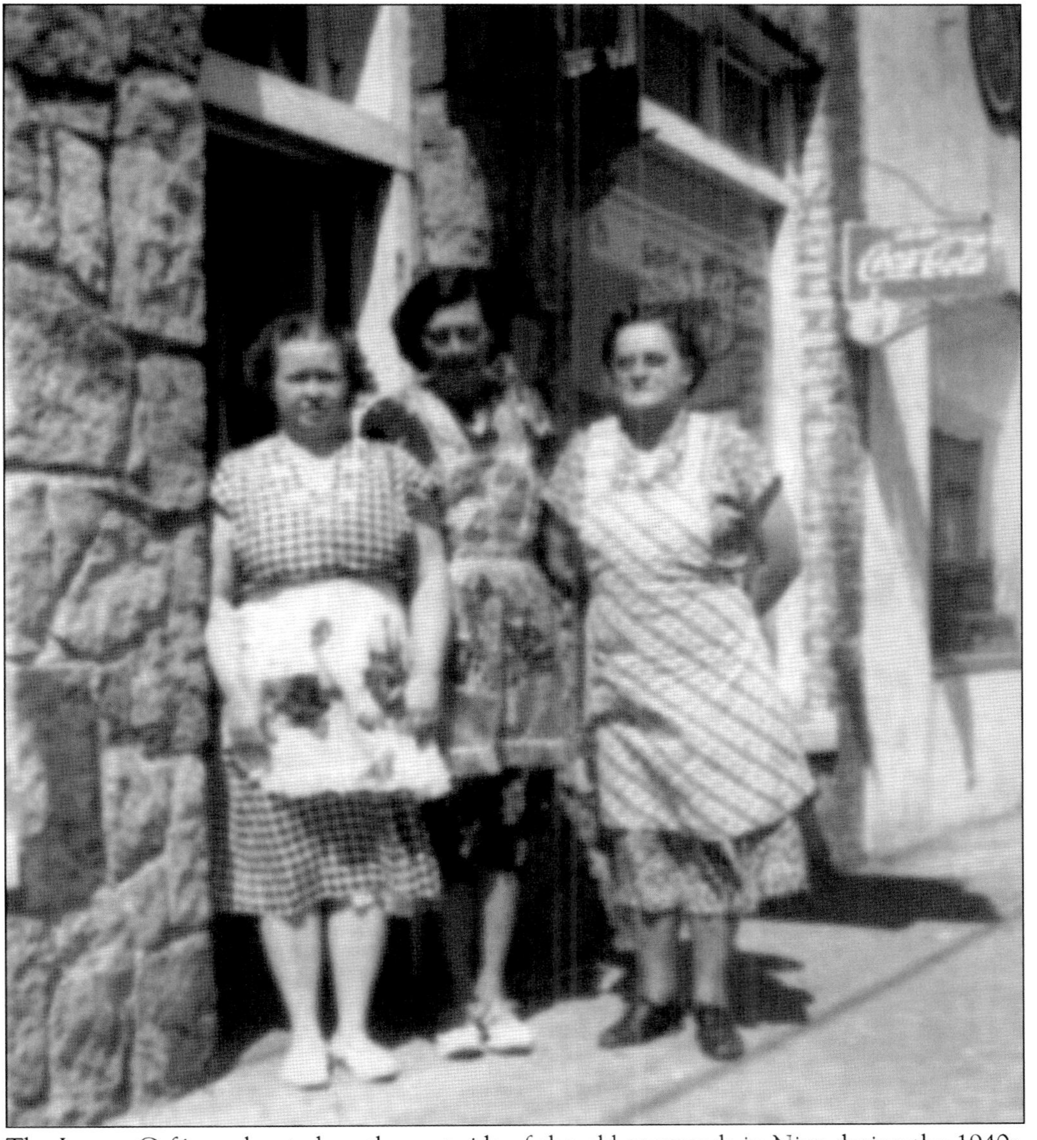

The Inman Café was located on the east side of the old crossroads in Nixa during the 1940s. Hester Ann (Aven) Jackson, on the far left hand side of this photo, is the only identified person. Hester was married to Herbert C. Jackson, and they were the parents of Joretta (Jackson) Fitzpatrick.

According to *A Photo History of Nixa & Vicinity* by Wayne Glenn, this photo of the Inman Café could have been the old "Soda Stiffler" café. Glenn states that after Soda's heart attack after the War, "Ollie Aven Inman opened a new café at that former site." He continues, "This was the era of three of four cafes at once in downtown Nixa, as the whey plant and cheese factory workers, milk haulers, and truckers provided a major customer base for cafes with good cooks like Ollie."

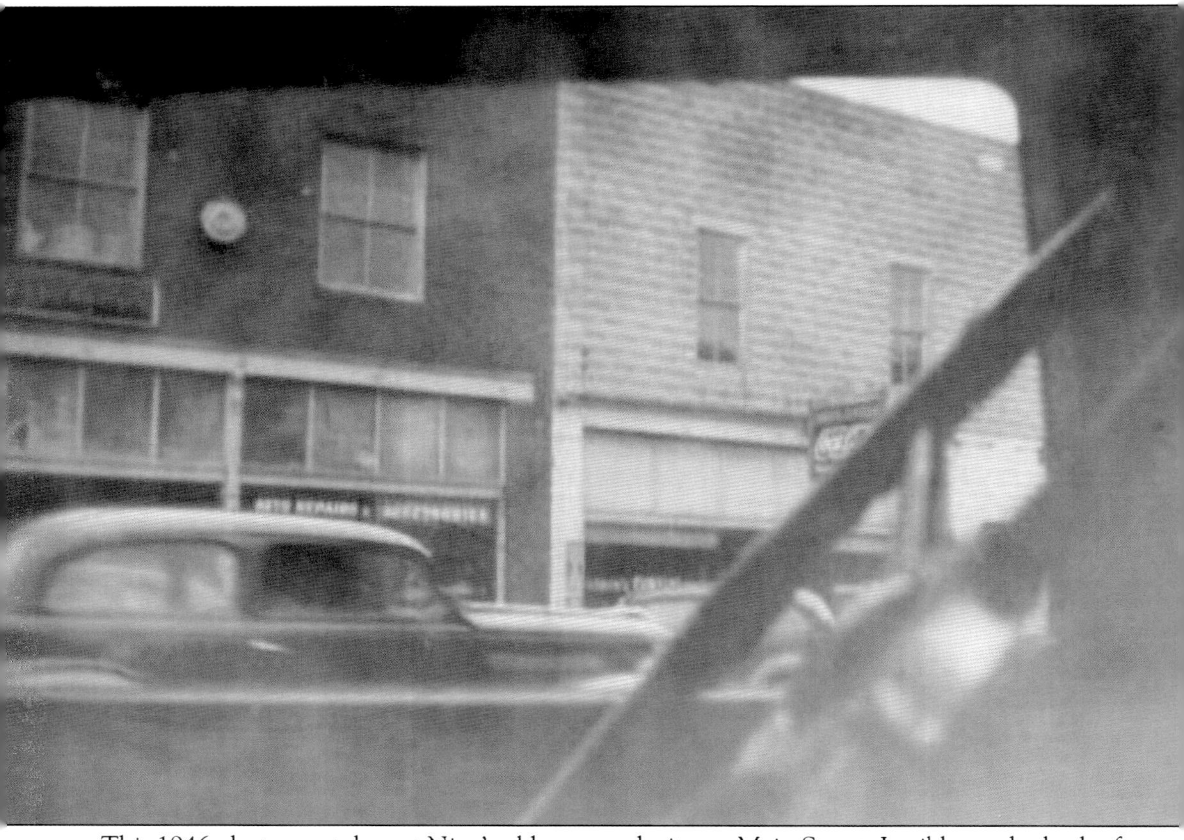

This 1946 photo was taken at Nixa's old crossroads site on Main Street. Legible on the back of this photo is, "Taken out of a man's car named Ralf ?, during 1946."

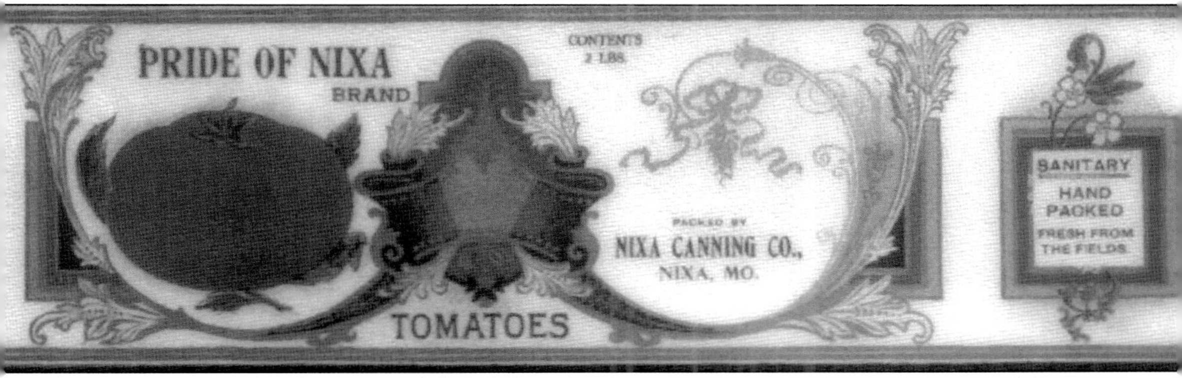

These are Nixa Canning Factory labels. The Nixa Canning Factory was one of the town's first major businesses. Wayne Glenn writes in *A Photo History of Nixa & Vicinity*, "This was a large building located about three-quarters of a mile east of the crossroads on the north side of the narrow road that led to Ozark."

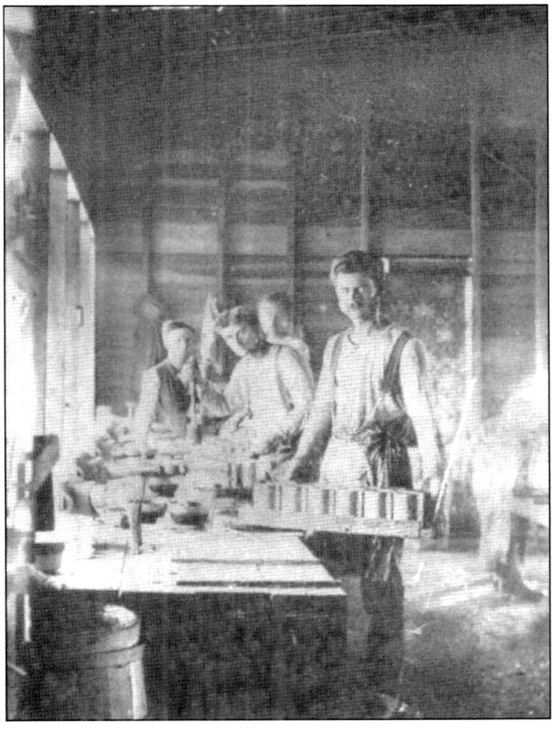

The Nixa Canning Factory was established in Nixa around 1898. The only man identified in this group is Fredrick Wilson Inman, who is in the foreground.

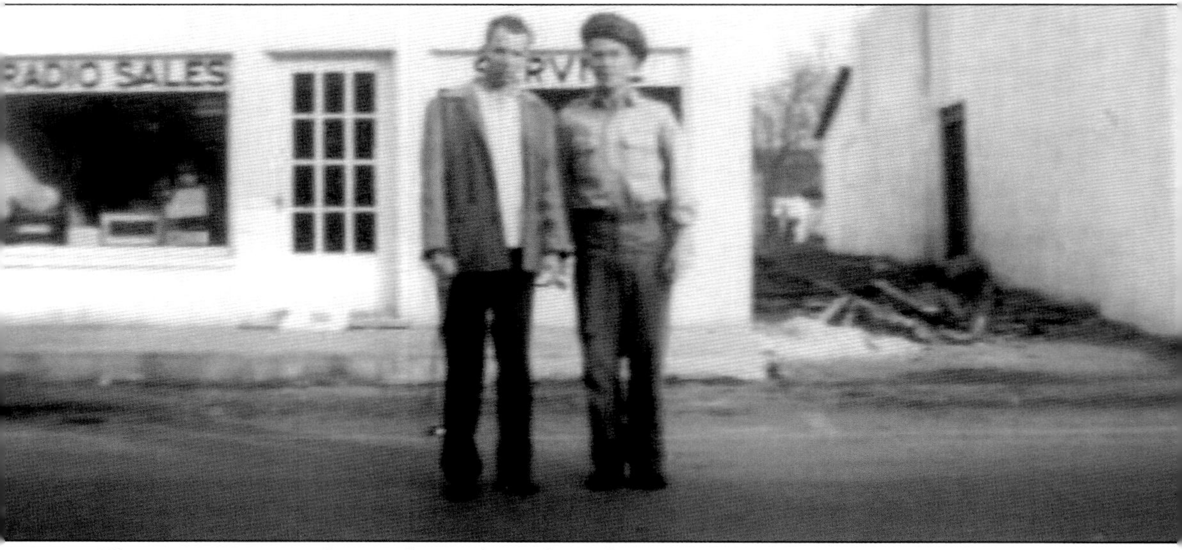

These two men standing in front of a Radio Sales store in Nixa are unknown. The photograph was taken sometime in the 1940s.

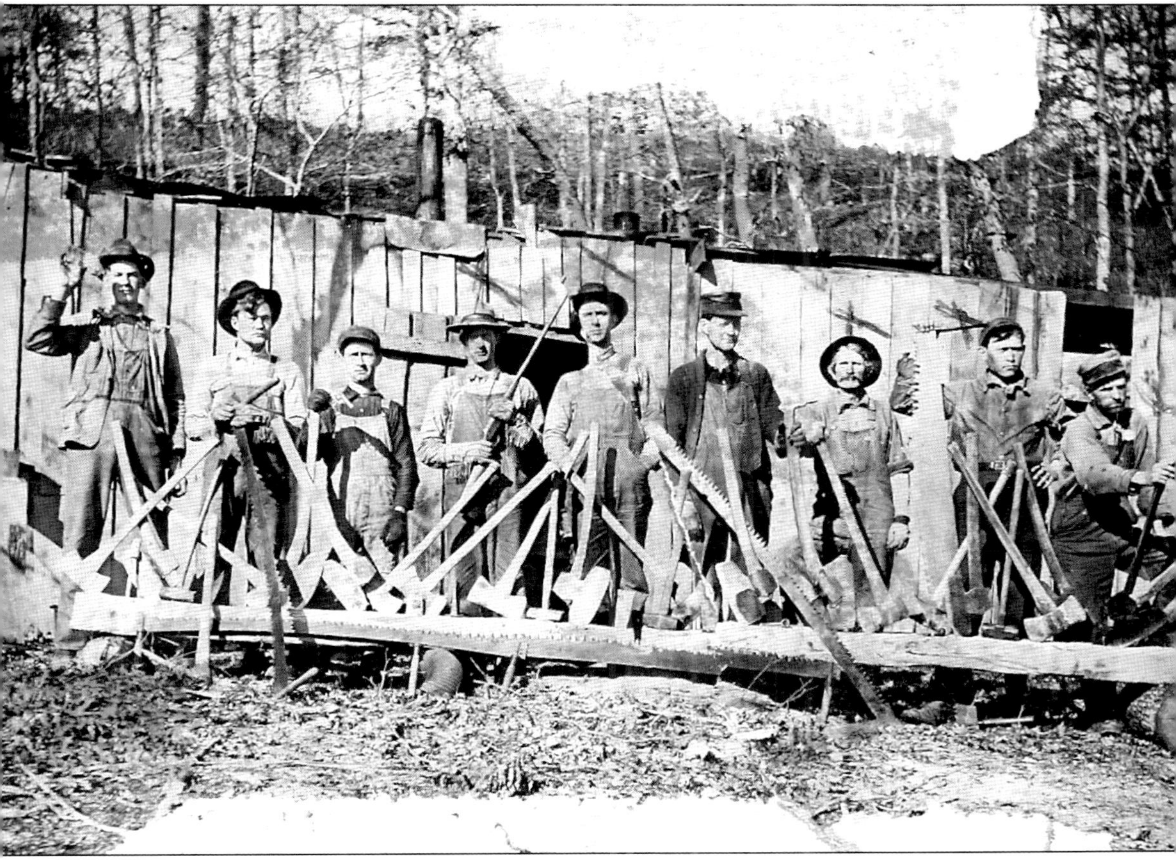

These Chadwick men are making railroad ties in 1917. Second from the left is Harve Lewis, and third from the left is Charles Lewis. It is unclear who the rest of the men are, but they include Jake Lewis, Wesley Lewis, and Riley Lewis, who were all sons of Charles Lewis. Also in the photo is Charles' son-in-law Frank Whitlock.

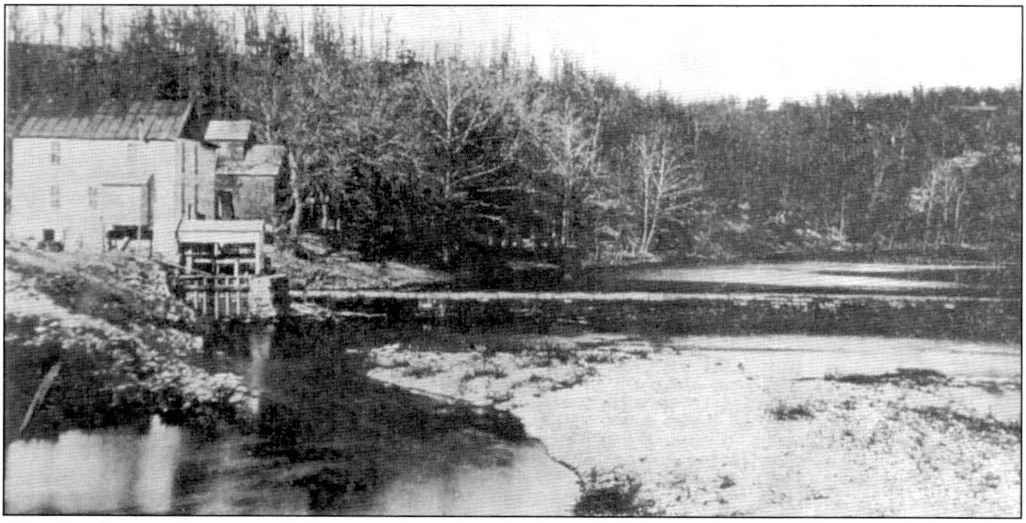

The Linden Mill in Linden, Missouri operated from 1833 to 1921. The Lindenlure Hotel extended out over this mill's pond at the extreme right and beyond this photo.

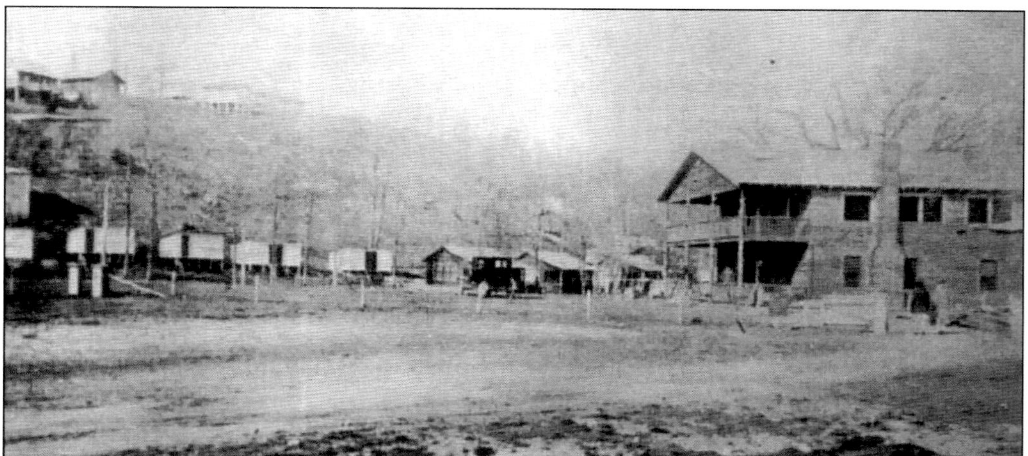

In this photo you can see the front portion of the Lindenlure Hotel. Cabins were built later to supplement the housing, which had been provided in the main building of the Linden Mill.

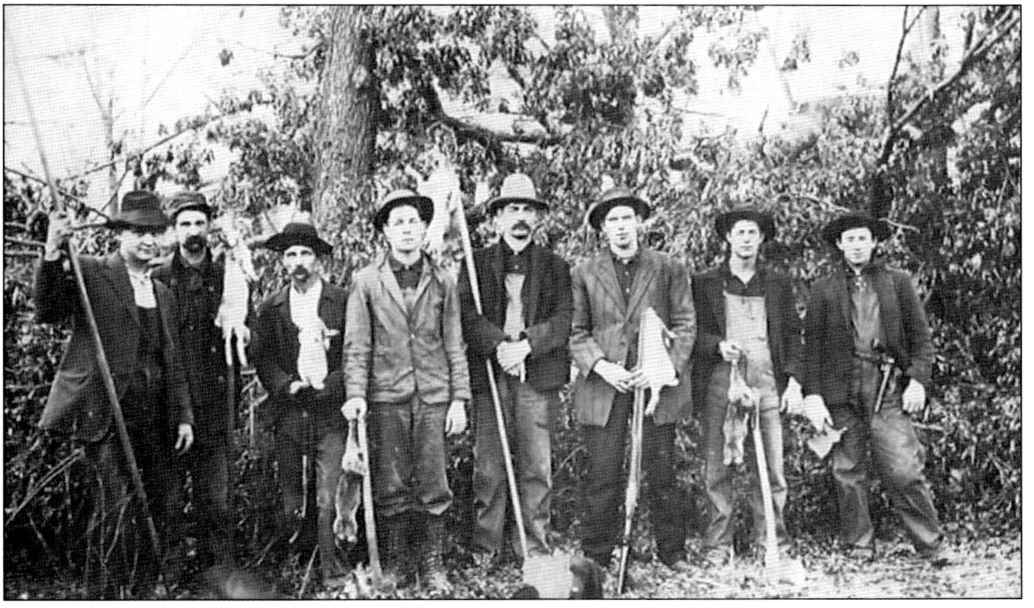

This *c.* 1862 photo shows hunters in Sparta. Pictured from left to right are Sam Weatherman, unidentified, John Henry Smith, unidentified, James McTeer, Moses Bond, and two unidentified. In those days, hunting was, if not a necessity, still an important source of food.

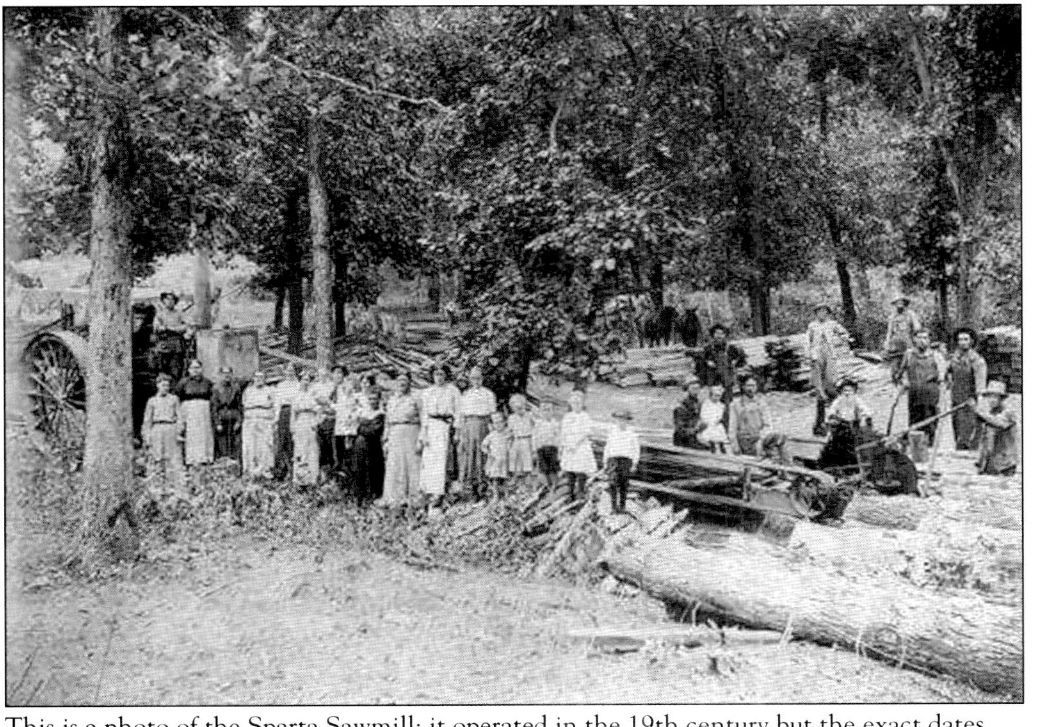

This is a photo of the Sparta Sawmill; it operated in the 19th century but the exact dates are unknown.

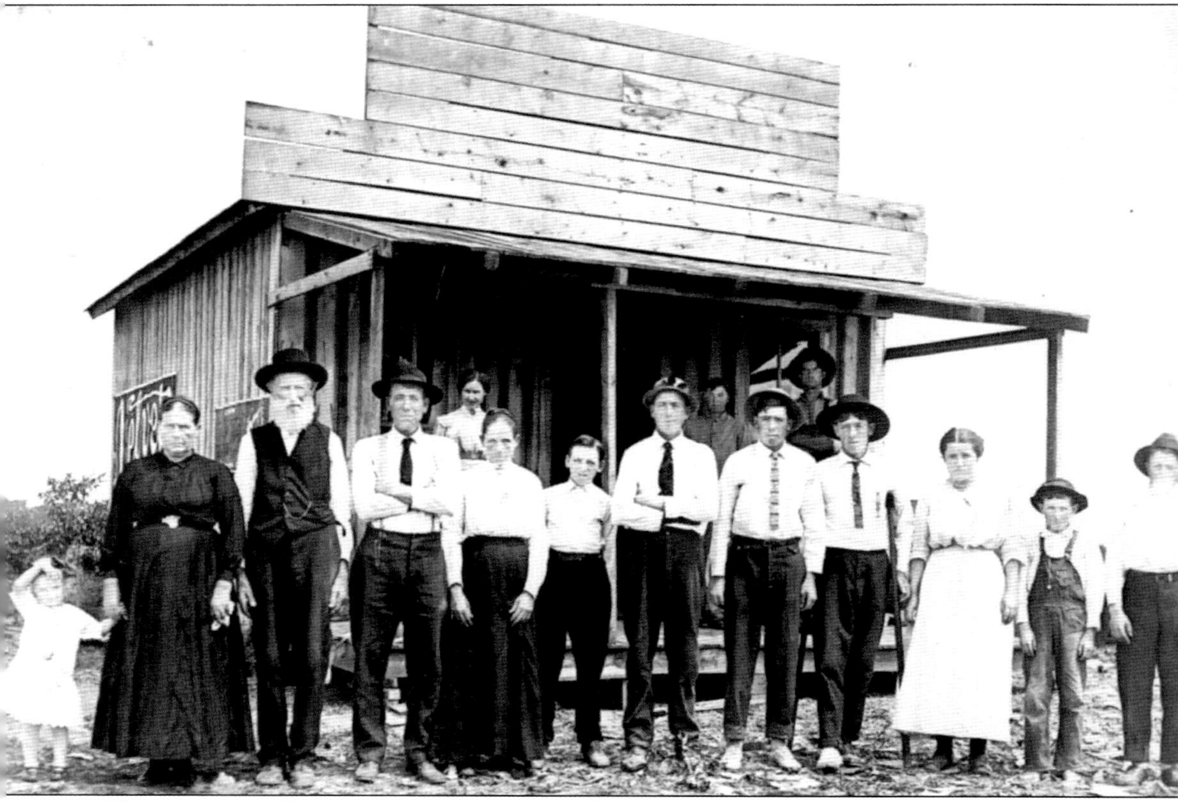

The Moses Bond Store in Sparta is pictured here in 1913. None of the individuals in the photograph are unidentified.

Five

SCHOOL DAY MEMORIES

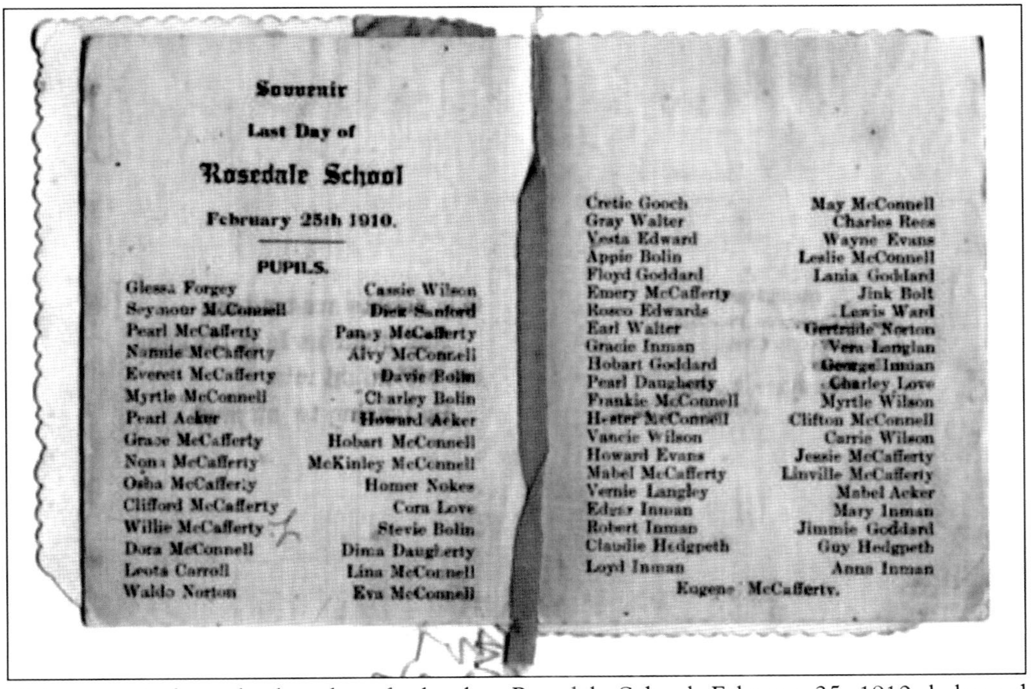

Souvenir

Last Day of

Rosedale School

February 25th 1910.

PUPILS.

Glessa Forgey	Cassie Wilson
Seymour McConnell	Dick Sanford
Pearl McCafferty	Pansy McCafferty
Nannie McCafferty	Alvy McConnell
Everett McCafferty	Davie Bolin
Myrtle McConnell	Charley Bolin
Pearl Acker	Howard Acker
Grace McCafferty	Hobart McConnell
Nona McCafferty	McKinley McConnell
Osha McCafferty	Homer Nokes
Clifford McCafferty	Cora Love
Willie McCafferty	Stevie Bolin
Dora McConnell	Dima Daugherty
Leota Carroll	Lina McConnell
Waldo Norton	Eva McConnell

Cretie Gooch	May McConnell
Gray Walter	Charles Rees
Vesta Edward	Wayne Evans
Appie Bolin	Leslie McConnell
Floyd Goddard	Lania Goddard
Emery McCafferty	Jink Bolt
Rosco Edwards	Lewis Ward
Earl Walter	Gertrude Norton
Gracie Inman	Vera Langlan
Hobart Goddard	George Inman
Pearl Daugherty	Charley Love
Frankie McConnell	Myrtle Wilson
Hester McConnell	Clifton McConnell
Vancie Wilson	Carrie Wilson
Howard Evans	Jessie McCafferty
Mabel McCafferty	Linville McCafferty
Vernie Langley	Mabel Acker
Edgar Inman	Mary Inman
Robert Inman	Jimmie Goddard
Claudie Hedgpeth	Guy Hedgpeth
Loyd Inman	Anna Inman

Eugene McCafferty.

This souvenir from the last day of school at Rosedale School, February 25, 1910, belonged to Cora L. Love. As often happens in small rural schools, many of the students were related, evidenced by those who shared the last names of McCafferty, McConnell, and Inman. Cora Love is listed on the left page, and Charley Love is listed on the right. Interestingly, the names are not listed in alphabetical order, and the last day of school would have been in February.

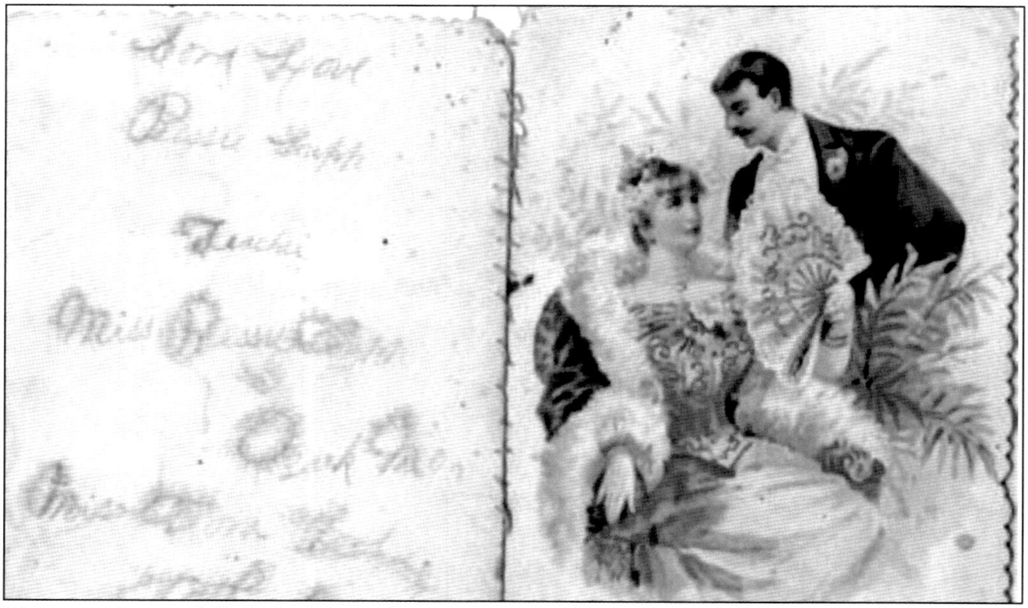

This is a photo of Cora Love's graduation announcement. She graduated from Nixa's public school. The handwriting appears to have the names Cora Love and Bessie Clapp. The rest of the writing is difficult to make out. It is believed that Bessie Clapp was the teacher. The ornate illustration would appear out of place on a modern graduation announcement.

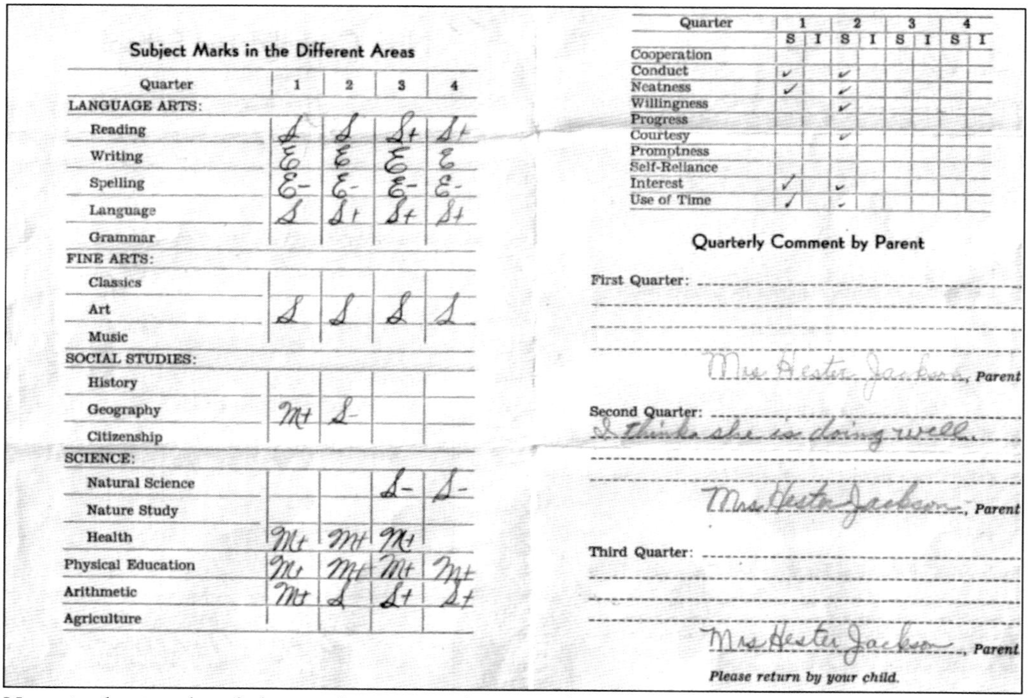

Subject Marks in the Different Areas

Quarter	1	2	3	4
LANGUAGE ARTS:				
Reading	S	S	S+	S+
Writing	E	E	E	E
Spelling	E-	E-	E-	E-
Language	S	S+	S+	S+
Grammar				
FINE ARTS:				
Classics				
Art	S	S	S	S
Music				
SOCIAL STUDIES:				
History				
Geography	M+	S-		
Citizenship				
SCIENCE:				
Natural Science			S-	S-
Nature Study				
Health	M+	M+	M+	
Physical Education	M+	M+	M+	M+
Arithmetic	M+	S	S+	S+
Agriculture				

Quarter	1		2		3		4	
	S	I	S	I	S	I	S	I
Cooperation								
Conduct	✓		✓					
Neatness	✓		✓					
Willingness			✓					
Progress								
Courtesy			✓					
Promptness								
Self-Reliance								
Interest	✓		✓					
Use of Time	✓		✓					

Quarterly Comment by Parent

First Quarter:

Mrs Hester Jackson, Parent

Second Quarter: I thinks she is doing well.

Mrs Hester Jackson, Parent

Third Quarter:

Mrs Hester Jackson, Parent

Please return by your child.

Here is the inside of the graduation card pictured above. Notice the grading style, which included many satisfactory marks indicated by an S..

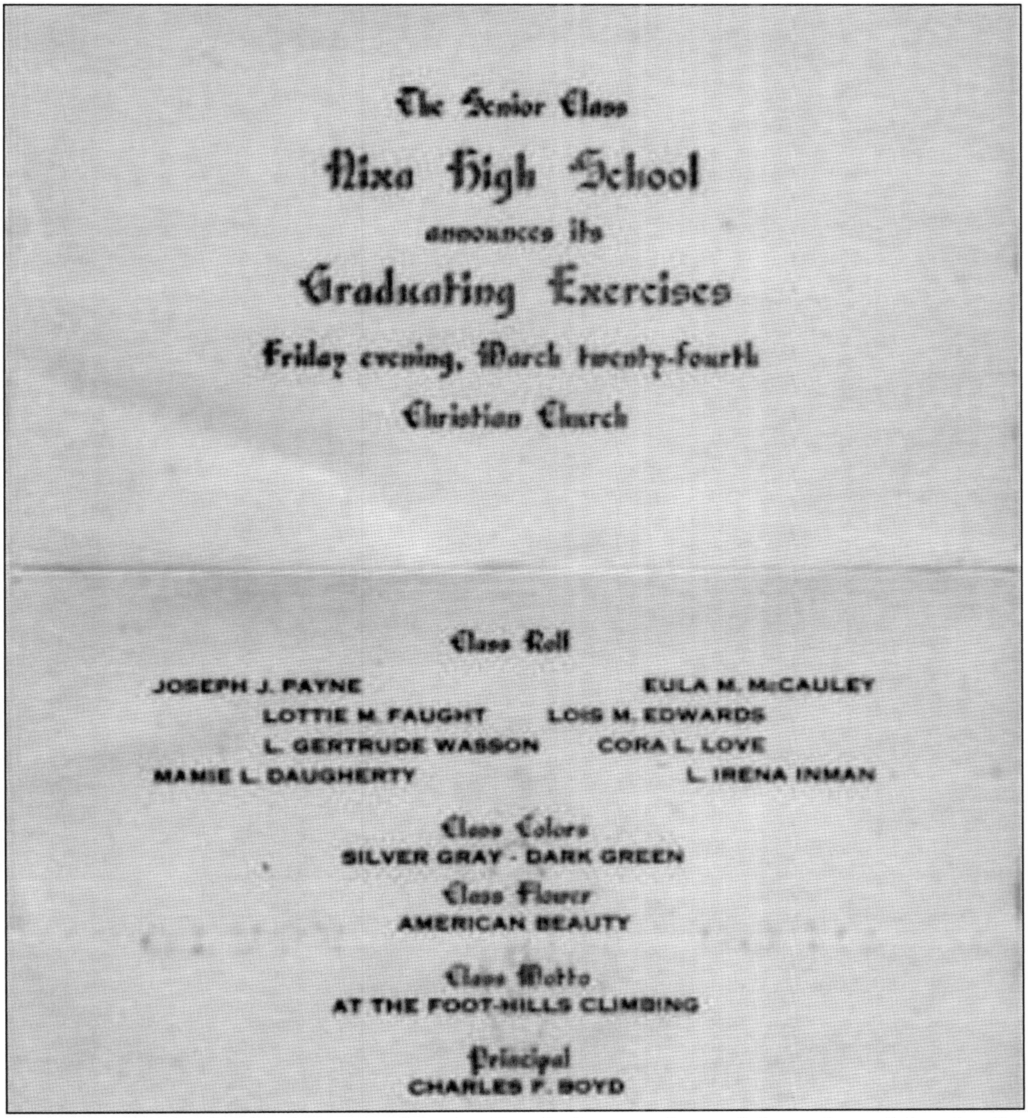

The Senior Class

Nixa High School

announces its

Graduating Exercises

Friday evening, March twenty-fourth

Christian Church

Class Roll

JOSEPH J. PAYNE	EULA M. McCAULEY
LOTTIE M. FAUGHT	LOIS M. EDWARDS
L. GERTRUDE WASSON	CORA L. LOVE
MAMIE L. DAUGHERTY	L. IRENA INMAN

Class Colors

SILVER GRAY - DARK GREEN

Class Flower

AMERICAN BEAUTY

Class Motto

AT THE FOOT-HILLS CLIMBING

Principal

CHARLES F. BOYD

This is another high school souvenir kept by Cora L. Love and passed down through her family. It reads:

Cora's graduation from Nixa High School
March 24, 1916

The Senior Class
Nixa High School
Announces its
Graduating Exercises
Friday evening, March twenty-fourth
Christian Church

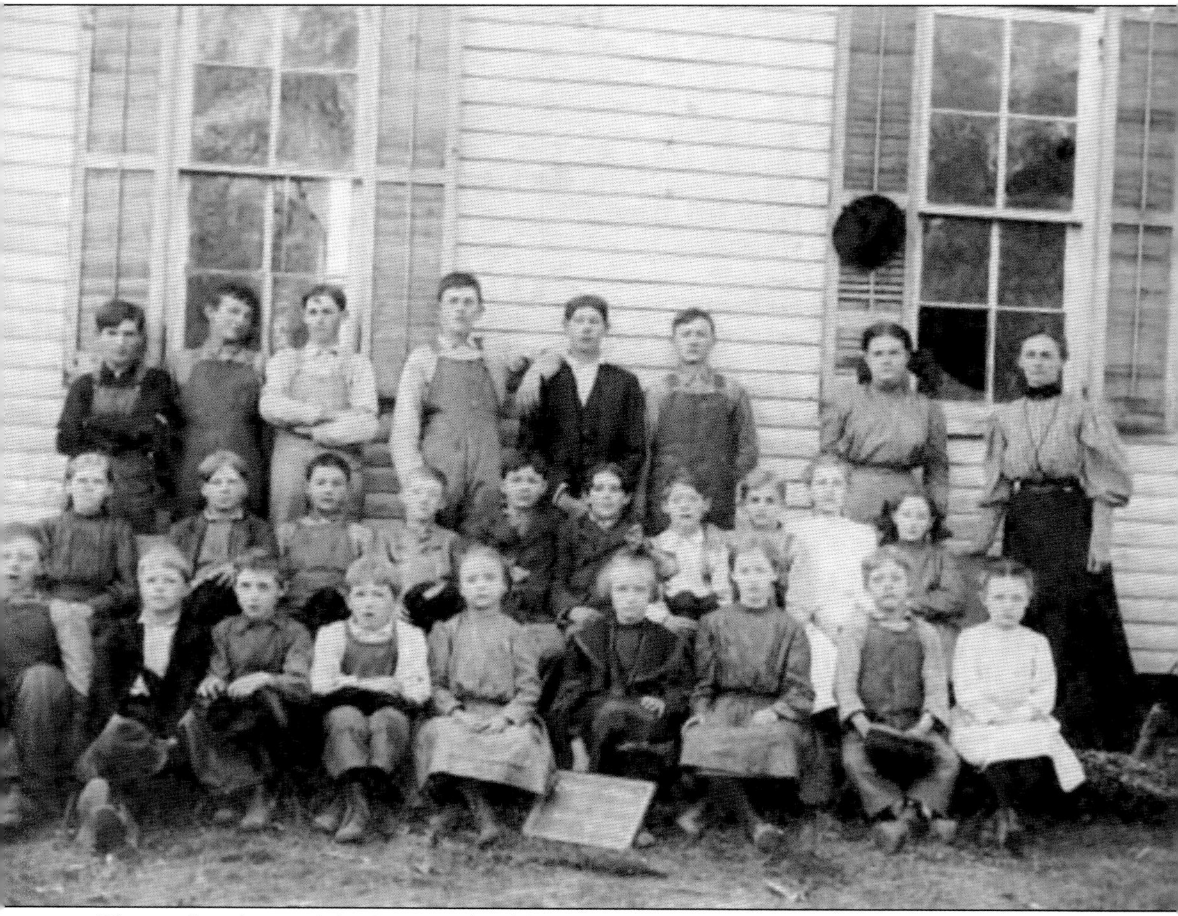

This is the photo of the Berea School located in the Nixa area before the Nixa Schools had been consolidated. This photo had been taken on either November 9 or November 12, 1909. The teacher in this photo is Mary Inman who was the daughter-in-law of Nicholas Alexander Inman, and the wife of Frederick Inman. She was the mother of Fredrick Waldo Inman, second row, eighth student from the left, and Irene Jane Inman, front row from the left. The other children in this photo are unidentified.

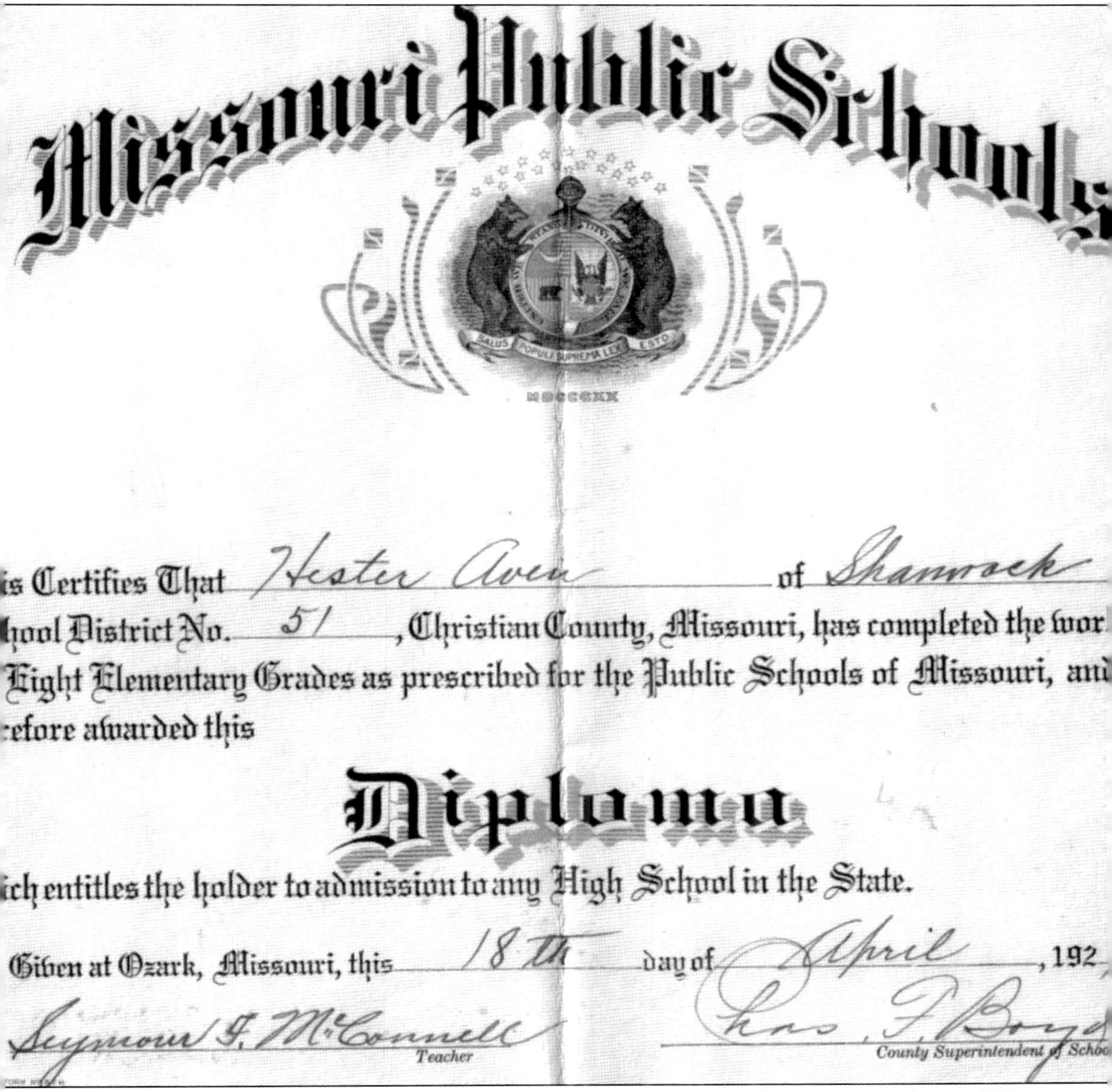

Missouri Public Schools

SALUS POPULI SUPREMA LEX ESTO

MDCCCXX

is Certifies That Hester Aven of Shamrock
hool District No. 51, Christian County, Missouri, has completed the wor
Eight Elementary Grades as prescribed for the Public Schools of Missouri, and
refore awarded this

Diploma

ich entitles the holder to admission to any High School in the State.

Given at Ozark, Missouri, this 18th day of April, 192

Seymour F. McConnell, Teacher

Chas. F. Boyd, County Superintendent of Scho

This photo is a diploma made out to Hester Ann (Aven) Jackson of Nixa on April 18, 1927 from Shamrock School which was in district No. 51.

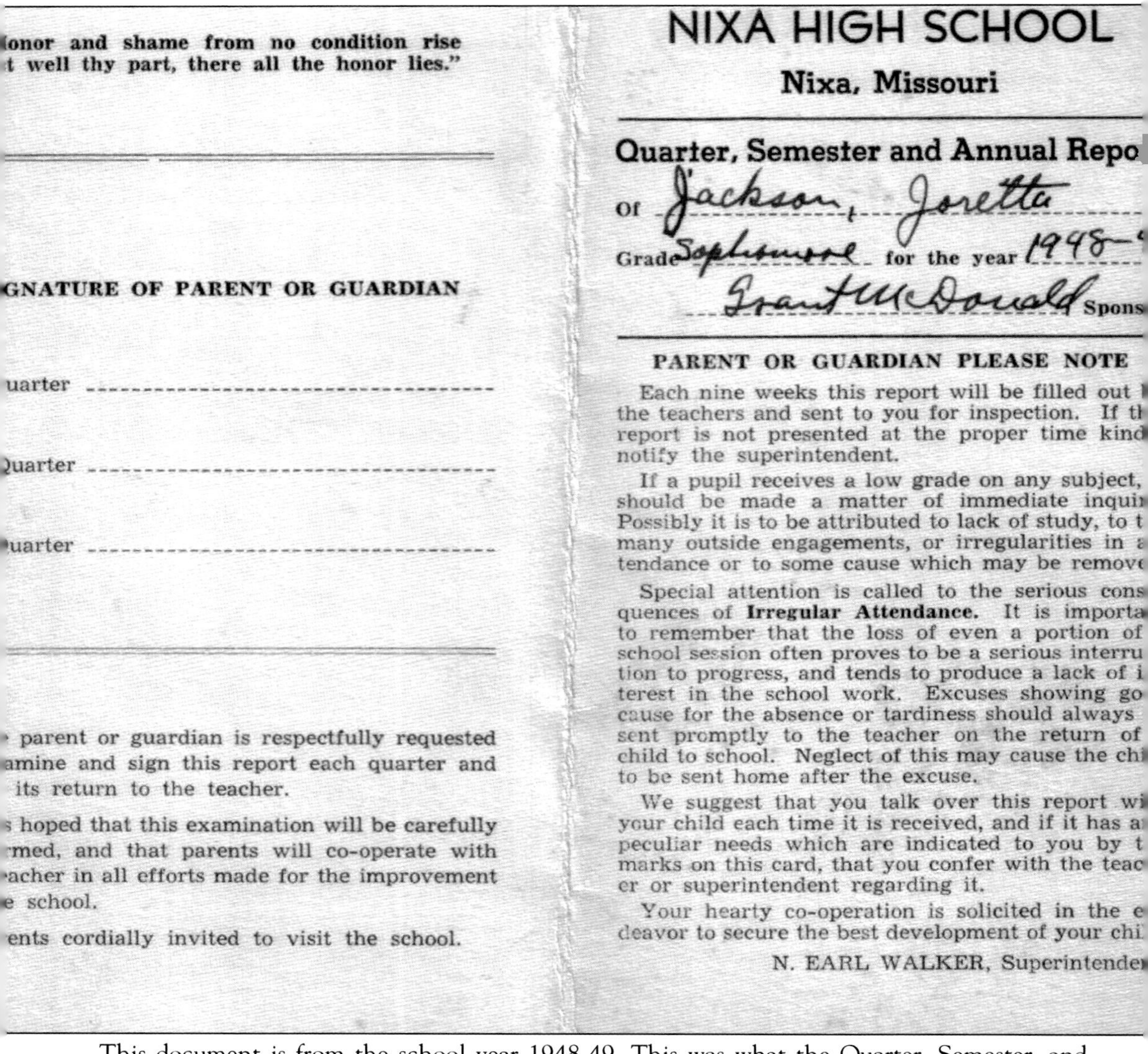
ionor and shame from no condition rise
t well thy part, there all the honor lies."

GNATURE OF PARENT OR GUARDIAN

uarter

Quarter

uarter

parent or guardian is respectfully requested amine and sign this report each quarter and its return to the teacher.

s hoped that this examination will be carefully rmed, and that parents will co-operate with acher in all efforts made for the improvement e school.

ents cordially invited to visit the school.

NIXA HIGH SCHOOL

Nixa, Missouri

Quarter, Semester and Annual Repo

Of Jackson, Joretta

Grade Sophomore for the year 1948-

Grant McDonald Spons

PARENT OR GUARDIAN PLEASE NOTE

Each nine weeks this report will be filled out the teachers and sent to you for inspection. If th report is not presented at the proper time kind notify the superintendent.

If a pupil receives a low grade on any subject, should be made a matter of immediate inqui Possibly it is to be attributed to lack of study, to t many outside engagements, or irregularities in a tendance or to some cause which may be remov

Special attention is called to the serious cons quences of **Irregular Attendance.** It is importa to remember that the loss of even a portion of school session often proves to be a serious interru tion to progress, and tends to produce a lack of i terest in the school work. Excuses showing go cause for the absence or tardiness should always sent promptly to the teacher on the return of child to school. Neglect of this may cause the chi to be sent home after the excuse.

We suggest that you talk over this report wi your child each time it is received, and if it has a peculiar needs which are indicated to you by t marks on this card, that you confer with the teac er or superintendent regarding it.

Your hearty co-operation is solicited in the e deavor to secure the best development of your chi

N. EARL WALKER, Superintende

This document is from the school year 1948-49. This was what the Quarter, Semester, and annual reports looked like. This grade card is for Nixa resident Joretta "Jo" Fitzpatrick, the daughter of Herbert C. and Hester Ann (Aven) Jackson. Jo later became the the wife of Billy "Bill" Jean Fitzpatrick.

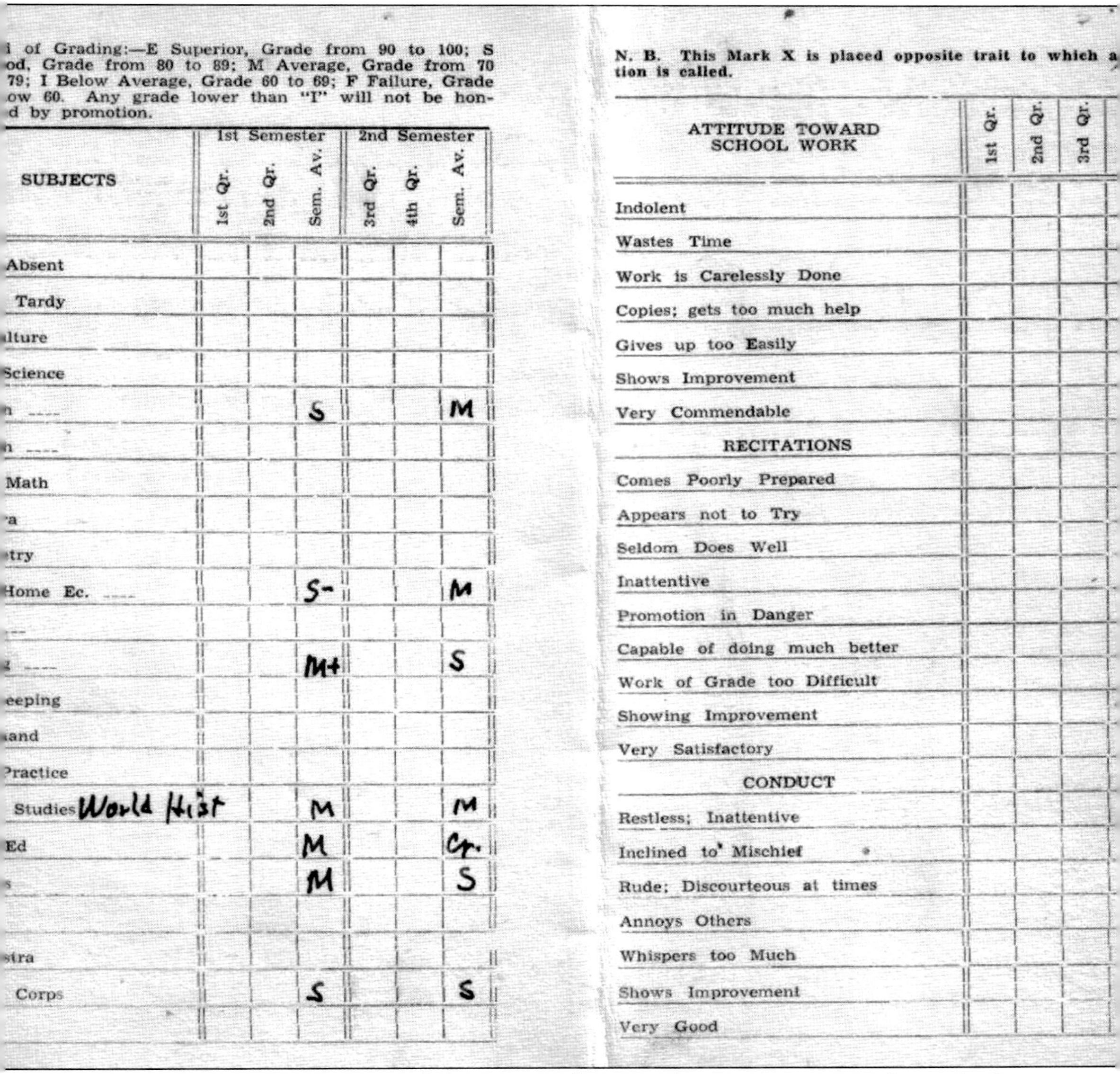

i of Grading:—E Superior, Grade from 90 to 100; S od, Grade from 80 to 89; M Average, Grade from 70 79; I Below Average, Grade 60 to 69; F Failure, Grade ow 60. Any grade lower than "I" will not be hon- d by promotion.

SUBJECTS	1st Semester 1st Qr.	2nd Qr.	Sem. Av.	2nd Semester 3rd Qr.	4th Qr.	Sem. Av.
Absent						
Tardy						
lture						
Science						
n ----			S			M
n ----						
Math						
a						
try						
Home Ec. ----			S-			M

----			M+			S
eeping						
and						
Practice						
Studies World Hist			M			M
Ed			M			Cr.
			M			S
stra						
Corps			S			S

N. B. This Mark X is placed opposite trait to which a tion is called.

ATTITUDE TOWARD SCHOOL WORK	1st Qr.	2nd Qr.	3rd Qr.
Indolent			
Wastes Time			
Work is Carelessly Done			
Copies; gets too much help			
Gives up too Easily			
Shows Improvement			
Very Commendable			
RECITATIONS			
Comes Poorly Prepared			
Appears not to Try			
Seldom Does Well			
Inattentive			
Promotion in Danger			
Capable of doing much better			
Work of Grade too Difficult			
Showing Improvement			
Very Satisfactory			
CONDUCT			
Restless; Inattentive			
Inclined to Mischief			
Rude; Discourteous at times			
Annoys Others			
Whispers too Much			
Shows Improvement			
Very Good			

This is the inside of the report card showing the letter grades. It is interesting that only the semester averages are filled out and not the quarter grades.

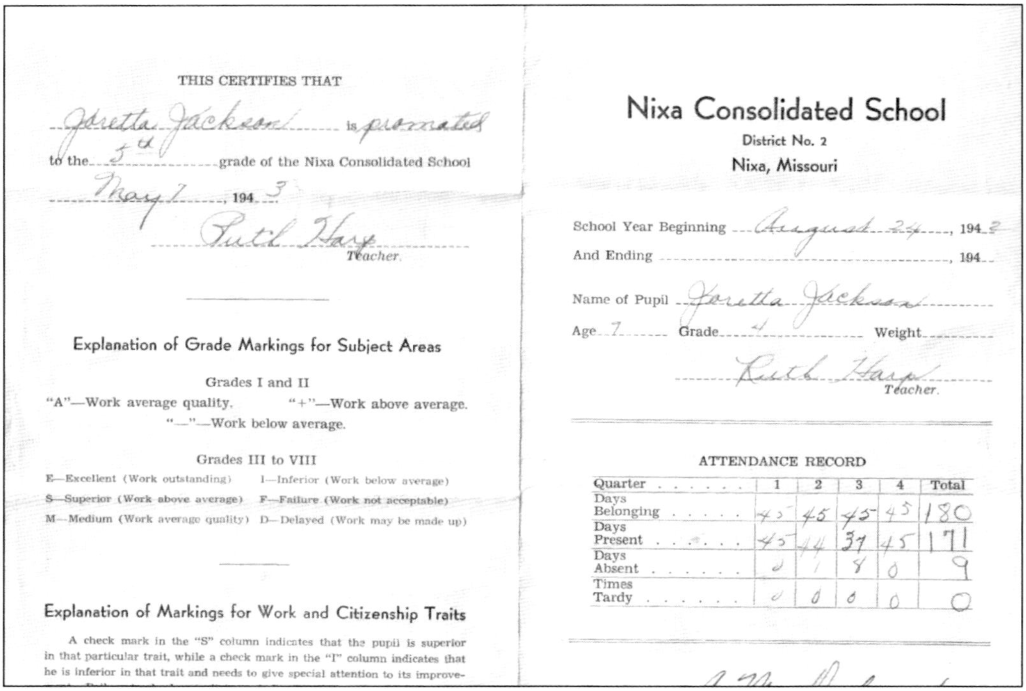

THIS CERTIFIES THAT

Joretta Jackson is promoted

to the 5th grade of the Nixa Consolidated School

May 7, 1943

Ruth Harp
Teacher.

Explanation of Grade Markings for Subject Areas

Grades I and II

"A"—Work average quality. "+"—Work above average.

"—"—Work below average.

Grades III to VIII

E—Excellent (Work outstanding) I—Inferior (Work below average)

S—Superior (Work above average) F—Failure (Work not acceptable)

M—Medium (Work average quality) D—Delayed (Work may be made up)

Explanation of Markings for Work and Citizenship Traits

A check mark in the "S" column indicates that the pupil is superior in that particular trait, while a check mark in the "I" column indicates that he is inferior in that trait and needs to give special attention to its improve-

Nixa Consolidated School

District No. 2

Nixa, Missouri

School Year Beginning August 24, 1942

And Ending , 194

Name of Pupil Joretta Jackson

Age 7 Grade 4 Weight

Ruth Harp
Teacher.

ATTENDANCE RECORD

Quarter	1	2	3	4	Total
Days Belonging	45	45	45	45	180
Days Present	45	44	37	45	171
Days Absent	0	1	8	0	9
Times Tardy	0	0	0	0	0

This is the outside part of a grade card from Nixa's Consolidated School District No. 2. This grade card is from August 24, 1942 and belonged to Joretta "Jo" (Jackson) Fitzpatrick.

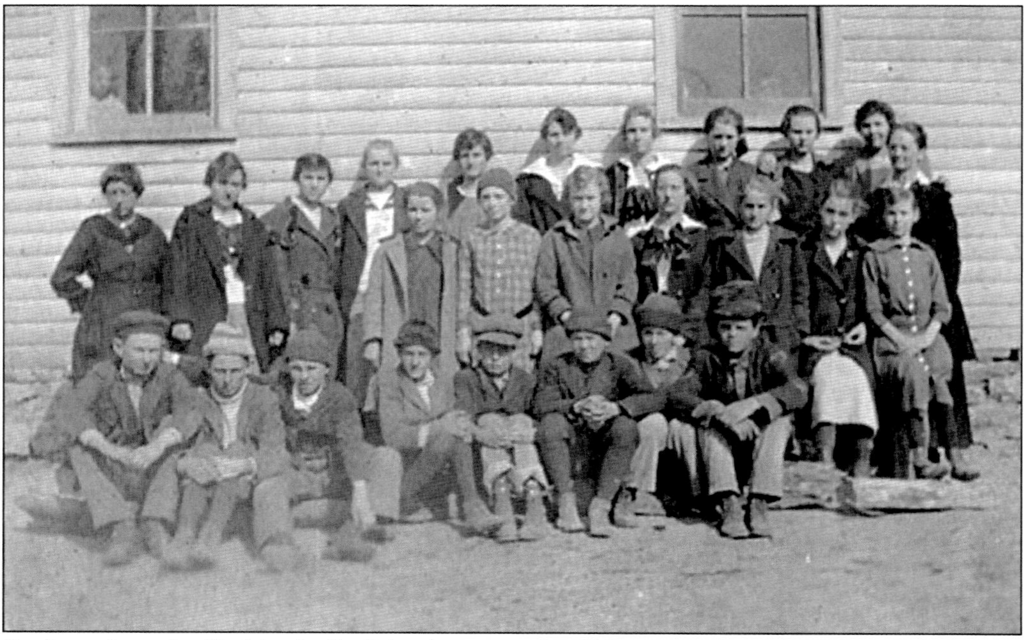

Students from the Highlandville School, just south of Nixa, pose for a class photo. The year is unknown.

Six

Nixa Goes to War

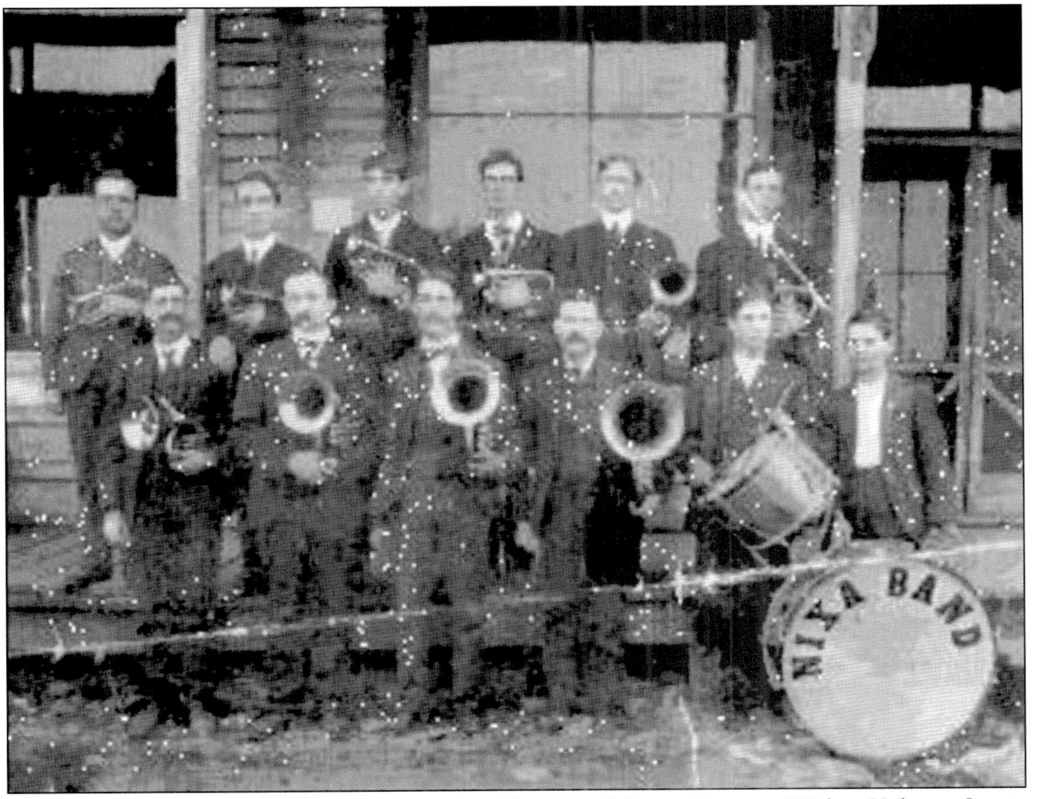

The 1905 Nixa Band was, from left to right: (front row) Jonas Parsons, Walter Keltner, Lewis Brokaw, John Bedingfield, Arthur Brokaw, and Harvey Nokes; (back row) Lum Kerr, Leo Kerr, Jim Thornton, Clarence Brokaw, Tom Welch, and Leslie Clay. Nixa's patriotic town bands kept spirits high through two world wars.

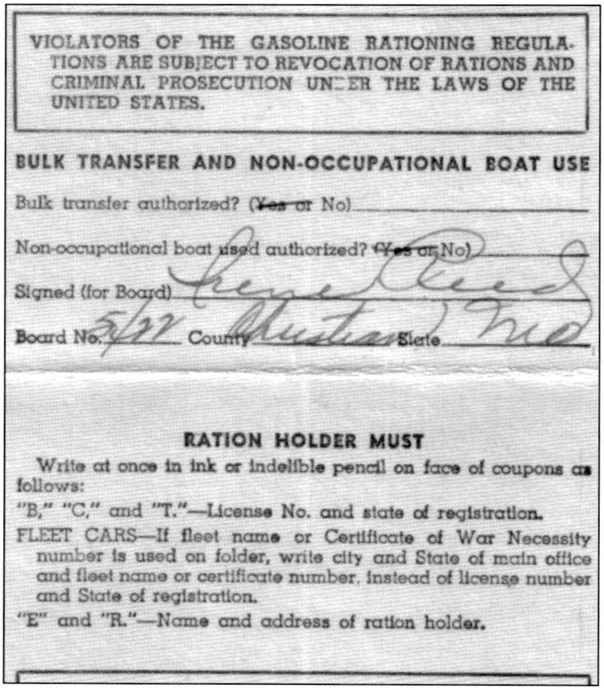

VIOLATORS OF THE GASOLINE RATIONING REGULATIONS ARE SUBJECT TO REVOCATION OF RATIONS AND CRIMINAL PROSECUTION UNDER THE LAWS OF THE UNITED STATES.

BULK TRANSFER AND NON-OCCUPATIONAL BOAT USE

Bulk transfer authorized? (~~Yes or~~ No) ________

Non-occupational boat used authorized? (~~Yes or~~ No) ________

Signed (for Board) ________

Board No. ____ County ____ State ____

RATION HOLDER MUST

Write at once in ink or indelible pencil on face of coupons as follows:

"B," "C," and "T."—License No. and state of registration.

FLEET CARS—If fleet name or Certificate of War Necessity number is used on folder, write city and State of main office and fleet name or certificate number, instead of license number and State of registration.

"E" and "R."—Name and address of ration holder.

Shortages caused almost everything to be rationed during World War II. This document explains the rules and limitations for using gasoline. The warning at the top shows how seriously rationing was taken.

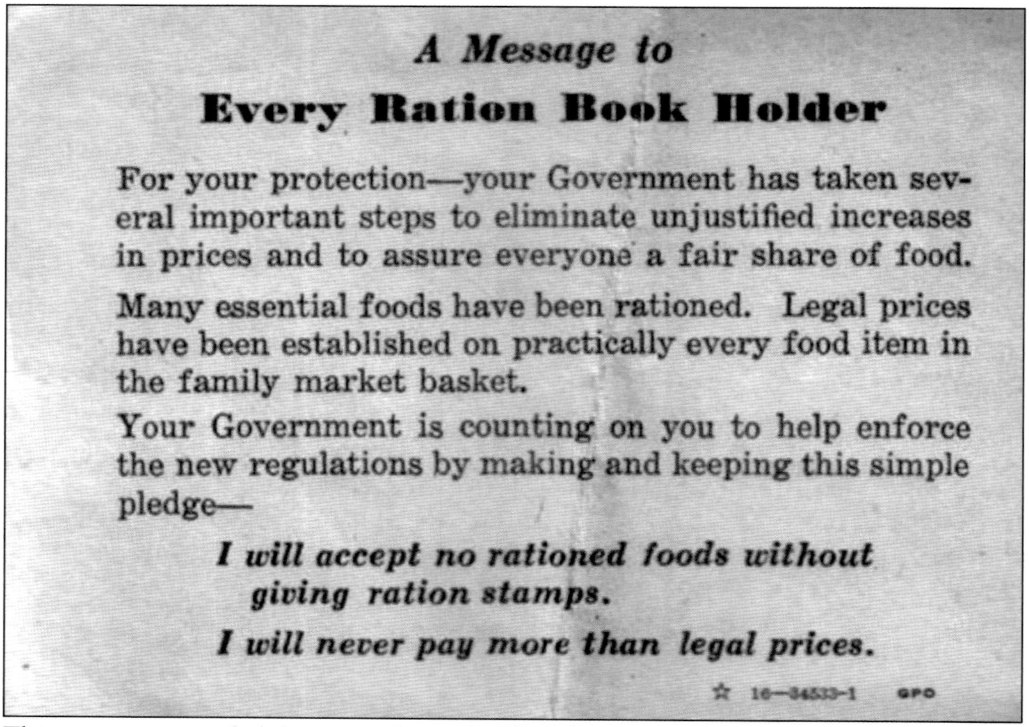

A Message to

Every Ration Book Holder

For your protection—your Government has taken several important steps to eliminate unjustified increases in prices and to assure everyone a fair share of food.

Many essential foods have been rationed. Legal prices have been established on practically every food item in the family market basket.

Your Government is counting on you to help enforce the new regulations by making and keeping this simple pledge—

I will accept no rationed foods without giving ration stamps.

I will never pay more than legal prices.

☆ 16—34533-1 GPO

This message was included in every Ration Book as the government called upon the citizens to help with the war effort.

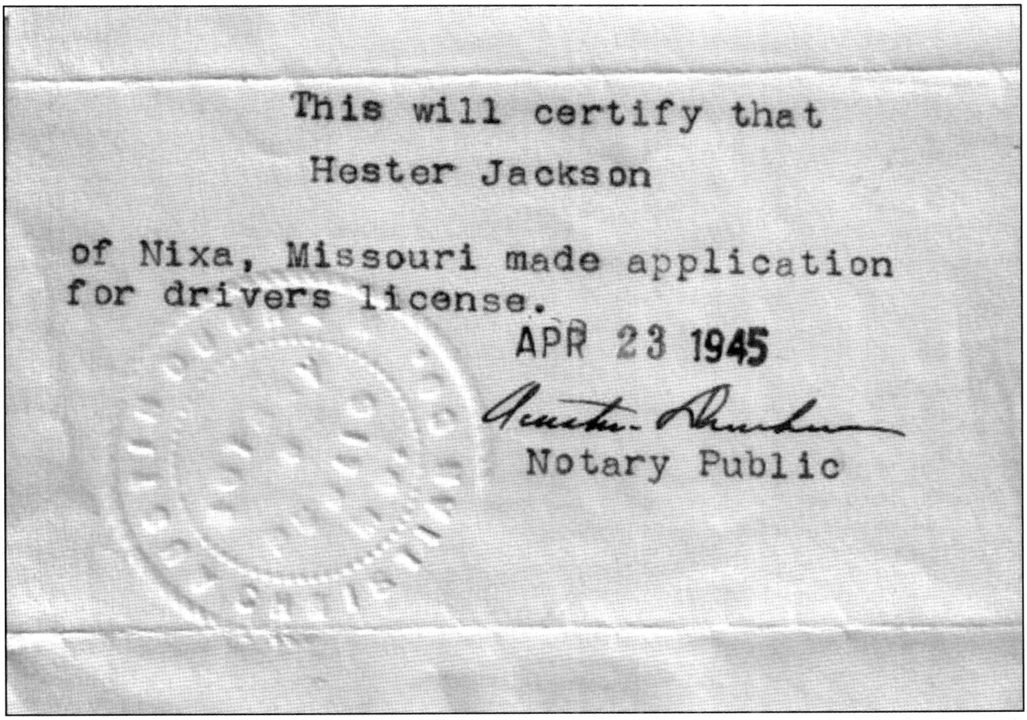

This will certify that
Hester Jackson

of Nixa, Missouri made application for drivers license.

APR 23 1945

Notary Public

During World War II, even applications for drivers licenses had to be certified and notarized. Hester Jackson made this request on April 23, 1945.

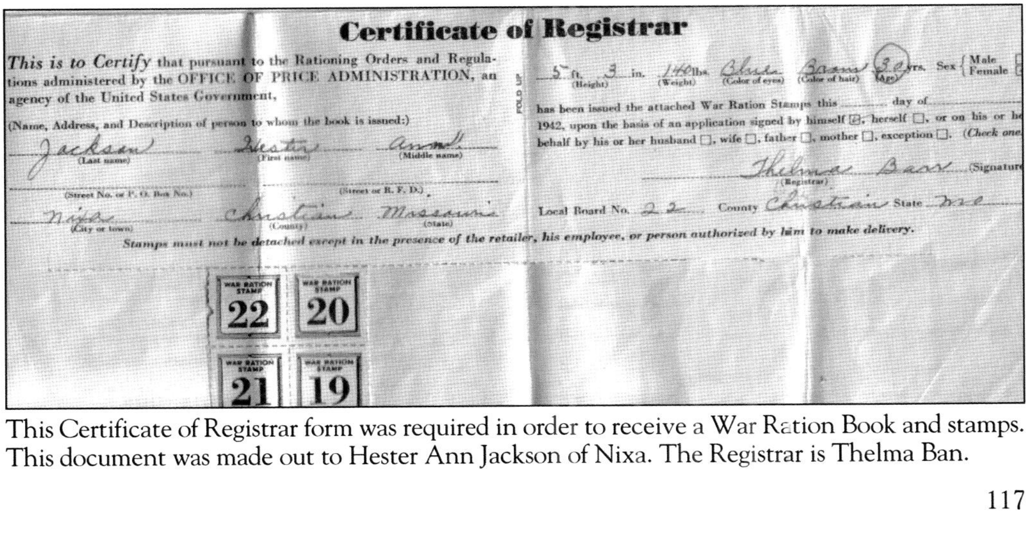

Certificate of Registrar

This is to Certify that pursuant to the Rationing Orders and Regulations administered by the OFFICE OF PRICE ADMINISTRATION, an agency of the United States Government,

(Name, Address, and Description of person to whom the book is issued:)

Jackson (Last name) Hester (First name) Ann (Middle name)

(Street No. or P. O. Box No.) (Street or R. F. D.)

Nixa (City or town) Christian (County) Missouri (State)

FOLD UP

5 ft. 3 in. (Height) 140 lbs. (Weight) Blue (Color of eyes) Brown (Color of hair) 30 (Age) yrs. Sex {Male / Female

has been issued the attached War Ration Stamps this ______ day of ______ 1942, upon the basis of an application signed by himself ☑, herself ☐, or on his or her behalf by his or her husband ☐, wife ☐, father ☐, mother ☐, exception ☐. (Check one

Thelma Barr (Registrar) (Signature

Local Board No. 22 County Christian State Mo

Stamps must not be detached except in the presence of the retailer, his employee, or person authorized by him to make delivery.

WAR RATION STAMP 22 | WAR RATION STAMP 20 | WAR RATION STAMP 21 | WAR RATION STAMP 19

This Certificate of Registrar form was required in order to receive a War Ration Book and stamps. This document was made out to Hester Ann Jackson of Nixa. The Registrar is Thelma Ban.

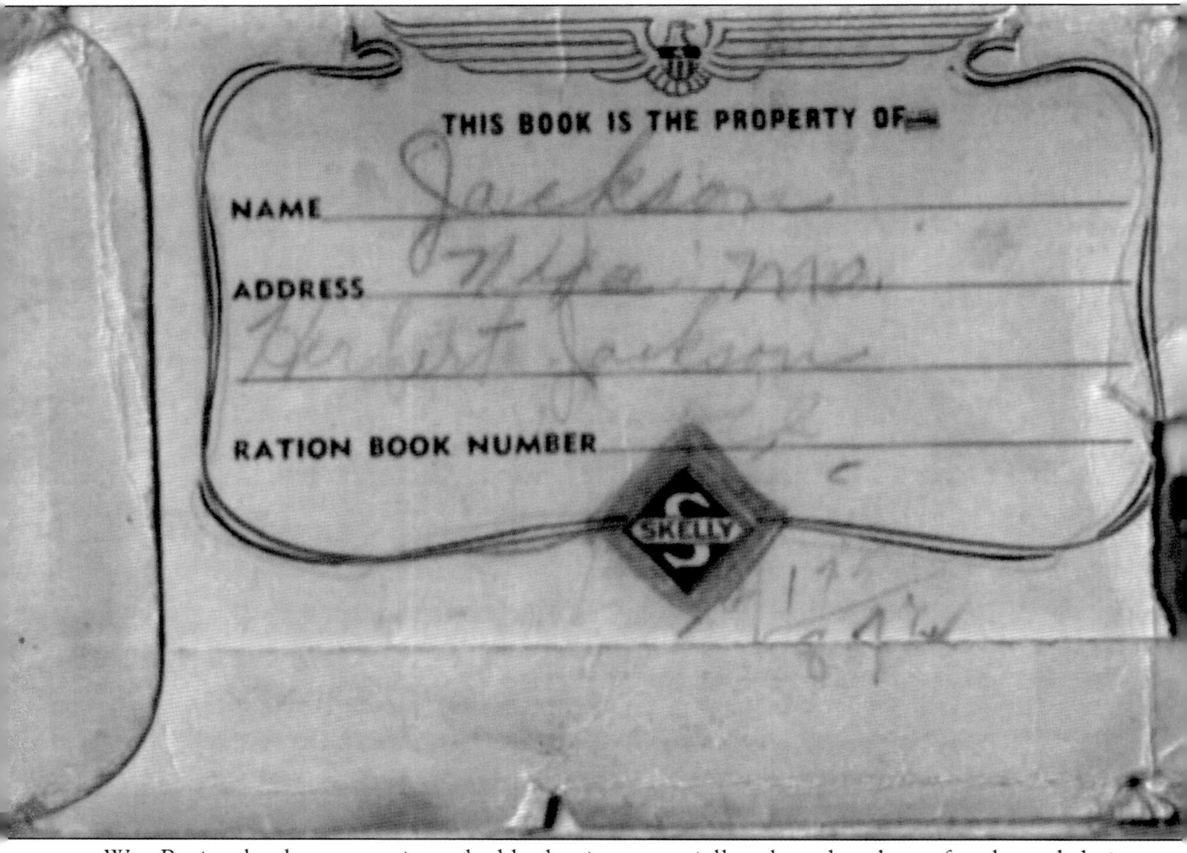

War Ration books were quite valuable, having essentially taken the place of cash, and their covers identified the owner and his address, so it could be returned if lost.

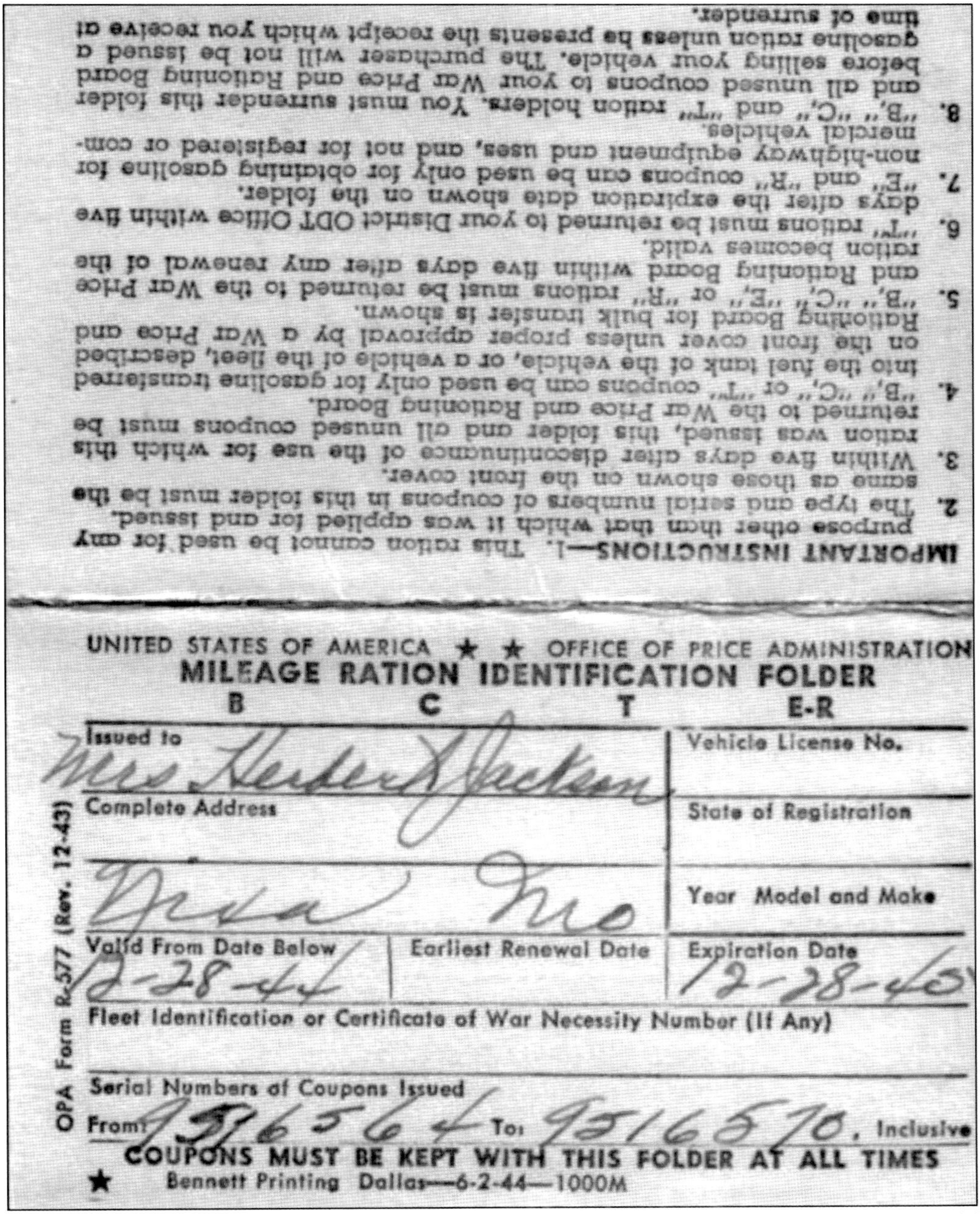

IMPORTANT INSTRUCTIONS—1. This ration cannot be used for any purpose other than that which it was applied for and issued.

2. The type and serial numbers of coupons in this folder must be the same as those shown on the front cover.

3. Within five days after discontinuance of the use for which this ration was issued, this folder and all unused coupons must be returned to the War Price and Rationing Board.

4. "B," "C," or "T" coupons can be used only for gasoline transferred into the fuel tank of the vehicle, or a vehicle of the fleet, described on the front cover unless proper approval by a War Price and Rationing Board for bulk transfer is shown.

5. "B," "C," "E," or "R" rations must be returned to the War Price and Rationing Board within five days after any renewal of the ration becomes valid.

6. "T" rations must be returned to your District ODT Office within five days after the expiration date shown on the folder.

7. "E" and "R" coupons can be used only for obtaining gasoline for non-highway equipment and uses, and not for registered or commercial vehicles.

8. "B," "C," and "T" ration holders. You must surrender this folder and all unused coupons to your War Price and Rationing Board before selling your vehicle. The purchaser will not be issued a gasoline ration unless he presents the receipt which you receive at time of surrender.

UNITED STATES OF AMERICA ★ ★ OFFICE OF PRICE ADMINISTRATION

MILEAGE RATION IDENTIFICATION FOLDER

B C T E-R

Issued to: Mrs Hester A Jackson

Complete Address: Nixa Mo

Vehicle License No.

State of Registration

Year Model and Make

Valid From Date Below: 12-28-44

Earliest Renewal Date

Expiration Date: 12-28-45

Fleet Identification or Certificate of War Necessity Number (If Any)

Serial Numbers of Coupons Issued

From: 951564 To: 951570, Inclusive

COUPONS MUST BE KEPT WITH THIS FOLDER AT ALL TIMES

★ Bennett Printing Dallas—6-2-44—1000M

OPA Form R-577 (Rev. 12-43)

This document was used for identification purposes to order a War Ration Book during World War II. It is dated December 28, 1944 and was filled out by Nixa resident Mrs. Hester Ann (Aven) Jackson.

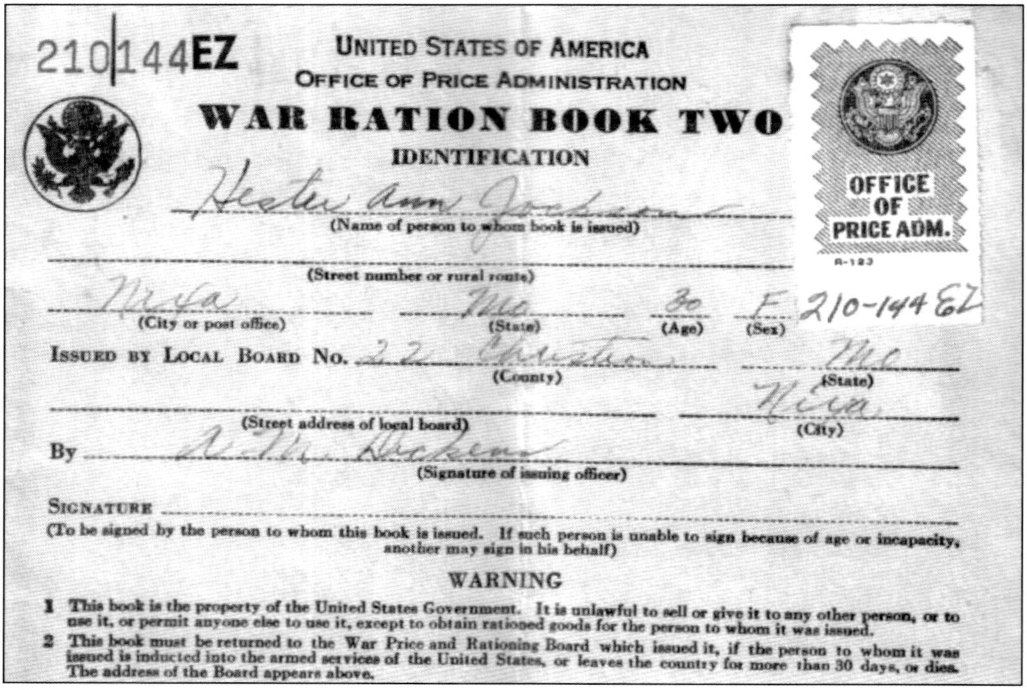

210|144EZ

UNITED STATES OF AMERICA
OFFICE OF PRICE ADMINISTRATION

WAR RATION BOOK TWO

IDENTIFICATION

OFFICE OF PRICE ADM.

R-123

Hester Ann Jackson
(Name of person to whom book is issued)

(Street number or rural route)

Nixa (City or post office) Mo (State) 30 (Age) F (Sex) 210-144 EZ

ISSUED BY LOCAL BOARD NO. 22 Christian (County) Mo (State)

(Street address of local board) Nixa (City)

By A. M. Jackson (Signature of issuing officer)

SIGNATURE
(To be signed by the person to whom this book is issued. If such person is unable to sign because of age or incapacity, another may sign in his behalf)

WARNING

1 This book is the property of the United States Government. It is unlawful to sell or give it to any other person, or to use it, or permit anyone else to use it, except to obtain rationed goods for the person to whom it was issued.
2 This book must be returned to the War Price and Rationing Board which issued it, if the person to whom it was issued is inducted into the armed services of the United States, or leaves the country for more than 30 days, or dies. The address of the Board appears above.

This document is from Hester Jackson's War Ration Book (Two). Note the warning that the book is the property of the United States Government.

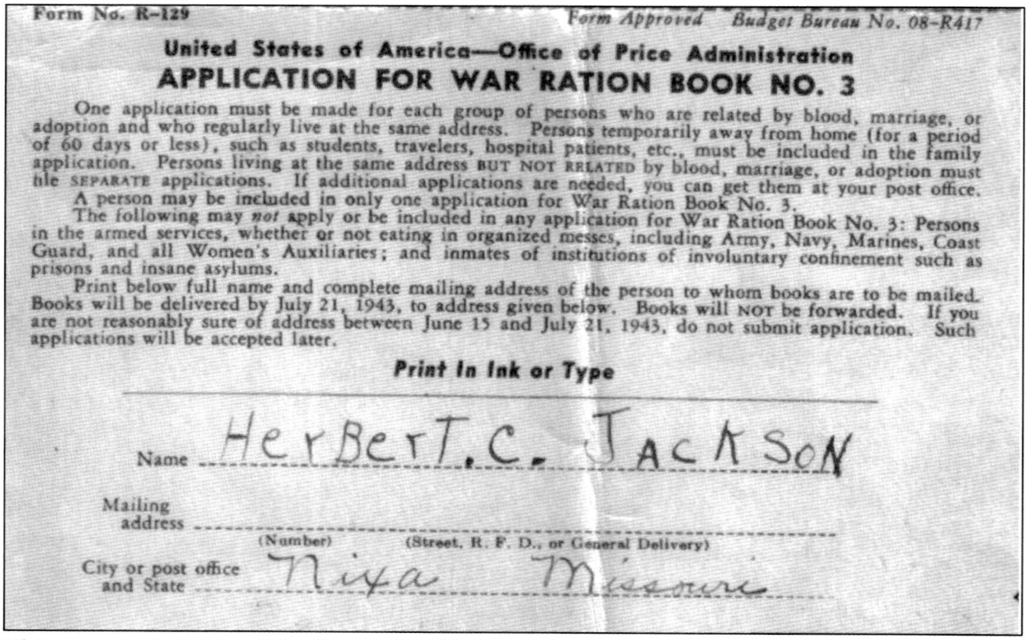

Form No. R-129 *Form Approved Budget Bureau No. 08-R417*

United States of America—Office of Price Administration

APPLICATION FOR WAR RATION BOOK NO. 3

One application must be made for each group of persons who are related by blood, marriage, or adoption and who regularly live at the same address. Persons temporarily away from home (for a period of 60 days or less), such as students, travelers, hospital patients, etc., must be included in the family application. Persons living at the same address BUT NOT RELATED by blood, marriage, or adoption must file SEPARATE applications. If additional applications are needed, you can get them at your post office.

A person may be included in only one application for War Ration Book No. 3.

The following may *not* apply or be included in any application for War Ration Book No. 3: Persons in the armed services, whether or not eating in organized messes, including Army, Navy, Marines, Coast Guard, and all Women's Auxiliaries; and inmates of institutions of involuntary confinement such as prisons and insane asylums.

Print below full name and complete mailing address of the person to whom books are to be mailed. Books will be delivered by July 21, 1943, to address given below. Books will NOT be forwarded. If you are not reasonably sure of address between June 15 and July 21, 1943, do not submit application. Such applications will be accepted later.

Print In Ink or Type

Name HerBerT.C. JACKSON

Mailing address
(Number) (Street, R. F. D., or General Delivery)

City or post office and State Nixa Missouri

This was another part of the Ration Booklet used during World War II. This is the application that had to be filled out in order to receive War Ration Books by mail.

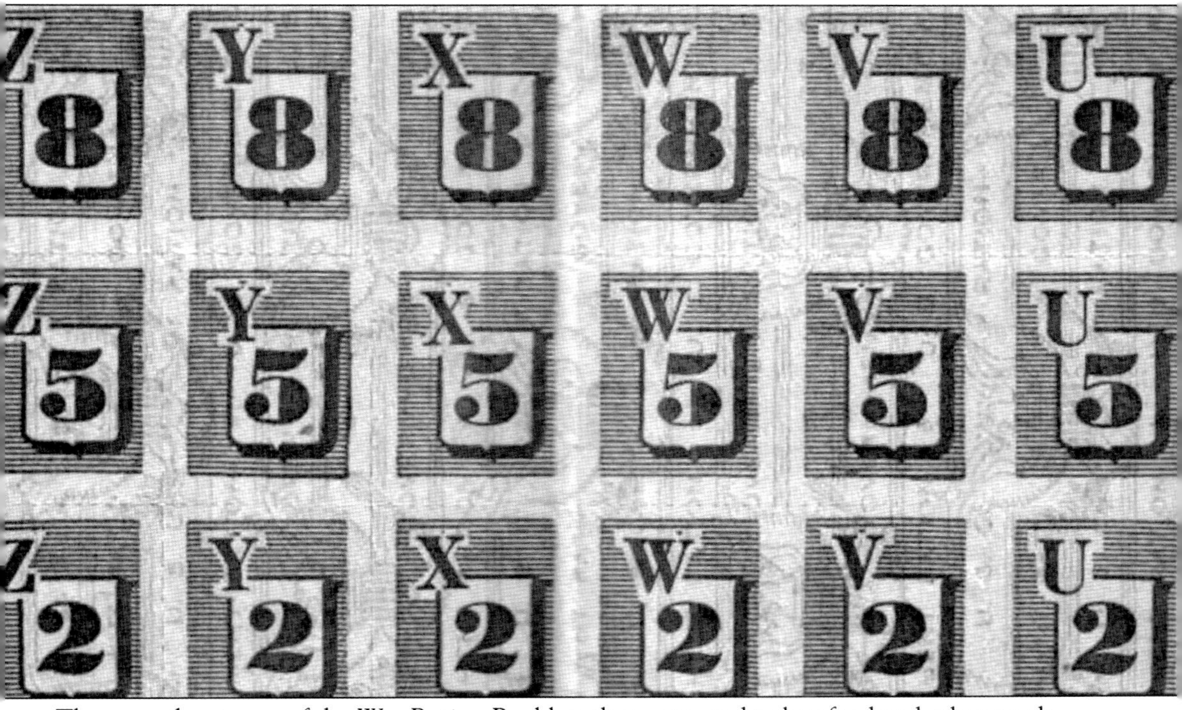

These are the stamps of the War Ration Booklets that were used to buy food and other goods.

This following documents show Bill No. 6—Ordinance No. 6 law's for the City of Nixa, which had been introduced by H.W. Stewart, and passed and approved on July 14, 1905 with J.B. Rice as the Chairman of the Board of Trustees and Leo S. Kerr as the Village Clerk of Nixa.

The strict, detailed rules and regulations in the ordinance, which pertain to public behavior in the city of Nixa, illustrate how much the times have changed in the last 100 years.

ime the chairman or trustees shall deem it proper or to the best interests of the village.

Sec. 2. That the Board of Trustees shall have power at any regular meeting to change the time of meeting, by ordinance, to any time that they deem best; provided, that all of the members of said board shall be present when said ordinance is passed.

Sec. 3. That all ordinances or parts of ordinances conflicting with this ordinance are hereby repealed.

Sec. 4. That this ordinance shall be in force from and after its passage, and approval by the chairman of the Board of Trustees.

Passed this the 14th day of July, 1905.

Approved this the 14th day of July, 1905.

J. B. RICE, Chairman of the Board of Trustees.

Seal—Attest: LEO S. KERR, Village Clerk.

BILL NO. 6—ORDINANCE NO. 6.

(Introduced by H. W. Stewart).

An Ordinance repealing Revised Original Bill, No. 8, Ordinance No. 8, and all amendments thereto, relating to misdemeanors, approved March 11th, 1903, and enacting a new Ordinance in lieu thereof.

Be it ordained by the Board of Trustees of the Village of Nixa, Missouri, as follows:

Section 1. That any person who shall, within the limits of the village, sell to any minor any cigarettes or cigarette wrappers, shall be deemed guilty of a misdemeanor.

Sec. 2. That if any three or more persons shall assemble within the village with the intent to do any unlawful act with force or violence against the property of the village; or against the person or property of any person; or being assembled shall agree to do any such unlawful act, and make any preparations or movements thereto, they shall each be deemed guilty of a misdemeanor.

Sec. 3. That if any person or persons shall, in this village, use violence, tumultous, offensive, threatening, profane or obscene language, they shall each be deemed guilty of a misdemeanor.

Sec. 4. If any person or persons shall, within the corporate limits of this village, wilfully disturb the peace of any neighborhood, or of any family, or of any person by any unusual noise and offensive or indecent conversation, or by threatening, quarreling, challenging or fighting, every person so offending shall, upon conviction, be adjudged guilty of a misdemeanor.

Sec. 5. Every person who shall, within the corporate limits of this village, wilfully, maliciously or contemptuously disquiet or disturb any camp meeting, congregation or other assembly, met for religious worship, or when meeting at the place of worship, or dispersing therefrom, or any school or other assembly of people met together for any lawful purpose whatever, by making a noise or by rude and indecent behavior, or profane discourse, within the place of assembly, or so near the same as to interrupt or disturb the order or solemnity thereof, or who shall wilfully menace, threaten or assault any person there, shall be deemed guilty of a misdemeanor.

Sec. 6. Any person who shall, within the corporate limits of this village, insult any female person, by the use of any profane, obscene or improper language, or indecent personal attitude or gesture, shall be deemed guilty of a misdemeanor.

Sec. 7. Any person, or persons, who shall be upon the streets, alleys, square or other public places in this village, in a state of intoxication, to the annoyance of any person or persons, or the inhabitants of this village, shall be deemed guilty of a misdemeanor.

Sec. 8. If any person shall, within the corporate limits of this village, carry concealed upon or about his person any deadly or dangerous weapon, or shall go into any church or place where people are assembled for religious, educational, literary or social purposes, or into any court room during the sitting of the court, or into any other public place, or to any election precinct on any election day, or into any other public assemblage of persons met for any lawful purpose, other than for militia drill or meetings, called under the militia law of this state, having upon or about his person any kind of fire arms, bowie knife, dirk, dagger, slug shot, or any other deadly weapon, or shall, in the presence of one or more persons, exhibit any such weapon in a rude, angry or threatening manner, or shall have or carry any such weapon upon or about his person when intoxicated or under the influence of intoxicating drinks, or shall, directly or indirectly, sell or deliver, loan or barter to any minor any such weapon, he shall, upon conviction, be punished by a fine of not less than fifty dollars ($50.00), nor more than one hundred dollars ($100.00); provided, that this section shall not be construed so as to prevent any officer of the United States, or the State, county or village from carrying or wearing such weapons as may be necessary in the discharge of his official duties.

Sec. 9. That any person or persons, within this village, who shall wound or maltreat in any cruel or unnecessary manner, any domestic animal, shall be deemed guilty of a misdemeanor.

Sec. 10. Whoever shall, within the village, ride or drive any horse, mule, cow, or any other animal, at any immoderate speed in any street, alley or other public place in the village, shall be deemed guilty of a misdemeanor.

Sec. 11. If any two or more persons shall assemble together upon any sidewalk, street crossing or street corner of the village, and there remain loafing or spending their time in idleness, so as to obstruct, hinder or delay travel thereon, they shall each be deemed guilty of a misdemeanor.

Sec. 12. Any person, or persons, who shall ride, drive or lead any horse, gelding, mule, ass, ox or cow along or across any sidewalk of the village, except public or private crossing thereof, or shall hitch any such animal so that it may stand upon any sidewalk of the village, shall be deemed guilty of a misdemeanor.

Sec. 13. Any person who shall, in this village, exhibit any jack, stallion or bull, on the public square, streets or alleys; or stable any such animal within fifty feet of any street, shall be deemed guilty of a misdemeanor.

Sec. 14. Any person who shall discharge any gun, pistol or other firearms within the corporate limits of this village, without the permission of the chairman, first obtained, shall be deemed guilty of a misdemeanor.

Sec. 15. Any person who shall post or exhibit in any public place in this village any indecent or obscene picture, written or printed matter, or shall sell or expose for sale within the limits of this village, any indecent or obscene books, pamphlets, papers or pictures, shall be deemed guilty of a misdemeanor.

Sec. 16. Any person who shall, in this village, deface or tear down any poster, bill, notice, advertisement, sign or bulletin board, shall be deemed guilty of a misdemeanor.

Sec. 17. Any person who shall, within the limits of this village, make any indecent, immoral or lewd exposure of his or her person, or cause or procure any person to make any such exposure in the presence or view of any person or persons, shall be deemed guilty of a misdemeanor.

Sec. 18. Any person, who shall falsely represent himself to be an officer of the village, or without being duly authorized by the village, shall exercise or attempt to exercise any of the duties, functions or powers of the village officer, shall be deemed guilty of a misdemeanor.

Sec. 19. Any person or persons, who shall obstruct or hinder or otherwise interfere with any officer in the discharge of his official duties, or endeavor to prevent the arrest of any person by any officer of the village, authorized to make such arrests, or attempt to rescue any person from the custody of any officer of this village, shall be deemed guilty of a misdemeanor.

Sec. 20. Any person who shall refuse or neglect to give aid or assistance to any officer of this village while such officer is in the discharge of his official duties, after being called upon for such aid or assistance, shall be deemed guilty of a misdemeanor.

Sec. 21. Any person who shall purposely and falsely raise any alarm of fire in this village, shall be deemed guilty of a misdemeanor.

Sec. 22. Any person who shall, within the village, deposit any ashes in any wooden box, trough or any other receptacle or vessel, which can be kindled into burning, within forty-eight hours after the same has been removed from the stove, furnace or fireplace, where they were formed, shall be deemed guilty of a misdemeanor.

Sec. 23. Any person or persons who shall, within the limits of this village, deposit any live ashes, containing coals or sparks, upon any lot, street, alley or square in the village where it will be liable to endanger the property of others, shall be deemed guilty of a misdemeanor.

Sec. 24. Any person or persons, who, within the limits of this village, shall purposely cause dogs, cocks or other creatures to fight, or shall attach anything to dogs or any other animals' tails, shall be deemed guilty of a misdemeanor.

Sec. 25. Any person or persons who shall, within this village, cast or throw any stone, club, ball or other missile in the public square, streets, alleys or other public places in this village, or at any railroad car, to the damage or injury of any person or property, or shall in this village do any other act which will cause any horse, mule, or any other

—25—

animal, to run away or become frightened so as to do any damage to any person or property, shall be deemed guilty of a misdemeanor.

Sec. 26. Any person or persons who shall keep within the limits of this village a bawdy house or an assignation house for the prostitution of women, shall be deemed guilty of a misdemeanor.

Sec. 27. Any person being the owner or agent of a building in this village, who shall knowingly allow such building or any portion thereof, to be occupied by any person or persons for the purpose of prostitution, shall be deemed guilty of a misdemeanor.

Sec. 28. Any person who shall knowingly rent or let any building in this village to be used as a bawdy house or assignation house, shall be deemed guilty of a misdemeanor.

Sec. 29. Every male person of the age of sixteen years or over, who shall visit in such bawdy or assignation house, in this village, shall be deemed guilty of a misdemeanor.

Sec. 30. Every male person of the age of sixteen years or over, who shall reside in such bawdy house or assignation house, for the purpose of assisting, aiding or abetting the owner or keeper thereof, or the women who live therein, cr resort to such house in lacivious practices, shall be deemed guilty of a misdemeanor.

Sec. 31. Every female person of the age of twelve years or over, who shall lodge in or resort to a bawdy or assignation house, in this village, for prostitution, or who, for the purpose of plying her vocation, shall stand in wait on any street, alley or other public place within the village, or shall do any other act for that purpose, shall be deemed guilty of a misdemeanor.

Sec. 32. Any person who shall, in this village, dig or cause to be dug, any excavation in or adjoining any highway, thoroughfare or other public place, and shall not during the night time cause the same to be fenced or covered with boards or red light signals of danger placed thereon, shall be deemed guilty of a misdemeanor.

Sec. 33. Any person, who shall obstruct, or cause to be obstructed, in any manner whatever, any street, alley, street crossing or sidewalk, or

—26—

first day of the week, commcnly called Sunday, shall be deemed guilty of a misdemeanor.

Sec. 35. That any person, or persons, who shall discharge or explode, or cause to be discharged or exploded, any fire cracker, Roman candle, skyrocket, or any other explosive known as fireworks; or any gun, pistol, or firearms within the corporate limits of the village of Nixa, shall be deemed guilty of a misdemeanor, and, upon conviction, shall be fined not less than one nor more than ten dollars for each offense.

Sec. 36. Every person who shall expose to sale any goods, wares or merchandise on the first day of the week, commonly called Sunday, shall on conviction, be adjudged guilty of a misdemeanor and fined not exceeding fifty dollars.

Sec. 37. The last section shall not be construed to prevent the sale of any drugs or medicines, provisions or other articles of immediate necessity.

Sec. 38. It shall be the duty of the marshal and police, in their official capacity, to enter any bawdy or assignation house, or any house used for the purpose of prostitution within the village, and to use force in accomplishing entrance, if necessary, upon the information or complaint of any creditable person, and arrest without process all persons found therein, and file complaints before the chairman against the arrested parties, and if any marshal or police officer shall neglect or refuse to make examination, as herein provided, his office shall be deemed vacated.

Sec. 39. Any person or persons, who shall, within this village, wilfully cut, hack, or otherwise injure any lamp post, window, docr, railing, post, sign or fence, or any ornamental shade or fruit trees, or any vine or shrub, or take away any fruit, flowers or vegetables, or throw cpen any gate, or blow out any street light, or do any damage to any telephone, telegraph or electric light line, pole or wire, or to property belonging to any other person, or to this village, or to land not his own, shall be deemed guilty of a misdemeanor.

Sec. 40. Every person who shall, in this village, set up or keep any gaming table or gambling device, at which any game of chance shall be played for money or property; or shall at any such table or device, or at any game of chance, bet, win or lose any money or property, either in specie or by anything representing the same, or shall suffer any table or

Sec. 41. If any person, minor or adult, shall climb upon, hang to, or in any manner attach himself to any locomotive engine or car, while the same is in motion or running into, out of, or through the village, who is not an employe or passenger thereon, shall be deemed guilty of a misdemeanor.

Sec. 42. Any owner or keeper of any billiard table, pool table, or any other table upon which balls and cues are used, or ten pin alley, or anything of a like nature, who shall permit or suffer the same to be played or used on the first day of the week, commonly called Sunday, shall be deemed guilty of a misdemeanor.

Sec. 43. Every person who shall convey, or attempt to convey, into the village jail, or other place of confinement, any disguised instrument, arms or other things proper or useful to aid any person committed, or to be detained or confined in such jail or other place of confinement, for any offense whatever, whether an escape be effected or not, shall be deemed guilty of a misdemeanor.

Sec. 44. Every person, who shall by forcibly breaking the walls or outer doors, window, or shutter of any window of the village jail, or other place of confinement in this village; or shall, by unlocking or breaking the lock or bolt of the door of the village jail, or other place of confinement, for the purpose of aiding, assisting, abetting or enabling the escape of any person, or persons, therein confined, shall be deemed guilty of a misdemeanor.

Sec. 45. Every person exercising or holding any office under the ordinances of this village, who shall be guilty of oppression, partiality, misconduct or abuse of authority, wilfully and intentionally in his official capacity, or under the color of his office, shall be deemed guilty of a misdemeanor.

Sec. 46. Hereafter it shall be unlawful for any minor under the age of eighteen years to loiter on the streets, alleys or other public places of the village after nine o'clock p. m.

Sec. 47. Any person who shall leave unhitched any team or other animal attached to any vehicle in the streets, alleys or other public places in the village, shall be deemed guilty of a misdemeanor.

Sec. 48. Any person, or persons, who shall charivari any person, or persons, in this village, by blowing horns, beating drums, kettles or pans, jingle bells, or by any other such means as are commonly used in a charivari, shall be deemed guilty of a misdemeanor.

—28—

Sec. 49. Any person who shall, in this village, bet any money or property upon any game played at, or upon any pool table, billiard table, or gaming table, or any gambling device of any kind; or upon any game of chance played with cards or dice; or upon any game of chance whatever; or play at pitch, throw or bet any money at or upon any game, commonly called "crackaloo," or shall induce or entice any other person to bet money or property upon any such game, shall be deemed guilty of a misdemeanor.

Sec. 50. Any person who shall, in the Village of Nixa, upon premises owned or occupied by him, keep open or in an unsafe or insecure condition, any cellar door, or cellar, or any door or grating, window or stairway, or vault opening into any sidewalk or highway of this village, or any cistern, well or ditches, whereby any person may be endangered by falling through or into such places, shall be deemed guilty of a misdemeanor.

Sec. 51. Any person who shall, in this village, keep or permit any gambling table, bank or device to be set up or used for the purpose of gaming in any house, building, shed, booth, shelter, lot, or other premises to him belonging; or by him occupied, or of which he has possession at the time, shall be deemed guilty of a misdemeanor.

Sec. 52. Any person who shall, in this village, run any foot race, or engage in rapid running upon any of the streets, alleys, or lots of this village; or who shall engage in foot-racing for money or property, shall be deemed guilty of a misdemeanor.

Sec. 53. Every person who shall, in this village, live in a state of open and notorious adultery; and every man and woman, one or both of whom are married and not to each other, who shall lewdly and lasciviously abide and co-habit with each other; and every person, married or unmarried, who shall be guilty of open, gross lewdness or lascivious behavior; or of any open, notorious act of public indecency, grossly scandously, shall, upon conviction, be deemed guilty of a misdemeanor.

Sec. 54. All persons who shall, knowingly, associate themselves with persons having the reputation of being thieves or prostitutes, with the intent in any manner whatever to aid or assist such persons in their nefarious callings, shall be deemed guilty of a misdemeanor.

Sec. 55. Every person, lawfully imprisoned in the village jail, or other place of confinement in the village, or who shall be in the lawful custody of the marshal, or other officer of the village, who shall escape, or attempt to escape from such jail or other place of confinement, or from the custody of such officer, shall be deemed guilty of a misdemeanor.

Sec. 56. All persons owning, controlling, operating, or managing threshing machines, cane mills, corn mills, saw mills, and steam engines of any kind, are required, in moving the same over the streets and public highways of this village, to lay down planks not less than one foot wide, two inches in thickness, and of such lengths on the floors, of all bridges and culverts situated on the public streets or highways of this village, while crossing the same for the wheels thereof to rest upon and run upon, and every person who shall violate the provisions of this section shall be deemed guilty of a misdemeanor.

Sec. 57. No information, trial, judgment, or other proceeding thereon for violating any of the ordinances of this village, shall be deemed invalid or in any manner affected by reason of the mis-statement, or failing to state the time when the offense was committed in any case where the time is not the essence of the offense; and if in any such trial the evidence shall show that the offense was committed at a time different from that alleged in the information, but within one year next before such prosecution was commenced, then such variance shall be deemed immaterial.

Sec. 58. No person shall be incapacitated from testifying touching any offense committed by another against any of the provisions of this ordinance relating to gaming, by reason of his having played or betted at any of the prohibited games or gaming devices, but the testimony given by such persons shall in no case be used against him.

Sec. 59. If two or more persons shall, in any public place, within the limits of this village, voluntarily or by agreement, engage in any fight, or use any blows or violence towards each other in an angry or quarrelsome manner; or do each other any wilful mischief; or if any person shall assault another and strike him in any public place, to the terror or disturbance of any other person, the person, or persons, so offending shall be deemed guilty of an affray, and upon conviction shall be punished as for a misdemeanor.

Sec. 60. That it shall be unlawful for any person or persons to engage in boxing, scuffling, dancing or wrestling upon any sidewalk, platform or street within the corporate limits of the Village of Nixa.

Sec. 61. That it shall be unlawful for any person, or persons, to approach within twenty feet of the village jail, except the officers of the law, without first obtaining a permit from the chairman of the Board of Trustees, or the Village Marshal.

Sec. 62. That a curfew bell shall be rung at nine o'clock p. m. each night within the corporate limits of the Village of Nixa, and that it shall be unlawful for any minor, under the age of eighteen years, to loiter upon any street, alley, vacant lot or commons within the corporate limits of the Village of Nixa after the ringing of the curfew bell, giving a reasonable time required for going home, unless the parent or guardian is with them or are on an errand of necessity. And any minor violating this ordinance shall be deemed guilty of a misdemeanor, and, upon conviction, shall be fined in a sum not less than one nor more than five dollars.

Sec. 63. That it shall be unlawful for any person, or persons, to conduct, permit or maintain, within the corporate limits of the village of Nixa, any disorderly house, wherein drinking, gambling, swearing, or any unusual noise, or offensive or indecent conversation is carried on; or quarreling, challenging or fighting is permitted to the annoyance of the public, shall be deemed guilty of a misdemeanor, and, upon conviction, shall be fined not less than one nor more than twenty-five dollars.

Sec. 64. Any person who shall be found guilty of any of the misdemeanors defined or prohibited in this or any other ordinance of the Village of Nixa, unless otherwise provided, shall be fined in a sum not less than one nor exceeding one hundred dollars for each offense, together with the costs of the suit; and such person may be committed to the village jail in default of the payment of such fines and costs, or any portion thereof, for a term not exceeding three months; or the chairman may order such fine and costs commuted to labor for a term not exceeding three months for any offense at the rate of one day for each fifty cents of such fine and costs.

Sec. 65. All ordinances or parts of ordinances conflicting with this ordinance are hereby repealed.

Sec. 66. This ordinance shall be in full force and effect from and after its passage and approval by the chairman of the Board of Trustees.

Passed this 14th day of July, 1905.

Approved this 14th day of July 1905.

J. B. RICE, Chairman of the Board of Trustees.

Seal—Attest: LEO S. KERR, Village Clerk.

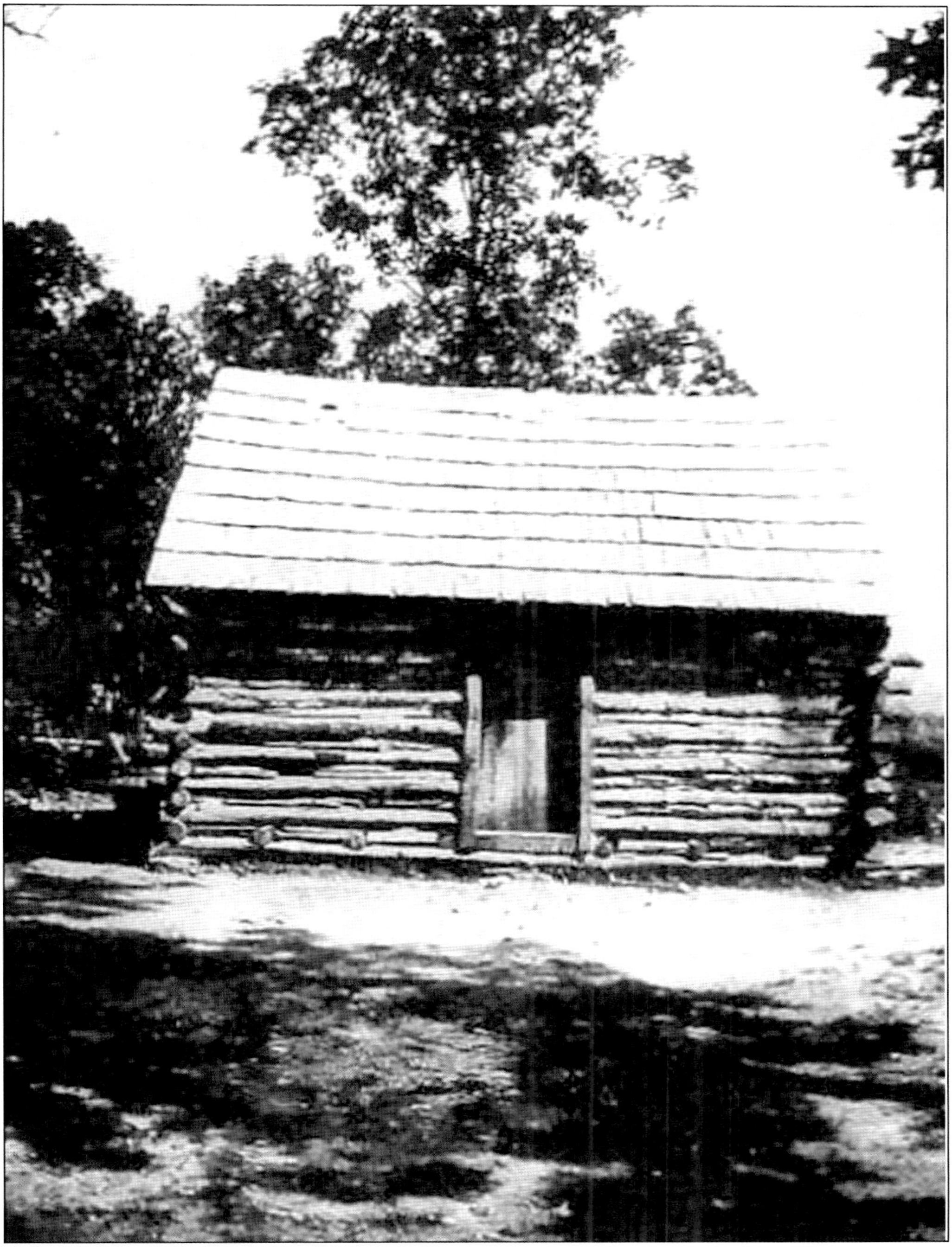

This is a family cabin from the early days of Christian County—it offers quite a contrast to the homes of today.

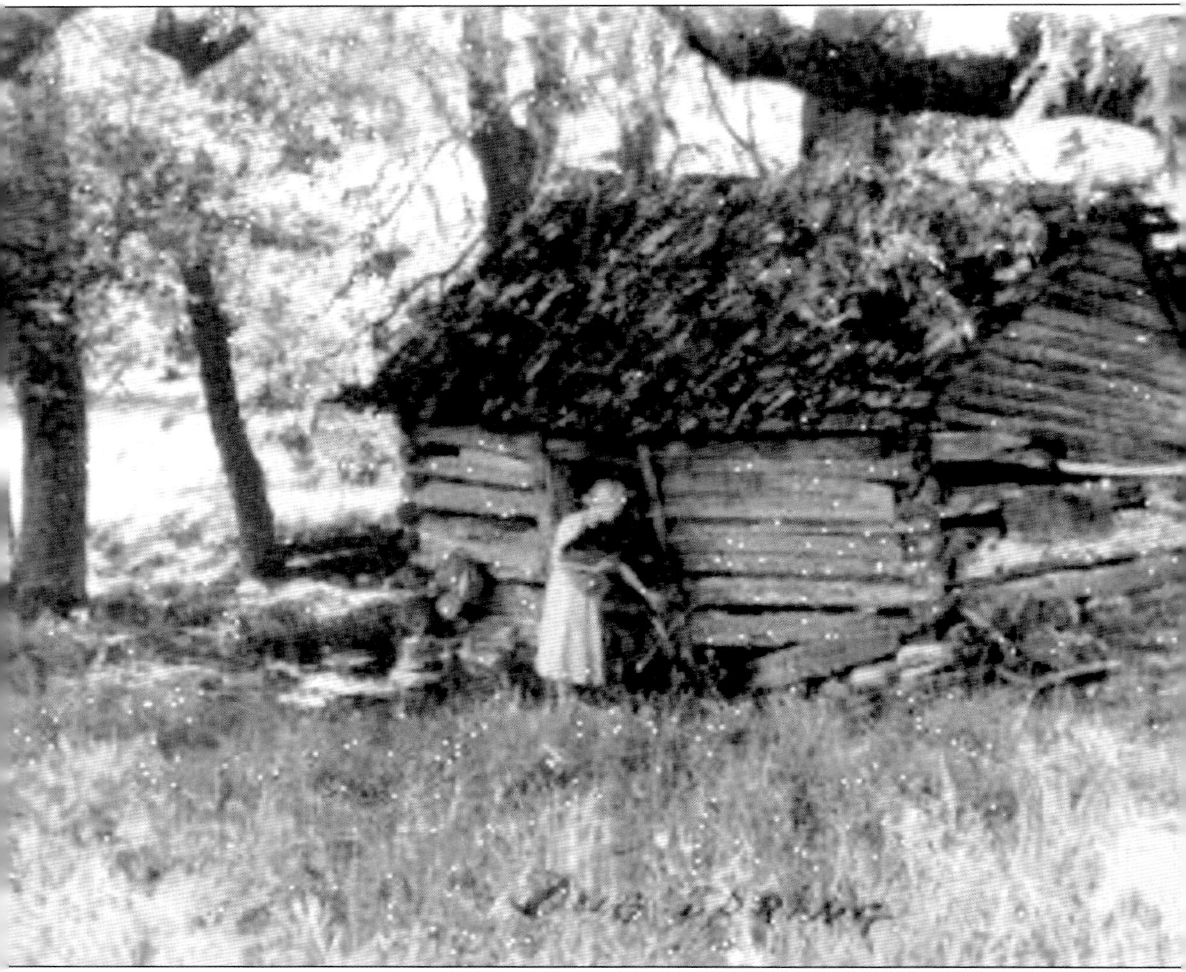

This log cabin was located at Dug Spring near Clever. The photo was taken during the first Civil War skirmish in Christian County on August 1, 1861. Pictured is Mrs. C.L. Brown at her cabin's front door.